THIS CLOSE
TO HAPPY

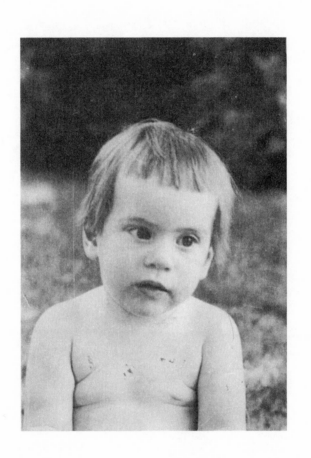

THIS CLOSE TO HAPPY

A RECKONING WITH DEPRESSION

DAPHNE MERKIN

FARRAR, STRAUS AND GIROUX   NEW YORK

Farrar, Straus and Giroux
18 West 18th Street, New York 10011

Portions of this book originally appeared, in slightly different form,
in *The New Yorker* and *The New York Times Magazine*.

Library of Congress Cataloging-in-Publication Data
Names: Merkin, Daphne, author.
Title: This close to happy : a reckoning with depression / Daphne Merkin.
Description: First edition. | New York : Farrar, Straus and Giroux, 2017.
Identifiers: LCCN 2016025616 | ISBN 9780374140366 (hardback) |
    ISBN 9780374711917 (e-book)
Subjects: LCSH: Merkin, Daphne—Mental health. | Postpartum
    depression—Treatment. | Postpartum depression—United States—
    Biography. | Depressed persons—Biography. | Women—Health and
    hygiene. | Psychotherapist and patient. | BISAC: BIOGRAPHY &
    AUTOBIOGRAPHY / Personal Memoirs.
Classification: LCC RG852 .M47 2017 | DDC 616.85/270092 [B]—dc23
LC record available at https://lccn.loc.gov/2016025616

Designed by Jonathan D. Lippincott

www.fsgbooks.com
www.twitter.com/fsgbooks • www.facebook.com/fsgbooks

1   3   5   7   9   10   8   6   4   2

To Michael Porder

Observe perpetually . . . Observe my own despondency.
By that means it becomes serviceable. Or so I hope.
—*The Diary of Virginia Woolf*, Volume V

All my watercolors fade to black.
—Annie Lennox, *Pavement Cracks*

THIS CLOSE TO HAPPY

PROLOGUE

Lately I've been thinking about the allure of suicide again—the way it says *basta!* to life, like an Italian grandmother sweeping out all the accumulated debris of daily existence, leaving a clean and unmarked surface. No more rage at the circumstances that have brought you down. No more dread. No more going from day to day in a state of suspended animation, feeling tired around the eyes—behind them, too—and making conversation, hoping no one can tell what's going on inside. No more anguish, that roaring pain inside your head that feels physical but has no somatic correlation that can be addressed and treated with a Band-Aid or ointment or cast. Most of all, no more *disguise*, no more need to wear a mask: "What, you, depressed? I never would have known."

They come on, such suicidally colored periods, at times like these—I am writing this in the winter, at my desk in New York City—when the days are short, evening starts early, the sky lacks light, and you have ceased admiring your own efforts to keep going. Although they can also come on when the day is long and the light never-fading, in early spring or

ripest summer. They come on because your mood, which
has been sliding perceptibly downward for weeks, even
months, has hit rock-bottom. You lie there in the sludge, no
longer bothering to flail around, marooned in a misery that
is no less easy to bear because there is nothing wildly terrible
to point to in the circumstances of your own life—on the
surface, at least—to account for it. And now this fatal tug
has made itself felt again, suggesting an end to your despondency, your inability to get with the program, a phrase you've
never liked in its brisk, gym-coach approach to what is after
all a complex situation—this matter of your life and how
much you want to submit to its terms—but all the same an
apt one.

   You have never understood the program, to be sure, what
it is that you are meant to be propelling yourself toward,
what long-term goal hovers before you that would suggest
the possibility of a successful completion. There is, of course,
the matter of your writing, a goal of a sort but also the impulse that keeps you going most reliably. Art is supposed to
be long and life short, or so the Latin saying has it. *Ars longa,
vita brevis.* But on a day like today, when everything seems
gray and thin, nothing gives you ballast. You are too worn
down to even pretend to know why you should put one foot
after the other: it is *life* that seems too long, endless. A clock
ticks somewhere in the silence of your apartment, empty
second after empty second, reminding you that time hangs
heavy when you have lost your way, like a vise around your
neck. You are reminded as well of one of your stays on a psychiatric unit, when you sat in the so-called Day Room with
some of the other patients and watched TV in the middle
of the afternoon, something you would never have done at
home and which made you feel entirely useless, like a piece
of clothing hung out to dry and then forgotten about.

How ever did you fill your days before this torpor came and claimed you? It is difficult to recall how you once went naturally from one activity to the next, writing and reading, indulging in virtual window-shopping on the computer, talking to your daughter, laughing over something with a friend, warming up a cup of coffee or tea in the microwave. It wasn't as though you were ever exactly a dervish of energy, spinning from one hectically scheduled event to the next—you are a stay-at-home sort at the best of times, someone who has to assemble the internal wherewithal to go out and meet people, no matter how open and receptive you seem—but before, you didn't question the whole ongoing shebang of making plans. Now you can no longer figure out what it is that moves other people to bustle about out there in the world, doing errands, rushing to appointments, picking up a child from school. You have lost the thread that pulled the circumstances of your life together. Nothing adds up and all you can think about is the raw nerve of pain that your mind has become—and, once again, how merciful it would be to yourself and others to extinguish this pain.

You might have become an addict, under different circumstances, retreating into the nullifying bliss of street drugs. Instead you take a prescribed regimen of legal drugs, tweaked occasionally by a well-meaning psychopharmacologist, and articulate your condition in fifty-minute sessions to people to whom you have paid large sums of money to listen to you over the years. You sit in their offices and discuss your wish to die the way other patients discuss their wish to find a lover. Never mind your daughter, your friends, your writing, the taste of something delicious, a new book, or the TV series everyone is watching: the things that are supposed to moor you to this world. Even those who know you best don't understand the glare bouncing off your eyes, the glare that prevents you from seeing up the road. Despair is always described as dull, when the truth is that despair has a light all its own, a lunar glow, the color of mottled silver.

1

A woman is standing in her kitchen, making a pot of coffee, spooning out the pungent overpriced ground beans from their snappy little aluminum bag into a paper filter, trying to remember what number tablespoon she was on—four? six? three?—before the dark thoughts began tumbling in, doing their wild and wily gymnastics: *You shouldn't, you should have, why are you, why aren't you, there's no hope, it's too late, it's always been too late, give up, go back to bed, there's no hope, the day is half gone, no, the day ahead is too long, there's so much to do, there's not enough to do, everything is futile, there is no hope.*

What, she wonders for the zillionth time, would it be like to be someone with a brighter take on things, with a more sustainable sense of the purposefulness of his or her existence? Someone possessed of the necessary illusions— that things make sense and will work out for the better, especially if you cultivate your own garden—without which life is unbearable? Surely that person would be sticking with the coffee, not leapfrogging to suicidal desires at the first promptings of despair? What, that is, would it be like

to be someone showered and dressed and more or less ready
to face the day, not jumping for joy but not hobbled by gloom,
either? For surely this is the worst part of being someone
who is at the mercy of her own mind the way she is, pickled
in the brine of self-hatred: the fact that there is no way out of
the reality of being her, no relief in sight other than through
forceful or at least conscientious intervention—talk therapy,
medication, attempts at forward-march thinking, remembering the starving and the maimed and the generally less
fortunate—until she's up and standing and has hauled herself forward to that point of preparedness other people seem
to arrive at with a naturalness of purpose that is utterly foreign to her.

The kitchen has a window that looks across a court-
yard to other buildings, other lives. It is done up in bright
antidepressant colors—orange and purple and aqua—and
the recessed spotlights are on but it feels cast in shadows all
the same. The woman in question has gone to great lengths to
make her apartment feel inviting, and other people always
respond positively to her choice of colors, art, and knickknacks; but when the wind of the dark season comes rus-
tling around her, all her attentive homemaking efforts are
to no avail. She has also gone to great lengths to create
a life that includes a close relationship with her daughter and
intimate friendships; a passionate interest in the surrounding culture in both its deeper and more frivolous aspects;
and meaningful work as a writer. She is appreciated for her
gimlet eye, her curiosity, her wry humor and warmth; from
the outside in, her life might strike others as good, if not
enviable. She knows this on some level but the knowledge
dries up as the wind howls through her, reminding her that
she feels barren and lost and quite without hope.

The plunge in mood can be sudden and steep, taking her unawares: one minute she's feeling more or less okay, the next like shooting her head off. It can occur on a Monday afternoon, for instance, when she's returned home from a dentist appointment to an empty apartment and the very motes in the air strike her as desolate. She feels isolated, stuck in a cave of grief, of ancient and permanent sorrow. And then, right on the wings of this feeling, gurgling up from somewhere inside her, comes the impulse to kill herself. It's so strong that she goes over to the wood block of knives that sits on the kitchen counter and takes one out, running its serrated edge across her thumb. She envisions herself slashing her wrists . . . no, filling a bathtub with water first and then slashing her wrists, isn't that the way to ensure death, the way Diane Arbus did it? To stop herself from thinking about it any further, she gets into her bed and lies there, waiting for the impulse to pass.

Then again, the dark season can take its own sweet time to make itself known, stretching out over weeks or even months until it announces itself as having irrevocably arrived. The particular afternoon alluded to here puts in an appearance in mid-March, but it could just as likely be a day in mid-December, or mid-August. The condition that envelops her respects no calendar; it arrives precisely when it feels like it. To the woman, it seems as if she has felt this way, in one form or another, for what feels like forever. She is always noticing the grime on the bricks, the flaws in her friends, the heartache lying in wait—the sadness that courses just underneath the skin of life, like blood.

Depression is a global problem, affecting 350 million people worldwide; in the United States 16 million people had at least one major depressive episode in 2012, and in

2014 there were more than 40,000 deaths by suicide. And yet this is a sadness that no one seems to want to talk about in public, not even in this Age of Indiscretion. At cocktail parties, for instance, you can talk endlessly about attending AA meetings or your stint in rehab without raising any eyebrows. But just imagine trying to tell the truth about how you feel at an upscale social gathering, where everyone's milling around, wine glass in hand, keeping a narrowed eye out for the next person, the person who isn't you:

"How are you?"

"Not fine. Very depressed, in fact. Can barely get out of bed. Have no idea what's happening in the world lately and don't much care."

Who wants to hear it? Has ever wanted to hear it? Will ever want to hear it? In spite of our anything-goes, tell-all culture, so much of the social realm is closed against too much real personal disclosure, too much ruffling of the surface. We live in a society that is embarrassed by interiority, unless it is presented in a shrill, almost campy style under the aegis of the recovery movement, with its insistence on dramatic personal testimony. Rigorous self-reflection—a sober and nuanced wrestling with personal demons—has gone out with the great, vexed Victorians, like John Ruskin, Thomas Carlyle, and Matthew Arnold.

Nor is the private realm particularly conducive to airing this sort of implacable feeling, no matter how affectionate or willing to listen friends are. Depression, in its insistence on its own stubborn one-note reality, becomes boring for other people to hear about, patient as they may initially be. *Take a yoga class*, they advise, or *Get a massage. Just don't go on and on about it*, is what they don't say, but you can see the resistance to joining you in your gloom in the set of their jaw.

When the woman finally disappears once again into the murky haze of the dark season—it has crept in as it always does, an invasion of negative thoughts that take over her interior, unnoticed by others, making no sound, raising no alarms except to she who hosts it, and by then it's too late—its malignant work is done and there is no one to intervene on her behalf.

This woman has a child named Zoë, a vivid daughter in her twenties with whom she laughs until the tears run in the emotionally incestuous way of mothers and daughters. She worries that Zoë has, willy-nilly, been placed too much in a caretaker role, keeping one eye out for a mother who was first hospitalized for depression six months after her birth—and again when she was not yet four, and then again when she was in her late teens. The woman loves this daughter with all her might but often feels that if she really loved her she would free her from the presence of a mother who is too much shade and too little sun, the better to let the girl flourish.

The woman is me, of course, but she might be anyone suffering from an affliction that haunts women almost twice as much as men, even though it is, curiously, mostly men who write about it. (They are also four times more likely to kill themselves than women are, though they are diagnosed as depressed and populate psychiatric units in far smaller numbers than women.) It's always interested me that notwithstanding the far greater statistical occurrence of depression in women, men seem to cast larger shadows than women even here, as though their illness were evidence of a cultural rather than personal distress. In the male version of the depression narrative, the blackness of mood arrives mostly like a pox, without warning. There are exceptions to this model, such as the accounts by Andrew Solomon and Edward St. Aubyn, but usually there is no indication of gloomy temperamental leanings; instead the finger is pointed at a specific precipitating cause outside the self, such as the aftereffects of a significant death, or withdrawing from alcohol or a sleeping pill—or, again, of being diagnosed with a serious illness. One minute you are puttering about, being a highly successful writer or scientist; the next, you are seriously contemplating jumping off the Brooklyn Bridge. Or, conversely, there is no external cause at all: like Chicken Little, you wake up one morning to discover the sky is falling.

In the second instance, the writer suddenly adduces the possibility of a hitherto overlooked genetic shadow; a schizophrenic uncle or a suicidal third cousin is conveniently recalled. Either way, the subject is spared the need to expose his own vulnerability or examine his problems; everything is linked to circumstances outside his own psychology. William Styron took this road in his poignant but strangely contextless memoir *Darkness Visible*, where he linked his depression almost entirely to going on the wagon. And then there is the British biologist Lewis Wolpert, who, toward the end of his memoir *Malignant Sadness*, mentions the many readers who have thanked him for openly discussing his personal experience with depression but adds the crucial qualifier: "I must admit that I am not free of the stigma, for I prefer a biological explanation for my depression rather than a psychological one."

Men, that is, have cannily figured out how to sidestep the implication of moral failing that attaches to mental illness— as well as the specific criticism of self-indulgence that is attributed to more introspective accounts of this condition—by insisting on a force outside themselves, or on a purely genetic susceptibility. The female version, by contrast, tends to tip the other way. As epitomized by Anne Sexton's poetry and Sylvia Plath's *The Bell Jar*, female sufferers tend to take ownership of the condition of depression, accepting that it springs not only from errant biology but from a yawning inner lack—some elusive craving for wholeness or well-being. This writing is usually highly interior almost to a fault: the world in which the narrator moves when she is not depressed is given such short shrift that it tends to fall away entirely.

In the autobiographical novels of Jean Rhys, for instance, Rhys's dysphoric heroines prowl the dingier neighborhoods of Paris in a state of such inner malaise that the reader is left with little other than a hermetic atmosphere of intense despair. The risk with these narratives is that they end up consuming any flicker of vitality and in the process threaten to alienate the reader's patience and sympathy. This brings us back to the gender divide once again, which suggests that women's depression is an entirely idiosyncratic matter, an accumulation of bereft responses to unlucky incidents— failed love affairs, thwarted work, bad childhoods—that has little to teach us as a paradigmatic model, with conclusions that might be drawn and applied to someone other than the depressed person under scrutiny.

As for the affliction itself, it has been called different names at different times in history—*acedia*, melancholia, malaise, *cafard*, brown study, the hypes, the blues, the mean reds, the black dog, the blue devils, the dismals, Lapp sickness, *Anfechtung* (the term the Hutterites use, meaning "temptation by the devil")—and has been treated as a spiritual malady, a failure of will, a biochemical malfunctioning, a psychic conundrum, or sometimes several things at once. (The French, with their aptitude for elegant packaging, have

devised a whole moody philosophy of "abjection," as expli-
cated by psychoanalytic thinkers like Julia Kristeva, in lieu
of anything simpler. Both abjection and depression involve
an impossible state of mourning for the lost maternal object,
although, in her book *Black Sun: Depression and Melancholia*, Kristeva posits depression as a discourse with a learned
language rather than strictly a pathology to be treated.) The
condition arouses, depending on the circumstances, pity,
hostility, suspicion, sympathy, contempt, disregard, respect, or
some unsorted-out combination thereof.

It's one thing, that is, if you're a suitably heroic or accomplished figure: Winston Churchill, valiantly waging war
against Hitler while fending off bouts of melancholy by way
of painting and bricklaying (although it seems to have been
his wife, Clementine, who suffered more deeply from depression, eventually seeking out ECT—electroconvulsive
therapy, or as it has come to be known, shock therapy—
in her latter years); or Abraham Lincoln, wrestling with self-
doubt and despair while pursuing his vision of a republic
free of slavery. It's another thing entirely if you're one of
millions of anonymous sufferers who are living as best they
can while they fend off similar demons. Like the painter
from Chapel Hill who's read my articles about depression
that have appeared over the years in *The New Yorker* and
The New York Times Magazine, and once wrote me: "The
black dog has followed me since my late teens and sleeps
beside my bed. He put my father in the hospital."

I have received letters, some of them eloquent and some
nearly inarticulate, from a thirty-five-year-old inmate in Sing
Sing; an ancient golfing buddy of John Updike's; and a "melancholic old English professor" whose daughter died at the
age of twenty-nine, after being in and out of locked wards.

Then there was the pseudonymous "Lisa," whose communication arrived in an assertive priority mail package and consisted of several pages torn from a yellow legal pad across which she had scrawled in a childlike print a list of "Hints from Heloise"–type suggestions for staving off depression, some of them commonsensical and some mystifying ("avoid every bit of grapefruit" and "avoid all songs with words"). Although the rush of recognition from others who have suffered doesn't do much to relieve the immediate anguish, coming as it does from someone who has survived on his or her own highly particular terms, there is solace in the knowledge that company can be found, even in the dark.

For years now, I have been on the lookout for a report from the battlefield that matched my own experience of depression and have failed to discover one. I am writing this book in part to fill that void, to describe what it feels like to suffer from clinical depression from the inside, in a way that I hope will speak to both the sufferers and the onlookers to that suffering, whether friends or family. Although the past two decades have seen a significant number of books that have taken up the issues of depression, both unipolar and bipolar, including Styron's *Darkness Visible*, Susanna Kaysen's *Girl, Interrupted*, and Kay Redfield Jamison's *An Unquiet Mind*, it seems to me that these characterizations tend to bracket the episodes of breakdown or incapacitating depression within unimpeachable demonstrations of the writer's otherwise hyperfunctioning existence. (It is worth noting in this regard that *Darkness Visible* begins when Styron is on his way to Paris to receive a prestigious award, and that the book's subtitle is "a memoir of madness.")

This characterization allows the reader to see depression as fascinatingly rare and abnormal, rather than as the

all-too-common, unexotically normal psychological alba-
tross it often is, against which one tries to construct a flour-
ishing self. Whether this is done out of a self-protective
impulse or out of a wish to protect the reader is hard to say,
and I'm not sure even the writer would know.

What I do know is that, as I experience it, the stigma
surrounding depression remains very real. There is something about the state that is both shameful and self-implicating
in a way that other illnesses aren't. It does not, for example,
fit neatly in with the literature of addiction and recovery,
and it offers the reader no vicarious thrills, mostly because
its symptoms are rarely florid enough to alienate or even titil-
late people. If there is something intangible about mental
illness generally, depression is all the harder to define because
it tends to creep in rather than announce itself, manifesting
itself as an absence—of appetite, energy, sociability—rather
than as a presence. There is little you can point to: no obscene
rantings, no sudden flips into unrecognizable, hyper-energized
behavior, no magical belief systems involving lottery numbers or fortune cookies. It seems to me that we are suspi-
cious of depression's claim to legitimacy in part because it
doesn't *look* crazy.

Then, too, the very murkiness surrounding depression—
involving as it does both a biological and psychological
component—has made it the phenomenological whipping
boy of the ongoing heated nature/nurture debate about the
evolution and content of our respective characters. It has become a magnet for the worst projections of both our Puritan
heritage and our pill-happy contemporary moment, with
the unfortunate result being that it is both underdiagnosed
and overmedicalized. We veer, on the one hand, between
shooing depression away as a phantom illness amenable to

exertions of willpower (*put one foot ahead of the other*), and, on the other, treating it as an issue for the ministrations of the general practitioner, who is deemed as capable of dispensing antidepressants as he is of giving flu shots.

I first agreed to write this book fifteen years ago, in the wake of publishing a piece in *The New Yorker* about being hospitalized for depression. I believe it has taken me this long to actually get it done because in writing about depression I am doing battle with both my ongoing fear of depression's return and my actual recurring bouts of it. But I am also doing battle with childhood ghosts, with the inhibitions I carry about the value of my story and whether I'm allowed to tell it. The slaying of ghosts is never easy, and my ghosts are particularly authoritative, exhorting me to keep my head down and my saga to myself. Finally, though, I am writing this book in an effort to exert some mastery over my own experience by closely observing it. My hope is that I will improve my chances of survival if I am clear about what is at stake: my life as I have slowly begun to make it, not as it has been made by others. In the process, I am trying not only to shatter the sinister enchantment of my childhood but also to wrest my story away from my own earlier telling of it—a narrative that once may have felt necessary and true, but that has by now become its own sort of prison.

I try to think of my experience of depression as "the dark season," in part as a gesture of hope that it will depart just as it has arrived and in part as an effort at prettifying a condition that is wholly unaesthetic. When it comes, it doesn't help to remind myself that I've been here before, that the place isn't entirely new, that it's got a familiar stale smell, a familiar lack of light and excess of enclosure. It doesn't help to think of the poor or lost or blighted, of people being tortured in Syria, starved in the Sudan, or beaten in Baltimore. What I want to know is how I will ever get out from under, and whether there is really any other kind of season. You see, down here, where life hangs heavy like a suffocating cloak, I can't remember that I've ever felt any other way. I need to be reminded that there are reasons in the world to hold on, even if I have forgotten them; I tell myself if I can just hold on I will remember them, these reasons, they will come back to me.

2

Sometimes I feel doomed to tell the story of my family over and over again, like the injunction at the annual Passover seder to narrate the story of the Jews' liberation from Pharaoh's cruel dominion and their subsequent departure from Egypt. In the Hebrew text this retelling is described explicitly as a "mitzvah," a good deed. We are called upon to impart the tale once more by reading the Haggadah aloud, for ourselves and for our guests, so we will not forget the fraught historical circumstances that brought us from there to here, from slavery to emancipation. I think of my childhood as a kind of slavery—certainly an imprisonment of sorts—but am not sure, even all these decades later, that I have ever escaped, ever reached anything but the most transitory sort of freedom.

This story, like all stories, goes forward and backward in time. Unlike most stories, the past never stays safely in its recessed place. Instead, it haunts the present to such an extent that it threatens to overwhelm it, to render it inoperative. For instance: it is late at night—early in the morning, actually—sometime in the present, and I am on the phone, talking with one of my sisters about the Tragedy of Our Family. We have circled this bleak subject many, many times before, detailing the inexplicable and unbearable reality of growing up in our house. My sister uses words like "carnage" and "damage"; I murmur assent. No one else who grew up in our house is as interested in having this conversation, not any of our four siblings—or, for that matter, our assorted children—but the two of us are enraptured by this tale, hooked on its horror, although we know all of its twists and turns and, by now, have a pretty good sense of the outcome. All the same, it seems we will never have enough of evoking the look and feel of the barbed-wire infrastructure of our early life, gilded over by its Park Avenue façade.

How, we wonder once again, to explain our mother's insidious cruelty—her wish to "eat her own," as one sibling's psychiatrist once dramatically put it, a kind of pathology undetectable by others because she seemed to be so different on the surface. Although I can't say that my mother would have struck anyone who met her as sweet, exactly, she passed muster as a certain type of mother, cold and a bit detached, but not as an outright anomaly—a monster-in-hiding. No matter that she didn't have any of the identifying characteristics of a normal mother, one who looked out for her young and wished them a life as good as or better than hers. In truth, it might have been difficult to discern her essential warpedness any which way, because the concept of "mothers" comes at us with inherently positive signifiers. Mothers, that is, aren't expected to lunge at their offspring with jaws snapping.

"Your tears don't move me," she would tell me repeatedly when I cried as a little girl. And she'd warn, "You'll feel my five fingers in your face," right before slapping me.

She would also tell me in one and the same breath that I was potentially pretty but that I looked hideous—she pressed hard on the word, emphasizing the first syllable and rushing along the second, as in *hi*-dyus—if I wasn't in a cheerful mood. "I can't explain it," she'd say, as if analyzing a chemical reaction. "Something happens to your face when you're moody." (*Moody* was another favorite of hers.) "You just look hi-dyus." I walked around with great self-consciousness, trying to keep my features genial and harmonious, fearful that they'd collapse into a repellent image if I weren't careful.

Don't get me wrong: my mother wasn't overtly negligent or crazy. She could go through the motions well enough, albeit all at a remove: oversee a birthday party with a chocolate-frosted cake made by Iva the cook, consult with the pediatrician over the phone, arrange for someone to take us to the dentist. But the underlying message she conveyed was poisoned with envy and disparagement. "I think he might be gay," she once remarked cheerily out of the blue about my older brother, who exhibited no signs of homosexuality that I could detect but who for a brief period in his teens wore his sideburns long, in a style my mother deemed feminine. Or, when I rushed home to impart the news that a piece of fiction I had written had been accepted by *The New Yorker*, "Your nose looks big when you smile." I worried about my nose anyway—it was a classically ethnic nose with a slight, aristocratic bump and a downward tilt rather than the cute, upturned model—but it was this remark that convinced me to get it bobbed.

Most of all, she didn't want any of us to think we were important—certainly not as worthy of taking up space as she was. *Stop talking about yourself*, she'd regularly tell me throughout my childhood as I walked along with her, regaling her about some small grievance or triumph. And although she filled us with stories of her own limitless promise, if only her education hadn't been truncated by the Nazis, she liked to cut our fledgling aspirations down. When I used to wonder aloud to her, like the girl in the song "Que Sera, Sera," what I would become as a grown-up—for a while I saw myself being an actress—she'd dash my visions of my future by assuring me that I could always work at Woolworth's, the five-and-ten store on Lexington Avenue. I took her seriously, imagined myself doomed to a lifetime of drably ringing up purchases of buttons and cleaning products, wearing a 1950s-style waisted dress and practical flats. Later in life she observed, with great glee, as though her deepest dream for us had been one of downward mobility: "All my children married poor as church-mice."

Now, more than forty years later, comes this compensatory barrage of words, this microscopic parsing of our injured selves. I lie on my bed, propped up against pillows, as my sister and I talk and talk, past 3:00 a.m., vigilantly awake in our apartments across the park from each other. The city that never sleeps has gone mostly quiet, with just an occasional sound of traffic or sudden cry from a passerby. My sister and I share a moment of silence as we assess the cost to our lives of all that has gone wrong and the havoc it has left in its wake, making it all but impossible to thrive as an adult.

Although none of us has emerged unscathed, there is always the factor of individual resilience, more or less of it, helping to shape one's destiny. The "boys" (that is how I still think of my brothers, although they are in their fifties and sixties), for all their faltering and misdemeanors, seem to have done better than the "girls" (as I still think of my sisters and myself); they have put the past further behind them. As for me, I take large doses of medication just to get through the day, gulping down twenty milligrams of this and seventy milligrams of that, dopamine enhancers, mood stabilizers, and uppers, a handful of pills in various colors, shapes, and sizes that alter the chemistry in my brain in ways nobody quite understands, which all the same should help explain how I am still here to tell the full, blasted tale.

If we could figure it out—what made my parents behave the way they did and why we responded the way we did, some of us more scarred than others, but all of us affected— would that help anything now? Then, too, I wonder: If we could unmake ourselves as we are, do away with all the misery, would we leap at the chance? Isn't it the essence of trauma to repeat itself, just as it is the essence of neurosis to resist change, to fear the step away from the familiar shadows and into the light? How would I have turned out if I hadn't turned out as I am? With all that bothers me about myself, it is too large a stretch to imagine myself as someone else, sent into the world on a current of love.

•

The thing about remembering is this: I am never sure how much credence to give my own memories, what is accurately recalled and what is a reconstruction after the fact. One of my brothers insists that he remembers the day he was born, but he is known within the family for being inventive with the truth, so I take this assertion with a grain of salt. Then there is the writer William Maxwell, who, in *So Long, See You Tomorrow*, a novel that shifts in and out of memoir mode, notes that "in talking about the past we lie with every breath we draw."

The reality is that some of us have longer—and more exacting—memories than others. (I am speaking here of affective as well as factual memory, the former involving emotional and visual recall rather than dredging up facts or other concrete bits of information.) It's a means of adaptation, really; some people survive by repressing or denying their own experiences while others try to master the indignities and humiliations of the past by storing them up in their minds, the better to revisit and replay them. I would place myself in this latter category; although there is much I don't remember, whole swaths of time that are lost to me, I believe it would be beneficial to forget even more—to let grievances and sorrows slip through my fingers rather than straining to hold on to them.

So here I am, just past a year old, in an ancient black-and-white snapshot, holding on to the side of the playpen I have been plunked in one afternoon in the garden behind our first summer house in Long Beach, an hour's drive from the city. Of course, someone must have taken the picture, but what it conveys to me is a sense of utter aloneness. The house is made of red brick with white trim, and stands imposingly on the corner of West Beach Street on a June or July day in the mid-1950s, under a white-hot sky. Playpens aren't much in vogue anymore—I don't think I put my own daughter in one more than a few times, despite my mother urging it upon me as something of a minor miracle of child care—and I can see why: they're little prisons, really, meant for the convenience of the caretaker and the displeased confinement of the child.

I am wearing cloth diapers fastened with safety pins

over which my belly pouts, and nothing else. My legs are slightly knock-kneed. My hair is still baby-fine and cut short, with the kind of mid-century, butchered-looking, mid-forehead bangs you don't see on children these days. I am reasonably cute-looking, with big brown eyes—the only inheritor among the six of us of my father's dark eyes instead of my mother's light ones, a detail that will make me feel unfairly singled out in the years to come.

It must have taken some effort to get myself into a standing position—I would have had to do it in carefully coordinated stages, pulling myself along with great concentration—and it would have been nice to be recognized for this feat but there are too many other children around to watch over and my mother is not the type to keep track of my progress, in any case. My mother, if she is around at all, sits far off in the garden, reading a novel in a lounge chair, or talking to one of the profusion of Israeli relatives who visit at my father's expense, eager to see how she has fared with a rich husband in Christian America. To the precise degree that she is unavailable, I crave my mother, wish she would come and pick me up, hold her face against mine. She does this very little. Instead I am handed over first to a baby nurse whose name I can't remember and who is a German immigrant, like my parents—efficient, undoubtedly, but not given to displays of affection—and then to Jane, the Dutch-born cleaning woman my mother had blithely hired to look after the six of us shortly before I was born, the scourge of my childhood.

I imagine I must have felt stranded in the playpen, stuck with myself. I'm sure there were familiar summery sounds in the background—lawn mowers humming, mosquitoes buzzing, and the occasional chirping of birds—but inside

my head I might as well have disappeared. How young do
the stirrings of anxiety begin, the feeling of being nowhere
and belonging to no one? I assume it started somewhere
around then, that default position of something akin to
vertigo, manifesting itself in an acute sense of placelessness.

It's a sense of primal existential dislocation that plagues
me to this day, so that I will find myself in midtown Manhattan in late afternoon, not twenty blocks from where I
grew up, and all the same feel like an uprooted alien. Take
Sixth Avenue in the mid-Fifties or Third Avenue in the
Forties: What streets are these, with all these soaring office
buildings, and, more confusingly, who am I? This core sense
of anxiety can happen anywhere outside the strictly circumscribed neighborhood of about twenty blocks that I think
of as familiar, almost as an annexation of my apartment. It is
as though I lack an inner compass, the sort that directs you
to the left rather than the right, or guides you when you get
out of the subway, so that you don't end up walking two
blocks in the wrong direction, as I frequently do, before you
realize where you are.

At some point I must have dropped to the floor of the
playpen and begun to cry; it's not a demanding cry but a
soft, useless wailing that expects nothing. I wonder how
long I sat there before someone came along to offer consolation, or whether I eventually gave up and curled myself to
sleep, perhaps with the help of a thumb or pacifier. Although
I was considered a rampant crybaby as a child and remember frequent bouts of tears in my twenties and thirties, these
days I cry rarely. Still, that lack of expectation of relief—of
the coming end of sorrow—has stayed with me, so that I
far too easily tend to fall into a mode of hopelessness when
something minor goes wrong. Where another person might

move to try and fix things, I sway in the wind, ready to be knocked over, prepared to give up. I admire other peoples' resourcefulness when their plans go awry—the ones who've persuaded themselves that "every bump is a boost," who pick themselves up, dust themselves off, and start over again—but I can't figure out a way to emulate them.

3

Self-inflicted death has always held out a stark allure for me: I am fascinated by people who have the temerity to bring down the curtain on their own suffering—who don't hang around moping, in hopes of a brighter day. I know all the arguments about the cowardice and selfishness (not to mention rage) involved in committing suicide, but nothing can persuade me that the act doesn't require some sort of courage, some steely embrace of self-extinction. I can't help but notice, as I continue to shove myself forward, trying to give my life purpose, trying to write this book about living despite a wish to die, that other people have been giving up—some of them famous, like Robin Williams, and Philip Seymour Hoffman, and some of them not.

Two poets, for instance, killed themselves in the same year, separated by eight months, neither of whom I'd read at the time of their death, though I'm quite the avid reader of poetry. One, Deborah Digges, was fifty-nine, the same age that Virginia Woolf, the writer whose sensibility and novels mean the most to me, was when she decided to pack it in. Digges jumped off the upper level of a campus stadium.

She looks very pretty in the jacket photo that accompanies her last collection of poems, *The Wind Blows Through the Doors of My Heart*, a review copy of which arrived in the mail quite by macabre chance some time after she died. Young, too, almost girlish, certainly nowhere near her age; I wonder whether it was her favorite photo or whether she just never bothered to have it updated.

There are other things I wonder in passing: whether Digges's weekends, in particular, were as shorn of relief as mine. Did she hibernate, the way I do, sleeping away the best part of the day, waking up briefly in the late morning and again in the early afternoon only to thump the pillows back into life before returning to the haven of sleep, ignoring all attempts at plans, redoing my life in dreams, in which I retrieve dead parents and far-off lovers, find myself pregnant with the second child I never had, or married to a long-ago boyfriend who wasn't my type but whose type I wished I had been. Waking up to find myself in the same bed as always, my nightgown sticky with sweat.

This is the same bed on which I will lie, more than a year later, at 7:00 p.m. on a Thursday evening in early May, feeling there is nowhere lower I can go and wondering whether I have it in me to kill myself and what would be the most reasonable way to do it, should I leave a note, would it have an irrevocably terrible effect on my daughter, are nine stories high enough to ensure death (the actress Elizabeth Hartman, so poignant as the blind girl in *A Patch of Blue* and then as Priss in *The Group*, "fell" to her death from the fifth floor), is there the possibility of crashing into the pavement and ending up alive but maimed?

A friend of mine who lives on the upper end of the Upper East Side—"where it verges into Spanish Harlem," as she says—recently told me about a woman in her building who hung out in the lobby every morning with the doormen, together with her little dog. "I was obsessed with her roots," this friend explains. "She had two inches of gray, her hair parted down the middle, the rest of it was a very dark brown. And I kept looking at her with my lip curled, it really bothered me, I couldn't understand why she didn't do her roots. Then she jumped off the roof and I felt bad that I snarled at her every morning in the lobby and that I wouldn't talk to her because of her roots." I think about how I frequently let my own roots grow out and wonder if untouched-up roots are an indication among a certain class of women of increasing despair, like Marilyn Monroe's uncut toenails.

Then there was the forty-two-year-old poet I didn't know but had heard of who called it quits on Christmas Day, 2009. She taught at the 92nd Street Y, where for a number of years I taught classes in "The Art of Reading" and memoir-writing, so for all I know we may even have passed each other on the way in or out of the building, might have bonded, shared war stories. As reported in *The New York Times*, Rachel Wetzsteon was despondent over a love affair that had recently ended after three years. She was also known to suffer from depression, no surprise there. I wonder how she did it and ask a friend who I think might be privy to this piece of information. This friend emails me that the poet hanged herself, or at least that's the story.

The methodology always being of such interest to me, almost as much as the finality of the act. Who by fire? Who by water? Who by pills? Who by razor blade? Rachel Roberts, the gifted Welsh actress who starred in gritty British films of the 1960s such as *Saturday Night and Sunday Morning* and *This Sporting Life*, continued to pine away for

Rex Harrison and the glamorous life he offered her long after they were divorced and became an alcoholic, according to her heartbreaking posthumously published journals, *No Bells on Sunday*. At the age of fifty-three, she swallowed lye and then crashed through a glass room divider, committing a sort of double hara-kiri. Hanging oneself seems to require so much in the way of accurate logistics, I can't see myself taking that route. I worry specifically that I would kick the stool or chair away at the wrong moment and be left dangling, choking but not dead. Or perhaps the rope wouldn't be short enough, those kinds of mistakes. I don't think I am possessed of the steely will and planning ability of a David Foster Wallace, who reportedly taped his hands together before hanging himself.

Virginia Woolf's method, on the other hand, has always made eminent sense to me. Walking into the River Ouse, with a large stone—or several stones, no one seems to know for sure their number or their size—in her coat pocket to help weigh her down, going under for good, the bubbles coming up in a frothy rush and then a final stillness. (She had tried and failed to drown herself several days earlier, returning home drenched.)

"By the way, what are the arguments against suicide?" Woolf wrote on the 30th of October, 1930, in a letter to her friend the composer Ethel Smyth. "You know what a flibberti-gibbet I am: well there suddenly comes in a thunder-clap a sense of the complete uselessness of my life. It's like suddenly running one's head against a wall at the end of a blind alley. Now what are the arguments against that sense—'Oh it would be better to end it'?" I read somewhere that suicide remained a crime in England until 1961 and am taken aback at the fierce judgment of this view, not all that different in its implications from Samuel Johnson's definition in his *Dictionary of the English Language*, written a little more than two centuries earlier: "SUICIDE": "Self-murder, the horrid crime of destroying one's self." The word "horrid" seems so supremely condemning; it's enough to make one feel ashamed of harboring such impulses, much less acting on them.

On the other hand, there's nothing much to cozy up to in the Scottish philosopher David Hume's hyper-rational essay in defense of suicide, either, written in 1783, less than three decades after Johnson. Hume takes a scrupulously dispassionate, almost bird's eye approach to the problem, treating suicide as a minor ripple in a larger, impermeable ecosystem— pointing out that the loss of an individual life "is of no greater importance than an oyster." This equal-opportunity diminishment is the other side of, perhaps even a corrective to, the melancholic's habit of seeing nothing but his own despair writ large everywhere he looks. We have, for instance, Max Brod, Kafka's great friend, recording in his diary: "Took a walk with Kafka; the misery of the Turks reminds him of his own." (In October 1912 the Turks had been expelled from the Balkans and coverage of the ensuing atrocities had filled the papers.) Still, Hume's cool-as-a-cucumber version puts me on the defensive, makes me want to separate myself out from other potential suicides in keeping with Churchill's famous pronouncement: "We are all worms but I do believe I am a glow worm." To which I would add: "We are all oysters but I do believe I am a glow oyster."

The Jewish attitude toward suicide, as one might expect, is not all that different from the Christian view: both religions consider it a sin, and those who take their own lives are technically not entitled to Jewish burial and mourning rites. (The Hebrew term for suicide translates into a person "losing knowledge of himself.") But Judaism is quick to adduce mitigating psychological circumstances behind the act, such as an unsound mind, which allows for a softening of the laws that prohibit giving a suicide a Jewish burial or sitting shiva for him or her. I remember asking my mother anxiously about this when I was young and still religiously observant, worried that suicide would lead to an eternal homelessness, that I'd float around as lonely in death as I felt in life. *Alix Strauss*

In *Death Becomes ~~Her~~ Them*, an incongruously lighthearted and often inaccurate book about famous and notorious suicides, drowning is described as "the most mentally demanding and painfully agonizing" method of killing oneself. I wonder if this is true, since so many other passing details are incorrect. (Woolf, to the best of my knowledge, was not remotely "considered unattractive"; many, including her husband, Leonard, considered her beautiful. Ted Hughes's affair with Assia Wevill did *not* begin several months after he married Sylvia Plath but in the summer of 1962, six years into their marriage. And Anne Sexton's daughter Linda was not, in the full meaning of the term, her mother's "lover," although they did have an inappropriately eroticized relationship.)

While skimming this romp of a history for nuggets worth noting ("Monday is the most popular day to kill yourself, whereas Saturday is the least popular"), I discover that Woolf is described as possibly having suffered from a pathology known as "catabythismomania": "a morbid impulse to commit suicide by drowning." The word strikes me as almost comical in its specificity, like one of those German nouns that go on and on and describe an extremely rarefied condition that would seem to be *Unbeschreibliche*—beyond the level of articulation. Besides, does having a word for such a wish explain anything? Or does it merely reduce Woolf to an exotic and impenetrable specimen of being, taking her ever further away from the rest of us?

I prefer Alison Light's take on the matter, which offers a humanizing cultural perspective. "Women, apparently, are more likely to choose a suicide which leaves the body whole," she observes in *Mrs. Woolf and the Servants*. "Death by drowning, so often the fate of the fallen woman in the nineteenth century, so often idealized as a purgation and a rebirth after the dissolution of the body." I can see why drowning was viewed in such alluring terms: There is something about water—the ongoing flow of it, the tide coming in and then going out again, time and time over—that suggests a joining up with rather than a ceasing to be, a larger lament than one's own puny keening. The sound of the waves like a hushed conversation, one that has begun long before you entered the world and will continue to go on long after. (Freud, in his dream interpretations, posited water as a symbol of intra-uterine life—of the womb, which makes a poetic sort of sense, especially if one is thinking of a capacious-yet-cozy, imperturbable womb.) Still, the commitment to the act must be fierce—forcing yourself down into the numbingly cold depths, resisting the natural impulse to come up and gasp madly for breath, allowing the water to enter your lungs.

More recently—time keeps ticking, years have passed between paragraphs, and still I'm here at my desk, trying to make sense of things—a dauntingly tall (six-foot-three) and quite beautiful fashion designer named L'Wren Scott abruptly killed herself, at the age of forty-nine. I had lunch with her once at the Lambs Club on West Forty-fourth Street, several years earlier, when there was an idea afloat at *Elle* that I might write a piece about her. *Clever girl*, I thought to myself when I first heard the news: *Now you will never have to grow old and haggard, lose your luster, sit alone in a coffee shop as the afternoon drains into evening, hope someone will invite you to a concert or a movie to fill up your week.*

Her death was deemed newsworthy, unlike some other suicides, because of the glamour surrounding her. Not least, there was her boyfriend of more than a decade—none other than Mick Jagger, he of the strutting gait and rubbery lips—who had, or had not, depending on which account you read or believed, recently broken up with her. Then there was the matter of her recent financial troubles with her fashion label, which had left her six million in debt. But she had also been a force in and of herself, a girl named Laura Bambrough, the adopted daughter of Mormon parents, with inauspicious beginnings in Roy, Utah. What powers of self-invention she must have had, enough to catapult her out of Roy at the age of sixteen to seek her fortune as a fashion model in Paris. When did they begin to sputter out? Did she spend a lot of time concealing her depression, or was it something that came with little history—or little that was discernible to others?

On another point, I wonder at what moment suicide became a verb. I first heard it used that way—as in "she suicided"—from a psychiatrist I dated on and off for a period of years in my forties. When I first met this man he described himself as a sexual "phenomenon"; I wasn't sure what he meant by it but his undeniable virility certainly contributed to the trouble I had extricating myself from what was a doomed relationship from the get-go. In any case, I found the usage disturbing—dismissive, somehow— as though the wish to do away with oneself could be tied up

neatly in a sterile bundle of professional jargon. I came upon
that usage again recently in a short story in the journal *n + 1*,
in which a character who is inhabiting the body of a female
dolphin writes a letter to Sylvia Plath. "Men suicide to con-
solidate a reputation, women suicide to get one." Then, of
course, I went on to muse whether there was any truth in
this assertion beyond the cynical binary quip of it . . . the
assumption that women lag behind men even here.

Suicide may be called many things—impulsive, calcu-
lated, or even self-serving—but certainly in the moment of
its enactment it requires a radical daring, a willingness to
abandon the known for the completely unknown—other
than the knowledge that, as Ernest Becker puts it in *The
Denial of Death*, "one is food for worms." The notion that
taking one's life is a form of cowardice may have some truth
to it but it also serves to soften the blow the suicidee aims at
friends and family, underlining the blunt fact that, important or loved as these intimates may have been, they simply
weren't enough. Or it is the kind of thing said to a suicidally inclined person, in an attempt to make the act less appealing. Who, after all, wants to be remembered as a coward?

Still, considering how frightened most of us are at the
possibility of our own extinction—how little we discuss
the conclusiveness of death, preferring to cover over its
finality with timorous words like "passed"—it has always
seemed to me that choosing to take your own life demands,
yes, a degree of selfishness regarding the emotional pain in-
flicted on others who have to suffer the consequences of
your act, but also a special, aberrant sort of bravery. Not to
leave out the desperation, which must be of such strength
as to torpedo all other solutions. Or the not insignificant
matter of how much physical pain one would have to en-

dure on the way to death. Suicides don't seem to fret about
the possibility of physical pain, or at least I haven't read
much about this aspect of things. And yet if I were being
completely honest, I would have to say that it is this prospect, as much as anything, that has stopped me from, for example, jumping off a roof—perhaps a trivial consideration
in light of the insensate eternity that awaits, but there it is.

I should also add, in fairness, that there is a side of me
that gives myself credit for keeping on keeping on—that
recognizes the courage, although it might be of a more
ordinary sort, it takes to hold on to life in the face of the
wish not to be here. It would be untrue, as well as inherently stupid, to say that I have contempt for people who
choose *not* to kill themselves. It's just that part of the allure
of depression for me has always been its negative bravura,
its splashy defiance in the face of what is on offer, its refusal
to be moved by the fact that there are no substitutes.

I'll have none of you, it says, not the wind or the stars or
human attachment or the slightly vacant quality of a late
Tuesday afternoon, when the streets are not yet full and
somewhere a siren is wailing. My own tendency has always
been to say *no* instead of *yes* to any number of invitations,
like an eternal two-year-old. I'm not proud of it but it's
who I am, standing guard against being pulled into experiences I'm not sure I will like. All the same, I've fought my
own suicidal wishes with as much strength as I can muster,
or borrow, and hope to keep doing so. I write this with
only a degree of conviction; if I were fully persuaded of the
wisdom of hanging around, I'd surely be a different person
and this would be a different book.

4

In the beginning, well, I imagine everything looked glistening, all the little children lined up in a row, with freshly shampooed hair smelling of Breck, equipped with wary eyes and tentative smiles. We were all reasonably good-looking and bright as could be; we must have struck others as a family of potential winners, abetted by money and the backbone of an Orthodox Jewish heritage. Who cared to look beyond the surface to the not-enoughness, the strange neglect that suffused our lives? I look back and can still feel the chill, but that kind of damage is invisible until it surfaces one day when you're least expecting it, tripping you up in subtle and not-so-subtle ways.

I was the fourth of six, the third girl, born thirteen months after my older brother, who in turn had been born fourteen months after the second girl, who was born the same amount of time after the oldest. After me, within five years, came two more boys. There were fewer than nine years from the first to last of us, with one miscarriage in between, jamming up the steady rate of reproduction. What a rush to get us out by two people—tough, transplanted German Jews who had found each other at a Manhattan dinner party that had been hatched by a cousin precisely with this intention in mind and who married relatively late, my mother at thirty, my father at a Jurassic forty-two. (For years my mother insisted that she had married at twenty-nine, as though that age implied a dancing youthfulness while thirty reeked of shameful elderliness.) Two people who didn't give a thought to things like optimal spacing and the child's need for his or her own primacy or period of adjustment. What my mother mainly cared about was keeping up in the race to procreate with her three siblings in Israel, who had gotten started well ahead of her, producing a classroom's worth of children—seventeen in all—among them. She may have begun late, with a demanding husband who clearly wasn't Daddy material, but she would show them.

I recognize that there is always the risk in a story like this one of alienating the reader, of coming off like a poor little rich girl, mewling piteously against a backdrop of plenitude. The very presence of money in someone's background tends to evoke envy and irritation—"What does she have to complain about?" or "What does she know of real suffering?"—and inures the reader to too much sympathy, elicits a certain disbelief about the possibility of other kinds of privation. Somewhere, even though we supposedly know better, we persist in believing that money buys happiness—or, at least, provides an immunity of sorts, warding off true misery.

And yet, there are deprivations that can be at least as injurious as material ones, difficult though it may be to understand them, strange withholdings—impoverishments, even—that can occur within a landscape of perceived privilege. You can, for instance, go to private schools and orthodontists and all the same suffer from a kind of insidious neglect, a lack of psychological investment in your well-being. Being a good parent requires a fair amount of emotional generosity and, in looking back, I don't think either of my parents possessed much, if any, ability to look beyond their own horizons to worlds in which they didn't occupy center stage. Perhaps this was because they both felt cheated out of their own destinies, my mother more vocally so than my father.

Then again, in terms of *yichus*, or pedigree, my mother's background was by far the more illustrious. She was a Breuer, not related to Freud's early colleague and mentor, Josef Breuer, but from a family that was known for its brilliance and Jewish scholarship. Her father, Isaac Breuer, was the grandson of the late-nineteenth-century German rabbi and thinker Samson Raphael Hirsch, whom many consider to be the creator of modern Jewish Orthodoxy; Breuer himself was a figure of intellectual prominence, a lawyer, philosopher, and writer and an early advocate of religious Zionism. My father's family were involved in mercantile affairs rather than the life of the mind, but were also known for their aptitude for Jewish learning. Because of the intrusion of Hitler's rise into their lives, both of my parents' families had to flee Germany in the 1930s—my mother's in 1936, my father's in 1939—and neither of them went to university. In my father's case, this lack of higher education had as much to do with his father's draconian insistence that he join the family fur business at age sixteen, despite his gifted student record, as with the looming Nazi threat. My mother, on the other hand, was prevented from attending Hebrew University in Palestine because of her father's affiliation with Agudat Yisroel, an ultra-Orthodox political party that opposed secular institutions.

All the same, my siblings and I were given to understand that this omission was a tremendous waste of their native abilities, that they both might have become entirely different beings—my businessman father a Kissingeresque eminence, my mother a great doctor—had their talents been given full rein. We all listened raptly to my mother's version of what-might-have-been, convinced that history had swindled them out of their sparkling prospects. Looking back, these alternative life-scenarios don't strike me as very persuasive, given my father's nonexistent diplomatic skill and my mother's lack of scientific aptitude and her dilettante approach to the things that interested her. But while I was growing up the sense of my parents' lost opportunities took up a good deal of space.

Was I looked on as a disappointment, a third girl instead of another boy? I was told that when my older brother was born, my father and grandfather practically did a jig in front of the hospital nursery, weeping for joy, sending crowing telegrams to far-off relatives, announcing the great event. Jewish families such as mine value sons, trumpet their entrance into the world with a bris, domesticating them for future family life. These occasions usually take place in the morning and feature blue balloons and tables groaning with bagels and lox as well as a *mohel* to perform the circumcision ritual. Girls are less noteworthy and I imagine my arrival after two sisters and one brother rather than another boy must have produced a sense of letdown.

But the presumed lack of excitement about my birth pales when set against the larger question: Who was there to take an interest in *any* of us? My father was preoccupied with work—he had decided to abandon the fur business for Wall Street sometime in the fifties—and Jewish community affairs, where he was involved in establishing a new Orthodox

shul on the Upper East Side. More to the point, he was a
man without a paternal bone in his body—and without much
interest in other people altogether, except for my mother.
He participated in no collective activities other than those
relating to Jewish life, and I don't believe he had any close
male friends; it's impossible to imagine him hanging out with
his contemporaries, shooting the breeze over a couple of
beers. In truth, I think he would have been perfectly happy
to have had no children, much less a gang of them, and I
realized fairly quickly that I and the homely details of my
existence held no allure for him whatsoever.

I knew little about him, beyond the basic facts that he
was born and grew up in Leipzig and that he was the kvelled-
over only son in a family of five sisters. That, and the fact
that he had served in the U.S. Army during World War II,
which I found hard to believe, although I have a faded
black-and-white photo of him standing in uniform, holding
a rifle like a man who knew how to use it. The workings of
political influence interested him, as did his weekly Talmud
class. He was constitutionally secretive about everything;
when I was younger I imagined that he was a spy in disguise, someone out of the KGB or CIA, who only appeared
to lead an ordinary existence but was really off stalking the
inner corridors of power. I suppose today he might be diagnosed as something of a schizoid personality, given his ob-
sessionality and emotional remove.

No, from first to last, my father wasn't the kind of father
I would have wished for—an image cobbled together from
the paternal figures I warmed to on television or in the movies, attentive and playful and full of wise counsel, like the
fathers on *Gidget* and *The Parent Trap*. I didn't like his
face, his thick lips and thick accent, and feared his read-

ily provoked rage. He would bellow at the top of his lungs when he was annoyed, even if the incitement was as small as a pencil that was missing from the neat lineup of finely sharpened Eberhard Faber #2 pencils he kept on his desk, next to a pile of small white notepads. There was something about him that seemed unappeasable when riled. I suspected him of being capable of great violence, although I only saw him erupt a few times (once, memorably, when he battled my naked older brother in the boys' bathroom about some perceived misbehavior and they both eventually fell into the bathtub, to my and my siblings' barely suppressed delight) and he rarely resorted to anything more forceful than shoving me forward or out of his way.

This dynamic might have changed as time passed— some men who are bored or mystified by very young children become intrigued by older ones—but it did not. My father was never to become intrigued by me. I don't think he ever knew the names of any of my teachers, and he couldn't tell my friends apart. He didn't teach me how to ride a bike (he couldn't ride one himself) or drive a car (he couldn't drive one himself) or lend himself to helping me master the world in any way, which is the role often attributed to fathers in the developmental histories of daughters. Then, too, he hadn't much use for feelings, which were what interested me the most, then as now. My habit of questioning everything wilted before his businesslike resolution, his focus on the bottom line. If I saw him as a remote, scary presence, he in turn regarded me as something of an incipient madwoman—a troublesome hysteric, at the least, given to tearful outbursts.

On those infrequent occasions when I would officially meet with him in his book-lined study with green felt wallpaper to discuss a childhood difficulty at my mother's urging,

I would invariably find my articulation of some finely honed conflict or other cut off at the pass. "Be decisive," he'd order me, in his commandeering style. "You've got to be decisive." I still remember an incident in my teens, when the very tall and angular psychiatrist I was then seeing, who approved of neither me nor my parents, called the house one morning to ask that someone take me to the hospital for psychiatric evaluation. "You take her!" my father answered, banging down the phone.

Still, I wanted him to find me smart, and to this end busied myself with world events at a younger age than I otherwise might have, dropping in casual references to the Vietnam War (he insisted on pronouncing it as "Whitnam") and student demonstrations at Friday night dinners and Shabbos lunches. When Israeli politicians came to visit, everyone from Menachem Begin to Chaim Herzog to a young and newly ascendant Bibi Netanyahu, I would try to appear both feminine and informed, like a Diane Sawyer in the making. I think in his own way my father was proud of me—when I started writing book and film reviews in my early twenties, he kept copies on file in his office—although I couldn't say for sure. I always had the sense that he eyed my literary aspirations warily, as something that would come at too high a cost and land me at the bottom of the river, like Virginia Woolf.

One of the few times I felt close to my father was on an occasion when I unexpectedly bumped into him in the outside world. It was such a rare and startling event that I remember every detail of it all these years later. I was in my early thirties and had gone into Rumpelmayer's, the old-fashioned tearoom in the St. Moritz Hotel on Central Park South, late one weekday afternoon to satisfy my always insistent sweet tooth with one of their delectable hot fudge sundaes. These were served in a silver bowl with a genteel mound of whipped cream, a sugar biscuit, and hot fudge dribbled over the top, together with a small pitcher of extra sauce. I sat at the counter, as I always did, having brought with me the latest issue of *The New Republic* to read.

Just as I was obliviously digging into my order I heard the discreet, mitteleuropean waiter say to the person on my right: "The usual?" Intrigued by the idea that there was someone who came in so regularly that he or she had a standing order, I looked up to see who this personage might be. It was none other than my father, stopping in on his way home from work to have a slice of the establishment's silky-smooth cheesecake. We greeted each other like fellow fugitives, escapees from an austere regimen, as we both hungrily devoured our illicit confections and went on to discuss the book review I was reading, which was by a friend I thought had an excessively orotund style. My father had an interest in language—he kept a list of words he liked or wanted to investigate further on the notepads on his desk—and I explained to him what I didn't like about some of the more finicky descriptions in the review. I knew my mother kept him on a fairly strict diet since he had a tendency to put on weight, and, sitting there at the counter, gobbling up our respective sweets and talking about writing, I felt a momentary kinship with him. It was as though I could glimpse, however briefly, the possibility of a closeness where none actually existed.

Years later I would find some of my relationship with him expressed in Franz Kafka's famous, importuning letter to his father, with its fearful, futile wish for a communion that cannot be. (As it turned out, Kafka gave his mother the letter to give to his father and she never passed it on.) From the very first sentence of this twenty-odd-page document—a manifesto, really, which Kafka described as "a lawyer's brief"—I felt my own father being invoked in all his indifference to me: "You asked me recently," Kafka begins, "why I maintain that I am afraid of you. As usual, I was unable to think of any answer to your question, partly for the very reason that I am afraid of you, and partly because an explanation of the grounds for this fear would mean going into far more details than I could even approximately keep in mind while talking. And if I now try to give you an answer in writing, it will still be very incomplete, because, even in writing, this fear and its consequences hamper me in relation to you."

Aside from being an absent parent, our father was our principal competitor for our mother's attention; he was, in effect, her best baby boy, the person she willingly fussed over, and she unfailingly placed his needs above our own. "Hermi comes first," she liked to tell people. "Then the children." The rigmarole of child care she left mostly to Jane, who scared all of us into a state of fearful compliance with ferocious spankings and a general air of fed-upness, which expressed itself in an abrupt manner and constant threats. "Don't you dare!" was her favorite way of forestalling behavior that went against her dictates, whether it was resisting leaving the playground or failing to get into bed at the appointed bedtime hour or even "talking back": Just who did we think we were?

Set against this joyless landscape, reading became my only true escape; it brought me as close as I ever came to a sense of pleasure. Going to the cozy, overheated public library way over on East Sixty-eighth Street on Friday afternoon to select a new batch of books—the latest *Mrs. Piggle-Wiggle* or another in Noel Streatfeild's *Shoes* series or in Edgar

Eager's *Half Magic* series—was one of the few unalloyed delights of my childhood. I loved everything about the library: the way books smelled, both musty and papery, and the fact that they never ran out, and the way the librarian stamped the due date on a card that was then inserted in a clever little pocket on the back. Reading was also—deliciously, confusingly—a pastime I shared with my mother. She had encouraged my and my siblings' reading in a wholehearted fashion she extended to few other activities and I can still remember the sense of excitement I felt when she bought me a book that she had liked as a child, such as *The Adventures of Maya the Bee*, which was translated from the original German and which she gave me for my tenth birthday.

So perhaps it was no wonder that I longed for Thursdays, Jane's day off, even if my mother disappointed me with her own unwillingness to hover, to minister lovingly to my hothouse needs. Inevitably, it didn't take long for her to become visibly tired of her understudy role, what with my siblings and me pulling hungrily at her. She'd soon enough become irate at one or the other of us—usually my older brother—and my dreams of reading out my English composition to her as she listened admiringly would be dashed. In any case, she was always in something of a hurry to get us finished with our homework and into baths and bed (although one of the pluses of my mother's being on duty was that we'd often skip baths) so that she'd be done with parenting for the night before my father came home.

The high point came at the end of the evening, when she would sing a few lullabies as we lay in our beds. My mother had a lilting, musical voice and her repertoire included a mixture of Hebrew, German, and English songs. Many of them, like "Goodnight, Irene," a Hebrew lullaby called "Numi

Numi," and another Hebrew song about a boat bringing
settlers to the new state of Israel, were inherently melancholic and I would wonder as she sang if she was feeling sad
about her own life—or, perhaps, her past. These occasions
offered a little-seen—and thus all the more tantalizing—
glimpse of my mother's tender side, and I wanted them to
go on forever. We weren't supposed to get out of bed while
she sang but once in a while I would slip out and sit in her
lap, the better to keep her company in case she felt lonely
(Was she lonely? Or was I? I could never tell these two things
apart), and to bring her back to the present and to me, who
loved her to the exclusion of all else.

5

The thing about depression is that it often starts young—younger than would seem possible, as though upon exiting the womb one is enveloped in a scratchy gray wool blanket instead of soft pastel-colored bunting. Although the diagnosis of "early-onset depression" remains a controversial one, the subject of long magazine articles arguing for and against its validity, these days more attention is being paid to the possibility of depression rearing its head even in preschoolers. But when I was growing up young children in the main weren't given the benefit of such consideration.

Still, although it seems to me that I've been wading through the muck of bleakness forever, I must have once upon a time slept the pure and consuming sleep of an infant who wakes up with a sense of alarm-turning-to-wonder. I don't think, that is, that I actually began as a melancholy baby, if I am to go by photos taken of me and the descriptions provided by others. True, there are photos where I look oddly pensive for one so young, gazing into the middle distance, but much of the time I look anything but melancholy as a child. At the ages of three and four, before everything began to darken, there is an impish quality to me; my eyes sparkle and my smile is wide. I was, in fact, more extroverted than my two sisters and considered charming by many of the adults I came in contact with at my parents' gatherings—the Purim *seudahs* and Passover seders that marked the Jewish calendar every bit as much as Rosh Hashanah and Shabbos dinners. On the other hand, who knows but that I was already adopting the mask of all-rightness that every depressed person learns to wear in order to navigate the world.

Who knows, either, what ancient familial forces hovered invisibly around the cradle in the form of inherited modes of temperament, pushing the scales toward one style of being in the world and not another. What part, that is, did genetics play? Was I more "programmed" for depression than I otherwise might have been, however suboptimal my circumstances were? Did some of the blame for my later bouts of depression—for surely part of the passion the nature/nurture argument continues to generate has to do with the wish to assign blame—rest with my biological loading, with my wiring, as much as it did with an unhappy-making environment?

In this respect I often think of the German therapist and writer Alice Miller, whom I described in a review of one of her books as the "guru of wounded inner children everywhere." Miller fervently believed that all adult pathology, even in its most extreme forms, like Adolf Hitler's or Saddam Hussein's, could be ascribed to bad or outright sadistic upbringing—"poisonous pedagogy," as she called it. From the very beginning of her career to her last book, she never went off-message, which was both her strength and her limitation.

Her first book, *The Drama of the Gifted Child*, published in 1981, was an account of the childhood trauma that was inevitable in even the most well-meaning of families. It emphasized the narcissistic parent's lack of empathy and the child's need to repress his or her emotions in response. Her book's message made use of a vocabulary previously only employed by psychoanalysts in the confines of their offices ("repetition compulsion," "maternal mirroring," "splitting," "the false self") and it evoked a passionate response in readers, eventually selling more than eight hundred thousand copies. It seemed there was almost no one who couldn't identify with the notion of having once been an unhappy captive in the hands of inattentive, neglectful, or outright abusive parents. Friends I considered to be paragons of mental health, or to have had *over*indulgent parents, treated as nothing short of revelatory the book's plainspoken insights into the unwittingly brutal behavior that Miller claimed is regularly shown the "tender, budding self" of the average child.

From the start, Miller's work met with resistance as well as admiration, particularly from those who carried the banner of biological determinism or who found her theories reductive. It didn't help that some of her assertions seemed questionable or that her case histories, even taking into account the general malleability of this genre, were loosely adduced and contoured to fit her theories. There is precious little resilience in the world according to Miller and scant allowance made for the ordinary imposition of parental influence—referred to disapprovingly in *The Drama of the Gifted Child* as "value selection"—in which one sort of behavior (sharing toys, say) is encouraged and another (grabbing another child's toy) is frowned upon and which, of necessity, favors the adult's view over the young child's.

In the mid-1990s when I was a staff writer at *The New Yorker*, Miller and I had a series of phone conversations about what she believed to be the journalistic resistance to her perspective. She insisted that most journalists identified with the parents rather than the child. I had gotten the go-ahead from Tina Brown, the magazine's editor, to write a profile of Miller, which ultimately proved impossible to set up, beginning with her refusal to disclose where she lived. (She listed her country of residence as Switzerland when she in fact lived in France.) Some years later, when I reviewed one of her books, *The Truth Will Set You Free*, for the Sunday *Times Book Review*, I gave her her due but also commented on the single-mindedness of her approach and the distortions it could engender.

We spoke once more in the fall of 2009; at her book editor's polite nudging, I had once again tried to contact Miller in the hope of writing about her. She didn't want to give out her phone number and she eventually reached me on a Sunday morning, when she suggested that I send her a series of questions that she would answer by way of an interview. The whole enterprise seemed too controlled and confining to be of any real interest and I let the opportunity slip; looking back, I think I had tired of the cat-and-mouse games she relished setting up. Miller died in May 2010 with her secrets intact.

•

These days the tide has changed and those who consider themselves sophisticated about mental health tend to lean toward a biological/environmental explanation of depression, while talk of bad parenting and dysfunctional families is mostly left for TV talk shows and twelve-step programs. It is almost as though it verges on the psychologically gauche or primitive to hold up one's parents to censure, especially if you appear to be all in one piece. The truth, of course, is far more nuanced than either stance allows for, but we seem as a culture to have trouble holding both points of view—nature and nurture—in our minds at the same time.

As is true of all families, if you looked hard enough at mine, there were troubled relatives on either side, tainted bloodlines to point to. My mother, in particular, preferred to stress hereditary weakness—"Jews," she liked to proclaim, "have tired genes"—rather than look too closely at her own contribution to her children's emerging psychological vulnerability. In keeping with this angle, she chose to highlight my father's family legacy of emotional disturbance (a cousin who had committed suicide; two nieces who led badly fragmented lives) while hiding her own family's history of psychological problems. These included her younger brother's schizophrenia, which she cagily covered up when referring to him, insisting that all that ailed him was a slight case of nerves and the tuberculosis that eventually killed him. I found out the truth quite by accident when I was already in my forties, during a seemingly casual conversation in my parents' Jerusalem apartment with my mother's younger sister.

What I do know is that, whatever ailed my parents, neither of them suffered from clinical depression. My father's withdrawal from emotional life suggested an autistic streak—or the schizoid quality I mentioned earlier—and while my mother might be said to have suffered from some primal discontent with the life she chose (she often looks grimly reflective in photos), she was never less than highly functional. Which, in turn, leads me to think that I was less, rather than more, fated to do battle with this illness, and that its origins lie with the cold and unnurturing atmosphere of my upbringing as much as anything else.

Still, we are left largely in the dark as to the whys and wherefores of our own emotional development except as we can fathom them through a process of retrospection, which is unreliable at best. I suppose that is why I harbor a documentarian's curiosity about my childhood, as though I might unearth some crucial piece of evidence if only I dig deeply enough or duck my head into the right cave, and thereby prove that what I believe to be true about my own history is not merely a subjective narrative but the definitive text, immutable as Scripture.

Given this impulse, it is curious that I have taken so few photos as an adult to help me retrieve objective (or, at the least, objective-seeming) information about what took place. I never rose to the occasion of videotaping my daughter's birthday parties and school events, and now that she has grown up I regret that I don't have scenes of her younger self to look at. Something in me resists the way photographs incriminate you as a participant, attesting that you were there at the scene of your own life, a life that can't be as intransigently unhappy as you paint it for yourself, at least not according to the photographs. There you are, leaning over a chocolate birthday cake aglow with candles as friends look on, or sitting in a black bathing suit at the side of a swimming pool one summer on Cape Cod, with your hand-some (soon-to-be-ex) husband—your red-haired, not-yet-two-year-old daughter paddling in her water wings near the pool's edge.

6

There were witnesses to what went wrong, I suppose, visitors to our orderly Friday night dinners who must have wondered at the iron discipline and the inordinantly well-mannered children. What they couldn't see was the ambience of near-terror that had us all in its grip, the tone of belittlement that marked our days. My Belgian maternal grandmother, who visited us regularly from her apartment near the sea in Tel Aviv, was the only person who ever tried to interfere in my mother's misguided arrangements, which included having the six of us eat lined up at a counter built against the kitchen wall, like a bunch of cabbies on a break. (My parents ate in regal splendor by themselves in the dining room, except for Friday night and Shabbos lunch, when we joined them. On Sunday evenings they tended to go out to eat, favoring the smorgasbord at a restaurant called Copenhagen, leaving us to eat mingy leftovers under Jane's watchful eye.)

Oma, as we called my grandmother, had the bluest of blue eyes and took a close interest in all of us, despite the fact that her relationship with my mother was uneasy at best—as opposed to my mother's worshipful attitude toward her deceased father. Oma wrote long, loving letters on old-fashioned airmail stationery, the kind that folded in on itself, like an elementary form of origami, and she dispensed the sort of homespun advice—"Marry your best friend, someone you can talk to"—that my mother never did. She had gone into the diamond business in Israel when she was left a widow in her fifties and supported her large family, an act that didn't seem to win her much in the way of goodwill from my mother. When she came for her once- or twice-yearly visits, she was put in the spare maid's room, which always struck me as begrudging. It was she who eventually persuaded my mother to exchange the counter we ate at for an ordinary kitchen table by insisting that we'd never learn good manners if we continued to eat and converse in serial fashion. She is also reported to have told a friend of my oldest sister, albeit many years later, that my parents should never have had children, that there was no love in our home.

Perhaps the oddest part of all was the overwhelming sense of deprivation that existed among us children, despite the backdrop of material wealth. I don't just mean emotional scarcity; what I'm referring to is a general lack of basic provisions. There was, for instance, never enough food to go around and a pervasive feeling of hunger, which would in turn lead me to fetishize food—to think about it and dream about it—from a young age on. My mother left all the cooking to Iva, but she oversaw the menus, jotting them down in her emphatic handwriting. Wednesday nights were fried fish, mashed potatoes, and spinach, and—joy of joys—ice cream for dessert. Thursday nights were my favorite: meatballs and spaghetti. Our vegetables were almost exclusively canned ones. My mother never went grocery shopping, preferring to order exclusively by telephone, whether they were basic supplies from Savarese, the small neighborhood market, or from the kosher butcher and bakery.

In later years I would often stand near her when she did her Thursday ordering on the kitchen phone, urging her to spring for more cheese Danish or the pareve almond cookies dipped in dark chocolate on either end that I loved. There were endless arguments with my siblings over who would get seconds at dinner, especially when it came to chicken or meat, which always ran out early. As for the lunches we took to school, they were singularly lacking in nutrition or forethought, slapped together by Jane and invariably featuring chocolate or multicolored sprinkles on white bread slathered with butter. I marveled at the care and time that went into my friends' lunches, the Baggies of cut-up vegetables and fruit that accompanied their tuna fish or egg salad sandwiches, fitted out with lettuce and tomato and sometimes a pickle.

When we were little we weren't allowed to go into the kitchen and get food for ourselves out of the refrigerator, and when we were old enough to do so there was never much food for the taking—especially by the middle of the week, when all the Shabbos leftovers were gone. I remember looking in vain on the nearly empty shelves for something to snack on when I came home from school. I eventually developed a ravenous sweet tooth and in my teens started saving up money to buy myself a quarter pound of brownies once a week at Versailles Patisserie, the small bakery on the corner of Sixty-fifth Street and Madison. I would bring them home in their white paper bag and hide them under my bed, as if in preparation for a famine.

During the summer my mother regularly skimped on

buying fresh fruit, ordering small amounts of plums and peaches and minuscule amounts of costlier items like raspberries and cherries. "Cherries are expensive," she insisted, which might certainly be true for families that didn't employ both a chauffeur and cook. I reacted to Brenda Patimkin's parents' fridge, overflowing with fruit, in Philip Roth's *Goodbye, Columbus* with every bit as much awe and envy as the working-class narrator.

Then there were our bath towels, ragged with wear, in different colors for each of us, kept in sad little piles in the hall closet. Mine were green, my sisters' were yellow and deep pink, my brothers' variously blue, orange, and gold. (Our parents' plush towels were kept in pristine condition in a closet in their bedroom.) We also wore undershirts and socks two days in a row, despite the presence of a laundress. I still remember the feel of those socks, stiff with dried sweat. The soap in the bathroom was always worn down to a sliver and for some reason two or three of us shared the bathwater when Jane gave us baths instead of its being run afresh.

In seventh grade I made friends with Mahla Kupferman, who had the longest eyelashes I had ever seen outside of a Barbie doll. Unlike my less sociable sisters, I started going away for weekend sleepovers as soon as my age permitted it, and the Kupfermans' was one of my favorite destinations. Standing in the front door, my mother would always remind me as I was about to get into the elevator, operated by one of the all-seeing Irish or Hispanic elevator men: "Don't put on your Orphan Annie act, no one wants to hear it." I was never sure what she meant by this but it must have had something to do with the longing I conveyed to join up with a family other than my own.

On Friday evenings before Shabbos, Mahla's entire family would gather in her family's spacious Mamaroneck kitchen and make an enormous salad in a wooden bowl, with everyone tossing in an ingredient dear to them; even Dr. Kupferman would get into the act. It was impossible for me to conceive of such casualness and togetherness in my own family, and I remember sobbing my eyes out before going home on Saturday night, after Shabbos was over.

Later on, when I was of an age to worry about such things, I fretted about having too few clothes and shoes to wear, at least by the standards of the private Jewish day school I attended, which was filled with the daughters of mothers, some of them Holocaust survivors, intent on giving their children the best and most of everything. And, indeed, my sisters' and my wardrobes were kept drastically pared down, in keeping with my mother's determination not to have us misled by the accoutrements of privilege. The first summer I went to sleep-away camp, an Orthodox Jewish one, with only two Shabbos dresses and four pairs of pants to last me over eight weeks, several girls in my bunk asked me, with wide-eyed curiosity, if my family was poor. Imagine their shock when I left camp after three weeks, beside myself with homesickness—the irony of being homesick for that home!—in the backseat of a chauffeur-driven Lincoln Continental.

I would continue to be homesick whenever I went away for extended periods of time for years afterward. I remember going to Harvard Summer School my junior year of high school and flying back nearly every weekend from Boston in order to go out to my family's beach house. I shared a dorm room on Harvard Yard with a friend from the city, both of us radiating an aura of virginal friskiness. No matter that I was meeting boys who were interested in me as I

trotted around the leafy campus in my shorts, my long legs
assiduously tanned, or that I had work to do for the two
courses I was taking, one in expatriate literature and one titled Currents in Jewish Thought, taught by the illustrious
historian H. H. Ben Sasson from Hebrew University. Nothing, it seemed, could hold a candle to what I had left behind.
My mother, who supported my forays out into the world
with one hand while pulling on the leash with the other,
bribed me by paying for my flights home and with offers of
ordering a strawberry shortcake, my favorite, for Shabbos. I
was sufficiently food-focused for this to have been a seduc-
tion but the real draw was my mother herself, whom I was
afraid to leave in the presence of my other siblings lest she
forget about me.

I desperately wished to be away from my mother yet felt
panicked whenever I stepped out of her orbit. Sometimes
this stopped me in my tracks completely: In my junior year
of college I applied to Cambridge, where I was accepted to
St. Catherine's. I had long dreamed of going to England,
home of my beloved Virginia Woolf and her fellow Blooms-
buryites, and studying under the tutelage of a brilliant
female don who would know John Ruskin's essays or George
Eliot's novels like the back of her hand, but when the time
came I couldn't get myself to leave. I couldn't imagine making it on my own, whether it was doing laundry or finding
my way around the campus. I saw myself going to pieces without my mother to glue me together, my voyage out ending
in tragedy rather than triumph. When I discussed this curious
fact with one of my psychiatrists he pronounced unblink-
ingly: "Abused children cling."

My mother's tight-fistedness didn't apply to my father,
who owned multiples of everything he considered impor-

tant, such as electric shavers, and whose clothes, including his underwear, came from Sulka's, the hoity-toity men's store. When it came to me and my siblings, her stinginess undoubtedly had something to do with her sense of guilt about marrying a rich man while the family she left behind in Israel—her mother, two brothers, and a sister—were striving to make ends meet. But I think she also resented her children being the natural beneficiaries of their father's wealth in a way that she wasn't—that she had to "work" for by virtue of looking after my father's every whim. The fact that we were born to the silver spoon that she could only claim by right of marriage infuriated her. To this end, she applied herself to undermining any tendency we might have had to take our background for granted. This approach had a positive aspect, to be sure—it was certainly a far cry from the arrogance with which the scions of privilege nowadays assume their entitled place in the world—except for the fact that it was so overdone that it ended up creating great inner confusion as to who we really were.

Were we, that is, the children of Hermann Merkin, Wall Street financier and Jewish philanthropist, or were we big-eyed orphans manqué, looking in through the bakery window while our empty stomachs rumbled? When you add to this my father's innate habit of secretiveness, which was exaggerated tenfold when it came to anything to do with money, it is hardly any wonder that I walked around in a daze, unsure what my father did—whether he worked with "chairs" or "shares," a confusion of terms that plagued me well past the age it could possibly be considered cute—and what my value as his daughter was. As time went on, I learned to disavow my own desires—for some trinket or other that seemed important to me, as well as for larger things—so as not to end up the object of my mother's derision. Better not to be caught out wanting than to wind up in a position of useless longing.

Nowadays I am surrounded by a deliberate pileup of possessions that I have chosen as an adult to make part of my life, all in an attempt to fill the drafty spaces within: books, magazines, hotel mementos, framed photos, *objets* of some and no worth, a pretty glazed bowl, a miniature teddy bear, and three tiny clay pots bought at a store in Sedona that sold wares made by local Native American tribes. As though mere things could address so primary a deprivation, offer a more than passing consolation. And yet these things, in their very thingness, help me stake my claim, firm up an identity that seems too tentatively hatched even now. I think of the line from a Philip Larkin poem "Absences": "Such attics cleared of me! Such absences!"

My mother, who liked uncluttered surfaces in her own home and was, indeed, a passionate, even ruthless, thrower-outer, hated my penchant for what she categorically dismissed as tchochkes. She would come to each of my apartments in turn and set about denuding them of knickknacks, instructing me to put them in a closet or get rid of them altogether. I acted as if I agreed with her about, say, an ancient, over-sized, and not particularly attractive striped candle that I had hauled with me from my college dorm days but would usually restore this and other such items to their proper place after she left. I really didn't know how to get rid of things that someone else might well view as junk, didn't know how to separate my own identity from the devalued object in question. I felt sorry for scorned things, as though they were a part of me. How could I abandon them?

7

These days, left to my own devices, I hold on to everything—scraps of paper, outdated bills, year-old magazines, business cards for places that no longer exist. Not to mention sweaters that no longer fit me as well as threadbare nightgowns. I have the temperament of a born hoarder, although I try for the sake of appearances to keep it under some semblance of control. Among all this stuff, I have pinned to the bulletin-board-like wall above my desk—already crowded with campaign buttons, mementoes, and snippets of prose—a photo that seems like a fossil in all its pre-digital simplicity. A black-and-white snapshot, that's all it was, to be pasted into a scrapbook, taken the summer I was two. I am sitting on a bed in a bedroom at our first summer house in Long Beach, in front of some busy, whimsical-looking wallpaper—crammed, my short legs dangling, between my two sisters and older brother. We are all wearing identical striped bathing trunks, T-shirts, and sneakers; there is no difference in dress between boy and girl. My hair is still cut in that same boxy utilitarian style, with a fringe of bangs that have been pushed to the side.

What to me is the most noteworthy detail in the photo, however, is the fact that I am looking straight ahead while my two sisters are looking at me balefully, without a trace of affection, as if I were an intruder in their midst. The two of them, born a little more than a year apart, were a pair from the beginning, sharing the light blue bedroom with the sloping ceiling on the third floor in the Long Beach house while I was stuck by myself in a room on the second floor behind Jane's room.

The nicest thing about that room was its linoleum floor in a confetti pattern; when I couldn't fall asleep, which was often, I would imagine myself crawling along the ocean floor, with the confetti transmogrified into magical fish that kept me company. Most of the time I was treated by my sisters as the tag-along third, more of an annoyance than anything else. In another family, I might have evoked some feelings of kindness or even protectiveness in an older sibling, but it wasn't that kind of family. Everyone was on the lookout for themselves, angling for a few drops of interest or warmth, and my efforts to insinuate myself into my sisters' affections usually ended in my being tearfully ejected.

And yet I suppose in many of the discernible ways I was a toddler much like any other, eager to go at the sound of the bell, the insistent clanging of a new day. Still, already by the age of four or five, racing around in my corduroy overalls and Keds sneakers, I believe I had begun to be leery about what lay in wait for me. Events had not conspired in my favor, for many reasons, including the fact that there was markedly little attention to go around and what there was left much to be desired. I would go so far as to say that the atmosphere at home was one of tactile starvation as far as we children were concerned: there wasn't much being picked up or hugging going on and, since my parents kept their bedroom door locked at night, no chance of snuggling with them in the early morning hours.

Once I had learned how to write I would slip notes with urgent communications to my mother ("I can't fall sleep. Need to talk to you. Will only take a few minutes, I promise") under my parents' bedroom door, in the mostly vain hope of getting my mother to emerge. Already as a very young girl I began having trouble falling asleep at night; I would lie in my bed, rigid with anxiety, until well past midnight. In truth, I moved through the world in a state of mortal dread: I worried about school, about friends, about my siblings, about my teachers, about the Lexington Avenue bus, about whether I was acceptable, about being alone. Then, too, one of the few chances I had of getting my mother to myself, however briefly, was during these episodes of insomnia, which surely contributed to their occurrence.

I must have longed for more physical contact of a reassuring kind, contact that I mostly found in playing obsessively with dolls. I see myself crooning over the soft-bodied baby doll my mother bought me, carrying it around with me in the most fixated of ways. At some point my mother received a notice from Bentley, the nonsectarian nursery school I was sent to, reporting that I masturbated excessively. I was shocked when she told me this decades later, apropos of I know not what, for I felt inhibited about masturbating as an adult and could not call up one memory of the experience. A psychiatrist I asked about it suggested that it was an indication of distress—and that the masturbation itself was an effort to soothe myself. The very thought of it, the naked need implicit in the action, makes me feel sad—and slightly ashamed—even now.

In the beginning . . . but it is so hard to get back there now that the damage is done, accommodations have been made, everyone's grown-up with children (and, in one instance, even a brood of grandchildren) of their own, and the parents are long dead. Yet the memories linger. Unhappy childhoods, as those who've had experience of them know, tend to stay with you, immune to displacement by the therapist's wand or later joys, threatening to cast a pall over all that would otherwise be sunlit.

I identified with miserable beginnings wherever I read about them, in two umitigatedly dismal children's books translated from the French, entitled *Nobody's Boy* and *Nobody's Girl*; another children's book about abandoned kids titled *Plippen's Palace*; and later on with Samuel Butler's great Victorian novel of liberation from paternal ill-treatment, *The Way of All Flesh.* There was also George Orwell's essay "Such, Such Were the Joys," about his early boarding-school experience of cruelty and snobbery, as well as Rudyard Kipling's autobiographical account of the harrowing interlude of neglect and abuse he was subject to at the hands of an English couple, the Holloways, with whom he and his younger sister were left while his parents were stationed in India. Kipling referred to the Holloways' home as the "House of Desolation," and for a while I borrowed this designation for my own.

It wasn't too long before I began dreading the beginning of the day, no matter what lay ahead, even a vacation from school; I would wake up with a sickening lurch in my stomach, wishing I were back in a dream. It didn't help that we were awakened during the week by a sullen Jane, standing in the doorway and flicking on the overhead light without preamble. Undoubtedly there are worse ways to be woken up than Jane's method—the nineteenth-century German judge Daniel Paul Schreber, who went crazy in midlife and whose *Memoirs of My Nervous Illness* were read and analyzed by Freud, was awakened by his sadistic father placing first cold and then hot water compresses on his eyelids—but there are surely also better ones.

My mother, meanwhile, was nowhere in sight. Rather than helping to get us up and out, she was sequestered downstairs with my father, both in their robes, enjoying a leisurely breakfast of orange juice, coffee, and warm Pepperidge Farm rolls at the dining room table, as they perused different sections of *The New York Times*. I loved to watch the way my mother generously buttered my father's roll before coating it with marmalade or raspberry jam and then repeated the same preparation for herself. In my mind it takes place in slow motion, attesting to the coziness of a scene that felt in such contrast to our abrupt awakening and subsequent rush to leave. It fell entirely to Jane to get the six of us dressed and breakfasted (although much of the time we skipped breakfast altogether), all of it done in near-silence so as not to disturb my parents.

As for school itself, in short order I did more than balk: I was wholly unwilling to attend, out of some combination of fear and separation anxiety; one of my sisters remembers my being literally dragged down the stairs and to the front door. I was among the youngest in my class—and young for my years, to boot—and easily intimidated. Still, it seems to me now that I was expressing early on a chronic depressive's wish to stay home, on the inside, instead of taking on the outside world in the form of classmates and teachers.

In any case, I felt I fit in nowhere, not with my older sisters, who shared a room, or with my brothers, with two of whom I shared a room until I was eight. I imagine some sexual hanky-panky of the milder sort must have occurred—I dimly recall one of my younger brothers strutting around, penis-proud—that would only have added to the atmosphere of distress I breathed in, day after day. My brothers were stronger than me and regularly beat me up, as did one of my sisters. Jane, with her general coldness and frequent recourse to corporal punishment, cast a long shadow. She kicked my older brother Ezra when angered, and sometimes locked him in the closet. Although he always emerged with a triumphant grin on his face, we had all heard him crying helplessly behind the door. The only adult in the house I felt was on my side was Iva, the cook, but she was powerless to protect me. By the age of eight I was such a traumatized specimen, such an anxious, constipated mess (I drank prune juice every morning, like an old man) and unstoppable fount of tears—I cried inconsolably about everything, from a girl in my class picking a fight with me to being late with homework, not to mention the raging insomnia that kept me up night after night—that even my relatively impermeable mother couldn't overlook the evidence.

8

At some point it was decided—unbeknownst to me, in the magical way adults went about such things—that I was to go into Columbia Presbyterian's Babies' Hospital for psychiatric evaluation. No one saw fit to tell me ahead of time what was in store but I remember the details leading up to my hospitalization with such vividness that it seems no time has passed: the itchy brown plaid wool blanket my mother covered me with as I lay on the couch in my father's study—a room that bordered on the sacrosanct—after I was kept back from school, having become distraught at not being able to locate a library book; the unfamiliar quiet of midmorning in the apartment after all my siblings had departed; the murmur of my parents' conversation drifting in from the dining room; the brief respite of peacefulness I felt as I dozed on the couch, thrilled to be released from school and the orbit of my siblings.

I can't begin to imagine how the hospital venture was explained to me but I remember that both my parents came along to check me in, an event that seemed amazing in and of itself, since my father rarely deigned to take time off

from the all-important "office." I felt scared but also excited at finding myself the sole object of parental attention.
I can recall standing with my father inside the looming
entrance to the hospital while my mother strode off down a
long polished corridor, her heels click-clacking, to look for
someone to help us, and his saying dryly, out of nowhere:
"Your mother likes being a big shot." I was both charmed
and confused by the remark, suggesting as it did a detach-
ment from my mother that I found impossible to imagine
ever being in possession of myself—and suggesting, as well,
that my father wasn't entirely as enamored of her as I thought
him to be.

It was my first time sleeping away from home, in itself
a momentous event. I wasn't sure whether I had been
taken to the hospital as a reward or punishment but I tried
very hard to make as little fuss as possible, just in case my
behavior was being evaluated by some unseen, Jane-like
presence. I was placed on a regular pediatric unit, where
I was given a pill to help me sleep through the night—
medication that I would continue to take after I left, and in
one version or another for decades to come. I immediately
warmed to the lack of routine and the benign staff, so different from what I was used to at home. I mostly wore pajamas and must have played with other children when I
was not being taken by one white-coated doctor after another for various psychological tests. I would wait for my
mother's almost daily visits with utmost concentration,
afraid that if I didn't focus on her arrival she would forget
about me.

After she had been coming for a few days, usually in the
late afternoon, I devised a way of keeping watch by the
elevator at the appointed hour, smiling at passing staff so

that they wouldn't notice I was outside the unit. My mother never stayed very long, she was always in a visible rush, and I cried frantically when she left, each and every time, convinced I'd never see her again. She would promise to bring me a present if I didn't cry the next time but crying was second nature to me by then, a seepage from my depths I couldn't stop even if I tried. Years later I would read a description of tearful seven-year-old Frederick in Elizabeth Bowen's short story "Tears, Idle Tears," whose eyes "seemed . . . to be wounds, in the world's surface, through which its inner, terrible, unassuageable, necessary sorrow constantly bled and as constantly welled up" and feel an instant kinship.

When I returned home after several weeks—even now I can call up the mixture of intense trepidation and equally intense relief that being away from home had induced in me—I was given the "job" of hanging up my father's coat when he came home from work on weekday evenings, for which I was paid a quarter. I presume the role of coat-check girl had been devised as a way of making me feel special, but it mainly served to arouse my siblings' ire. My mother had told them some vague story about my suffering from anemia and needing rest, which it was clear no one believed. My brothers explained my mysterious disappearance by referring to me as BOPS, short for "Brain Operation Post-Surgery." Just the mention of the word BOPS would send them into gales of uproarious laughter. What, I wonder, was my actual diagnosis? A case of an overly high-strung disposition thrust into an unnurturing environment? Of wrecked nerves from living under a "fascist regime," as one of my brothers once described our upbringing? Or, perhaps, a full-blown case of childhood depression, never mind what had caused it? Any of those findings might have been more or less accurate but all I was told at the time by my mother was that tests had shown that I had the intellectual ability to get into Harvard one day.

What I wasn't told was that my mother had been advised, by the psychiatrist who had been assigned to my case, to shut me in her bedroom when I cried; this had been deemed the correct intervention for the chronic tears that had gotten me to the hospital in the first place. I don't remember if she locked the door or merely closed it but I can feel it still now as a double humiliation, her rejection on top of my abject display of weakness—all conducted within full view of my smirking siblings.

She had also been advised to separate me from my brothers as far as the sleeping arrangements were concerned, so I joined my sisters in their room, much to their disgruntlement. In spite of our living in a duplex, the apartment wasn't particularly commodious in terms of square footage and there weren't enough bedrooms to go around. Aside from these hard-and-fast logistics, my mother didn't believe that children needed their own space in order to develop a better sense of self. I don't think she was persuaded, when you came right down to it, that a better sense of self was necessarily such a good idea to cultivate in one's child.

•

It was after this hospitalization that I started taking the bus uptown to Columbia Presbyterian once a week to see a brisk Texan child psychiatrist named Dr. Hanson. Dr. Hanson wore squared-off black glasses and looked a bit like Clark Kent; he was the very same doctor who had advised my mother to isolate me in her bedroom when I cried.

I was usually accompanied on these trips by Willie Mae, a
taciturn black woman who did washing and ironing for my
mother and rhythmically snapped her chewing gum in a
way I found mesmerizing.

In retrospect I think Dr. Hanson had no idea what
manner of uncuddly family he was dealing with, if only
because he had so little contact with anyone other than
me. He may have met my mother or talked to her on the
phone but I imagine she could spin things her way and
I'm sure my father was spared any involvement. How was
the doctor to know what I was up against, a member of a
clan that might look, at first glance, like a normal family,
but was anything but normal? How to explain the pathology that began with the strange, quasi-symbiotic union my
parents had forged (in which they spoke to each other in
their native German, a language neither I nor my siblings
ever managed to wholly penetrate, despite being privy to
it throughout our growing up) and spread outward from
there to affect every aspect of the hyper-regimented, sa-
distically tinged existence that went on behind the front
door of Apartment 6B? An existence that was largely run
by the merciless—and, to be fair, entirely overworked—
Jane.

This was the mid-sixties, before the popularization of
the family systems model of therapy, as espoused by theorists like Carl Whitaker and Nathan Ackerman, and no
one thought to address the problem at its root cause—
which was the nature of the family itself, as rotten at its
core as Hamlet's Denmark. Or perhaps it had been determined that my parents weren't the type to participate in
any kind of therapy. Instead it fell on me, a talkative, eager-
to-please young girl with shiny brown hair, implacably afraid

of everyone—my parents, my siblings, my classmates, my teachers, and most of all Jane—to explain what was wrong, why I cried all the time, what I was doing there in Dr. Hanson's office in the first place.

A particularly energetic psychiatrist I saw in my twenties—Dr. Harry Alpert, the same person who would coax me into trying antidepressant medication for the first time—went up to Babies' Hospital, foraged around, and found a note I had written while I was there that someone had thought to keep in a file. He gave it to me at one of our sessions, explaining that he had taken it because he believed it would help me to look upon myself more kindly by reminding me of all I had been through.

The note was written on a blue-lined piece of paper that had been ripped out of a small pad. At the top of the page, in keeping with my religious-school education, I had written "bet" "hay," the two Hebrew letters that stood for "Be'ezrat Hashem," With God's Help; I had been taught to append them to everything I wrote. (It seemed inconceivable to me that I had ever been so dutiful—so religiously compliant—but then again it is always difficult to try and reenvision oneself as an infinitely moldable child, before the revisiting and questioning that comes with adult consciousness sets in.) Then, in a very legible, surprisingly mature script for an eight-year-old, I explained that I was afraid to go home, and that I wanted to know why my mother was only nice to me when I was sick.

The girl who had written the note sounded sweet and fearful and overwhelmed. I remember feeling an initial jolt of sympathy for her, but I couldn't hold on to the sensation long enough for it to make a difference. She was a clue to what I would become but she also seemed like someone I

wanted to keep clear of, lest her manifest vulnerability con-
taminate me by association. Still, I folded up the note into
quadrants and put it in my wallet, as a sort of reverse charm,
an antidote to my own habit of self-belittlement, until I
eventually lost it.

9

"My time is up," I tell Dr. P. "I've hung around long enough. It's ridiculous," I add, warming to my case. "I should have been dead years ago."

Dr. P. is the latest in a long series of shrinks I have seen, a tall man with a full head of white hair who has read all of Proust three times (I myself have never made it past Volume 1) and loves classical music. I have alternately wished he were my father or my husband, but mostly I try not to put all my eggs in his basket, lest he fail me. He is advanced in years and when I'm not entertaining thoughts of offing myself I worry that he will die before our work, whatever it consists of, is done.

Many of our sessions revolve around my learned habit of distrust, my inability, as the analyst Wilfred Bion put it, to "link"—to maintain connections. I insist to Dr. P. that no one tries to stay linked to *me*, that, despite my covey of friends, I can go for a whole weekend without a phone call, that I'm tired of doing all the work. "You think you're not worth it," he reminds me. "You don't realize what an appealing person you are, how much people are drawn to you." His comments fly over my head, like a flock of birds up in the sky heading in the wrong direction.

"I want my mother back," I say. "Even though she was terrible." My mother has been dead for nearly a decade now, leaving me absolutely in the lurch. I used to think that she, demon-lover that she was, had succeeded in keeping me alive by finally coming through as a proper, mothering mother precisely when I was at my worst, thus making the whole descent into darkness worthwhile. At these times she would step up to the plate, envelop me with reassurances, cajole me, humor me, tuck me into the narrow bed in my old room at home and bring me cervelat sandwiches with mayonnaise and thinly sliced tomatoes on a tray, as though I were an invalid. It was as if my desperation brought out the best in her, the sliver of empathy that wasn't discernible otherwise. You can see the problem right there, the "carrot" that would materialize in front of me only when things had become truly unbearable.

Once upon a time—throughout my twenties, thirties, and forties—there had been my mother and the apartment I had grown up in to retreat to, my mother who always rose to drastic occasions in a way she never rose to ordinary life. Tough as nails, she had withstood any number of breakdowns, depressions, and crises in her children, all of whom appeared to be of less sturdy stock than she.

When my father died, in 1999, at the age of ninety-one, I felt bewildered that his absence had become finalized, the trail gone dry. I had never known him except in flashes and now I would never be able to form a fuller picture. My mother, by contrast, entered a period of intense mourning, after which she magically sprouted new sides of herself. She lost a bit of weight, dressed in a softer manner, went to

movies and the theater with friends, and traveled, going on
a cruise to Alaska with one of my sisters and two grand-
daughters and staying in her apartment in Jerusalem for
months at a time. She seemed released in some essential way,
even taking up the fiction writing she had mostly set aside
when she married. I had expected her to live on into an
indefinite future in which she would finally mutate into the
mother I yearned for her to be, but instead she went and
died, rather abruptly, in 2006, at the age of eighty-six, of
lung cancer. (Although both her father and my father were
smokers, she wasn't.)

Whatever was wrong with her as a mother, including a
striking deficiency of maternal impulse, she had been my
all—far more so than any man, including the one I married
and divorced. She was my North, my South, my East and
West. She had been larger-than-life for me in her presence
and she continued to consume me after she was gone. I
could make no sense of her death, not at the beginning and
not after the passage of time, and so I sat in Dr. P.'s office,
wanting my mother back, if only to shoo away my despair.
From childhood on, my episodes of depression had brought
her over to my side, wrested her attention away from my
father and my siblings, however briefly, to do battle on my
behalf. She did so in the only way she knew how, which
was by being ironic and minimizing, making light of the
darkness that engulfed me.

"Everything will be all right, you'll see," she would as-
sure me. And for the moment, at least, I was reassured. But
now she is in the ground and I am hideously alone with my
depression and there are no longer any secondary gains to
be reaped from my suffering. Being in despair no longer
means my mother will come flapping around me, loaning

me her feisty energy, her refusal to look too closely at anything. I am left to my own insufficient devices, staring into blackness.

"I don't want to be here," I say to Dr. P., a note of quiet fury in my voice. "I have never wanted to be here." By "here," I mean in this world, but I probably also mean in therapy itself, which I have found only really avails me when things are going relatively well. When I am in extremis, caught in an ancient snare of self-loathing, it fails, like everything else—feels like scratching one's nails against the wall of a cell.

"I don't know if this is helping," I say, hoping Dr. P. will intervene in some drastic manner, offer to bring me home with him at the end of the day, tuck me into bed. I wonder if he realizes that I am not all talk, that I have schemes up my sleeve.

"How would you do it?" Dr. P. has asked me, more than once, as though to prove how seriously he takes me.

Then there comes a moment, suicide or no suicide, when the session is over and I am called upon to leave the therapist's creaky old-shoe of an office, with the artifacts he has chosen to display and the piles of unopened mail scattered across his desk, everything sorely in need of a good dusting. I find it difficult to leave, each and every time. I am safe inside Dr. P.'s office—safe from strangers and, more importantly, safe from my family, who often materialize in my sessions. "Begone," he likes to say, quoting Glinda the Good Witch in *The Wizard of Oz*. "You have no power here." Outside the world awaits, impervious and unforgiving—notwithstanding Dr. P.'s assurances to the contrary.

10

Another recollection: I am eight, nine, ten years old, leaning over the banister, imploring my mother not to leave me in Jane's clutches. She is going on a trip with my father—to Europe or Israel—and, as is her wont, has told me only at the very last minute, perhaps to spare me anxiety. She will be gone for a week, ten days, two weeks, forever. My stomach churns and I feel jittery at the thought of her absence. No one will look out for me without her.

My mother is also not to be relied on—although on occasion she uses German endearments like *Schatz* or *goldige Kind*, she can turn on me at a moment's whim, is fearsome when angered, slaps me in the face or pinches me hard on my arms. But she is still all I have, intermittent as her presence is and unavailable as she is when she is around—all that stands between me and the hostile forces arrayed against me everywhere I turn. Who, I wonder nervously, will protect me from Jane? Certainly not any of my siblings, who are busy trying to look out for themselves. The six of us have never bonded together in an "us against them" fashion, the way some siblings in unhappy families do, never tried to defend one another. "Please tell Jane to be nice to me," I plead.

The first time I was left in Jane's care was when my parents took my three older siblings on a trip to Israel, leaving me at home with my two younger brothers. I must have been three or four and was already deeply afraid of Jane. My mother had brought me an uncharacteristically lavish present—a baby carriage for my beloved, ceaselessly disciplined dolls—to keep me distracted, but I was so upset that I went to bed early even though I was being allowed to stay up later than usual because of their departure. My brothers and I were already in pajamas when good-byes were made, and I felt it was best to get out of Jane's way. The baby carriage stood in the living room, untouched by me for days.

It is curious to me that I have forgotten so much else that has happened, and yet can still re-create the bleakness of those long-ago Sunday evenings, when Ed Sullivan's ritual good-night wave at the end of his weekly show—the wave that seemed to project directly from the middle of his peculiar hunched-over body rather than as an extension of his arm—signaled that the television around which the six of us, huddled in pajamas and leather slippers from Indian Walk (red for the girls, navy for the boys), was about to be firmly turned off. The gray-blue light of the black-and-white TV screen would wink out, like a firefly, and then there was nothing to be done but go up to bed and acknowledge that the weekend, which you hadn't liked all that much in the first place, was officially over and would now be followed by the advent of the school week, which you liked even less.

Given this immediacy of recall, it is all the more curious that I find it so hard to summon up Jane, to put the various images of her together into a lasting impression of a singular person whose life touched mine at all its crucial points. That was what we called her—Jane, blunt and American—

although she was in fact born and raised under the name
Adrienne in far-off Holland. I don't know when or why
she Americanized her first name, but it always intrigued me
that she held on to her original surname of Van der Ven,
so that she became Jane Van der Ven, as though half of her
belonged in a *See Spot Run* primer and the other half of
her in wooden clogs.

I could pull out any detail from the vast inventory of
yellowing sorrows that make up my childhood, and not one
of them would be of much help in filling out Jane's stringent outlines. None of these would serve, that is, to leave a
sufficiently weighty imprint, some warm doughy impression
that would make her feel real to me even in memory. Jane
was in the habit, for instance, of wearing incongruous
pastel-colored baby-doll pajamas summer in and summer
out, drawing my mother's chilly glare of disapproval at their
slutty abbreviatedness. She was proud of her figure, although
she was in fact the least sex-kittenish of women, one who
I believe died a virgin. She had taut legs and frighten-
ingly visible muscles in her arms, well before the Age
of Fitness had dawned, biceps you could win a boxing
match with.

Jane lived in a tiny maid's room upstairs, behind what
was called the nursery. She looked after the six of us with
very little help from my mother, and as a result was always
harried. On her day off on Thursday she went shopping,
scouring for bargain-priced clothes she would triumphantly
display when she got home. She would also report the details of her dinners out, where she mostly ordered seafood
dishes and savored an alcoholic drink or two. For a while,
when we had all been young, there had been a boyfriend, a
good-looking, somewhat dim-witted hulk of a guy named

Dick, who took my brothers to ball games and seemed to dote on Jane. There is a photo I still have of her wearing a red two-piece and matching lipstick standing shyly next to Dick on the sand in Long Beach, but at some point he ceased to be in the picture. Every so often Jane would have a female friend up to her room, but these visits grew rarer with the passing of time.

At night she liked to smoke while sitting straight up in bed and watching TV, hour after hour, the ashes piling up in a little blue-and-white ceramic dish she kept by her bedside. She read in exactly the same fashion as she watched TV, sitting straight up and smoking while she resolutely paged through a paperback novel she had picked up from around the house, never slumping against the pillows with what I considered to be a true readerly surrender. I don't know what powers of imaginative empathy or even simple identification she had, whether she ever saw herself through the eyes of a character she was reading about, envisioned herself leading someone else's life. It wasn't that she lacked discernment—she noticed the sort of little things about people, mannerisms and gestures, that suggested some kind of psychological attunement—but it seemed to me that she read very much from the outside in, refusing to get overly involved. This posture of disengagement fascinated me as much as it puzzled me: What was the point of reading if you didn't allow yourself to get immersed?

Which brings me to the crux of the difficulty in writing about Jane: I never learned during all those years how to read her from the inside out—never learned what made her, as they say, "tick." Jane woke me almost every grade-school morning and turned off the light every night when I was still young enough to have a bedtime. Yet she exists for me now as more of an absence than a presence—like a blur at the center of the portrait where a likeness should be, a snapshot that fails to develop, a character who never quite comes off the page. I cannot, for instance, remember her ever reading to me; or her taking my hand as a little girl, other than to drag me away from a playground swing or to pull me along faster than I was going on my own steam; or her leaning down and saying something sweet to me. But she must have, even if rarely.

The thing is, she left so few traces. We are all born to die, of course, and in the end few of us leave indelible marks; we exist mostly in the memories of others. But even erased or lost memories must be a clue to something, if only to a need or insistence on the part of the person doing the erasing. Why, then, do I insist on erasing Jane? What is making me so uneasy, back there in the far reaches of the past?

•

Jane came to work for my family in the fall of 1953, half a year after my older brother was born and seven months before I joined the group. It was during that brief, zealously domestic period when it was fashionable for even upper-middle-class American mothers to look after their children themselves. They might not do all the drudge work but they tended to be around and available, to dole out the eggs and toast at breakfast as well as the steak and peas at dinner. True, the word "bonding" hadn't yet achieved the pride of place that it would by the time I had my daughter in 1986, but I don't think my mother would have much bought into the notion even if it had. She ridiculed such ideas, like the emphasis on people being "warm," as being inanely American, lacking the rigor of her European background.

(My own mothering approach would be quite different—more overtly affectionate, for one thing—yet if I look back I recognize that I had my own difficulties in attaching to Zoë. The situation wasn't helped by my sliding into a post-partum depression shortly after she was born, but there was also the lingering influence of what I had imbibed about the maternal role from my mother and from watching my sisters with their children. I was afraid of making Zoë too important, of letting other people know how important she was to me, for fear—of what, exactly? I feared my mother's mockery if I made too much fuss over Zoë, but I also feared the intensity of my feelings for her, that they would show me up as a simpering fool.)

Jane was the second such person to be hired, part of a staff that included a cook, a laundress, a cleaning woman, and a chauffeur. An earlier full-time nanny—who was actually referred to as Nanny, as Jane was not, and who was properly trained in her calling, as Jane was not—had been hired before the birth of my sister Debra, the second-eldest. A slim, older woman, she gives off a dignified, almost regal air in the black-and-white photos where she appears, standing proudly, with her two identically dressed charges, one of them sitting up in a Silver Cross carriage. Nanny wore her hair in a gray bun, scarlet lipstick, and a starched white uniform (in contrast to Jane, who wore regular street clothes). Although she and Jane briefly overlapped, she left when I was still too young to have any memory of her.

I was, you might say, Jane's first "baby"; she became the designated caretaker just as I came into view. And yet while I suppose this might have translated into a greater attachment to me than to the other children, it in fact meant nothing of the kind. Then again, her own history didn't bode well:

she herself had been the third of sixteen children in what must have been a tightly run and hardscrabble Catholic household—her father had lost a leg during the Allied bombardments in World War II—and I don't think she had ever experienced much in the way of nurturing. Jane vastly preferred my two younger brothers to the rest of us but her capacity for rage was particularly focused on my older brother and me.

My parents traveled a great deal when we were young, my mother accompanying my father on business trips to Europe and to visit family in Israel; there were whole summers they were hardly at home. When my mother wasn't around, Jane could turn savage—could kick and punch as well as beat us—but somehow my mother must have known what was taking place and decided to go along with it. Once in a while, one of us would put up a show of resistance. My sister Debra, at the age of ten, kicked Jane back when she was kicked, but this only ended up in Jane's threatening to quit and leaving the house in a fury for several hours, to return by evening.

Which brings me to the inevitable questions: What was Jane, underpaid and overworked, doing taking care of us, with so much impatience and so little capacity for love or even affection? What were we to make of the instinct that had caused my mother to hire her in the first place, this dry well of a creature, transfiguring her from her former position as a cleaning woman who worked for cousins in London to the woman who scared the six of us into compliance?

Given that Jane was, in one sense, doomed to coexist with us just as we were unwillingly bound to her, she displayed a curious lack of interest in engaging with any of us. When I talk about Jane with one of my sisters now, she uses the word "schizoid" to describe her. And certainly there was that—a sense of chronic remove, an unwillingness, perhaps an inability, to connect. I'm sure I must have tried to elicit a convivial response from her when I was little, during those quick, silent baths she gave me in the tiny, dark bathroom off my brothers' room where all six of us were bathed. I attribute my compulsively hygienic grooming habits to a lingering sense of horror I have about that bathroom, which in my memory always smelled slightly fecal, despite its narrow window overlooking East Sixty-fifth Street. I can still see Jane wrinkling her finely modeled nose after one or the other of us had used the toilet to detectable odoriferous effect and uttering her verdict: "Stinky."

What I recollect most, though, about those grim, assembly-line baths is the cavernous sense of loneliness they induced in me, with just Jane, the gray-and-white-tiled floor, and the silent white-tiled walls for company. I was a fairly chatty child when in the right mood, given to asking a lot of questions, but somewhere along the way I gave up the effort at meaningful communication with Jane. I didn't splash around or laugh or pretend the bathtub was a swimming pool and duck my head under the water as my daughter would later do during her bath times. Instead I would sit in the minimally filled tub, my skinny legs thrust in front of me, and obediently hand my limbs over for Jane to scrub at with a washcloth and then stand up so she could swipe between my legs. She used a set of washcloths, actually—one for my top half and one for my bottom half, as though I were literally sawed in two. I continued to use two washcloths when I started bathing myself and only stopped living under their bifurcating rule sometime in my late twenties.

Beyond this, I can't remember feeling anything but fear

of and caution around Jane. She regularly administered full-scale, over-the-knee, British-boarding-school-style spankings to my siblings and me, sometimes with her amazingly strong hand and sometimes resorting to a Kent hairbrush. I know being a witness to these fervent spankings—especially those she gave to my second-to-youngest brother, who was the only one of us born with blond curls and who was Jane's clear-and-away favorite—affected me deeply, skewing my sexual tastes for years afterward. It eventually led me to write a much-discussed *New Yorker* essay about erotic spanking, where I examined the ways in which emotional pain could be transformed into a sexualized scenario, but I have blanked out on the experience of being spanked myself.

11

Undoubtedly in response to my own experience with Jane, I became obsessed with the idea of nannies, both real and fantastical. I devoured P. L. Travers's Mary Poppins series, and when I was in the fifth grade Mrs. Berle, the school librarian, helped me locate Travers's address in England so I could send her a letter in which I inquired whether she was planning to write any more books after the fourth, *Mary Poppins in the Park*. (She never answered me.) I loved reading about the Banks children, Michael and Jane, followed by the twins and then by baby Annabel. They all resided on Cherry Tree Lane with their fretful mother, their irascible banker father, the cook Mrs. Brill, the overwhelmed children's nurse Katie Nanna, and various other staff, until one day the "spit spot"–intoning, wryly affectionate, magic-spinning creature known as Mary Poppins arrived with the East Wind to take firm but loving charge of all of them. They seemed like a shinier and much cozier version of my own family, a tribute to a lapsed golden Edwardian moment. And whatever was wrong with Mary Poppins—there was an undeniable crustiness, even chill, to the original fictional character, as opposed to the sweet-as-spun-sugar version of her that Julie Andrews played on-screen—seemed minor compared to all that was wrong with, or merely missing in, Jane.

Later on, I read Jonathan Gathorne-Hardy's *The Unnatural History of the Nanny*, about the venerable British upper-class tradition of trained nannies, with its assortment of supremely good and horrifyingly bad examples, the sterling mother-substitutes as well as the evil anti-maternal stand-ins. It was here I first learned about Winston Churchill's beloved nanny, Mrs. Everest, who was the mainstay of his youth, his "dearest and most intimate friend," as Churchill described her in *My Early Life*. I thought his nickname for her, "Womany," was much the most moving appellation anyone could come up with, as though she stood in for all that was most female and nurturing about her sex. She in turn wrapped him in endearments like "Winny," "my lamb," and "my darling precious boy." I wondered who I might have become with a Mrs. Everest behind me, who worried whether Winny would catch a chill even as he stood by her deathbed. Then there were the nannies who sexually fondled their charges or maltreated them so egregiously—like Miss Paraman, who looked after the young Lord Curzon, beating him and his siblings savagely and making them parade around in conical caps with words like "Liar," "Sneak," and "Coward" emblazoned on them in enormous letters by the children themselves—that it's hard to believe no one called the police.

•

The particular incident that led to my own release from Jane's absolute domination occurred one Friday afternoon in early summer out at our second beach house, when I was twelve years old. I had loved our summer house in Long Beach, but I had switched my allegiance when we moved two years earlier to a house with—miracle of miracles—a swimming pool. This one was in Atlantic Beach, a small enclave tucked on the far side of the Atlantic Beach Bridge about an hour out of the city, frequented by a sprinkling of Mafiosi and a growing Orthodox Jewish community.

The house had an unsavory reputation that conspired to make it something of a white elephant, and my parents had bought it for a ludicrously low price. (The previous owner had been a doctor, and rumor had it that he used part of the house as an abortion clinic. There had originally been ramps to some of the rooms, and the house came equipped with enormous bathrooms, which gave the rumor some credence.) It stood at the end of the block, bounded by a high wooden fence, across the street from the ocean and the various pastel-colored beach clubs, each with its own booming loudspeaker alerting guests to missing children and mis-parked cars.

On this afternoon, Jane and the three youngest of us— along with a collection of cardboard boxes containing gro- ceries and various cooked dishes—had been driven to Atlantic Beach ahead of the rest of the family by Jimmy the chauffeur, who wore gold-rimmed glasses and a reddish toupée. The toupée fascinated me; I watched it carefully for signs of movement and wondered whether Jimmy wore it for his own vanity or to please his wife. Jimmy delivered the six of us to school every morning, on which trips he would regale me and my food-obsessed siblings with the details of his dinners, which always concluded with a slice of pie and a big "glash of milk," as he pronounced it. I loved the way he shuffled his *s*'s (probably because of dentures, as I think back on it now), softening the sibilance.

After dropping us off, Jimmy had returned to the city, where he would pick up my parents and the other kids and bring them back before Shabbos. There was still a chill in the air, enough to dissuade us from taking a dip—or perhaps Jane had forbidden it. In any case, she was busy in the kitchen, unpacking the various boxes of food, when my mother happened to call. While I was talking to my mother on the phone, my second-to-youngest brother—Jane's darling—grabbed the receiver out of my hand. Instead of giving in, as I usually did, something inside me rebelled and I snatched the receiver back. My brother hit me and I hit him weakly in return. He was stronger than I, despite being two years younger, but I didn't care.

We were still tussling when Jane suddenly intervened and turned on me with the ferocity of a wolf guarding her young. Pulling me off my brother, she dragged me into the downstairs guest bathroom to the right of the staircase. The former owners had fixed up this bathroom with gilded faucets, smoked mirrors, a marble sink, and fancy gold-printed wallpaper; although this nouveau-riche décor was emphatically not to my mother's taste, she had left the bathroom intact when she redid the rest of the house before we moved in. Here Jane began banging my head against the wall, even as I tried to push her off me. My uncharacteristic show of resistance, faint as it was, infuriated her even more and she banged my head with greater force. I imagined myself blacking out, the calm of a beach town on a Friday afternoon shattered by a screaming siren as an ambulance took me to a nearby hospital.

Again, I can't call up the pain or humiliation of it—it

seems to have happened to someone else, someone whom I have but the vaguest sense of inhabiting—so much as I can visualize the space in which it took place, my face bobbing somewhere in the smoked mirrors as Jane asserted her authority. What I remember best is how I focused on the details of the bathroom as though everything depended on them—particularly the two little glass bottles etched faintly in gold that stood to one side of the sink. They, too, had been left behind by the former owners and were probably once meant to hold cotton balls and Q-tips—I can imagine a whole other, more delicate kind of life they had been envisioned for—but now they stood empty. They were fragile, those bottles, and it surprised me that they hadn't broken once my family took up residence in the house.

When my mother arrived later that afternoon I reported the incident to her. I remember considering the thrilling possibility that she might actually fire Jane, although a part of me also suspected that Jane's abusiveness wasn't exactly news to her—that she knew who Jane was and what she was capable of. Indeed, perhaps the two of them were in cahoots, with Jane acting on my mother's orders. I felt distinctly uneasy telling my mother about the head-banging—would she think it was justified by something I had done?—and when I started crying midway through, I remember thinking that I should cry harder, or not at all, that this specific amount of tears was the wrong amount, would not elicit her sympathy.

My mother was not visibly upset by my story. Nevertheless, something in her must have responded to my efforts to defend myself in this instance—when there had been so much else that passed uncommented upon—because she clearly said something to Jane. After that day Jane no longer felt free to bend my will to hers with brute displays of strength; I became less afraid of her, although still wary.

Somewhere along the way I left Jane behind, in her mouse-hole of a room at the back of the nursery which became effectively her home. (One summer during high school my sister Debra and I, as part of our first trip to Europe, visited Jane's family home in Eindhoven, in the southern-most part of Holland, where her mother still lived with two aging daughters. My mother had suggested the excursion and I was curious to see what origins Jane had sprung from. I remember being made uncomfortable by the tiny, cramped house and the inedible food that we were served for lunch, food that had been prepared so as not to violate any of the kosher dietary restrictions but seemed all the same unpalatably alien. For a fleeting moment, I felt sorry for this tormentor of my youth, wondering at the constricting circumstances that had produced her.)

Jane inhabited two successive mouse-holes, to be exact, over the almost fifty years she lingered on in the apartment I grew up in. She eventually moved into the even tinier maid's room behind the kitchen, where she sat and smoked and ate skimpy cheese sandwiches and wrote birthday cards in her unmistakable forward-slanting handwriting. She never forgot the birthday of anyone in the family, not once during all the years, nor did she forget the birthdays of any of the next generation—the proliferating grandchildren who eventually came to a whopping twenty-one in total. That was touching of her, I suppose; just as it was touching that, like it or not, my family must have become more of a family to her than her original one.

Jane died at the age of eighty-eight one hot July day in 2004, after a brief hospitalization; she was a wizened ver-

sion of her former self by then, still hobbling around in my
mother's employ, still given to her meager, straight-backed
pleasures. I cried at her funeral, where she lay in full cosmeti-
cized glory in an open casket—so different from the Orthodox Jewish tradition I was familiar with, which dictated a
closed pine box without ornament. The service took place
in a little side room at the Frank E. Campbell Funeral Chapel
on Madison Avenue that my mother had paid for, with pitifully few in attendance.

I'm not sure whom or what I was crying for, those noisy
sobs erupting out of me; I remember my mother looking at
me incredulously. (Most of my siblings were in attendance,
but they managed to keep their emotions in check.) Perhaps
it had to do with the discrepancy between the elegant
milieu of Campbell's, where I knew the funerals of the rich
and famous were often held, and the barren reality of Jane's
life. Or perhaps I was crying in response to the words of the
resident clergyman who guided the brief service. This priest
spoke in the most gentle of Father Christmas affirmations,
to the effect that Jane—whom he compared unconvinc-
ingly to the biblical character Ruth—was an enterprising
spirit who had crossed the Atlantic to take care of us and
had loved all of us like her own. His sanguine belief was in
stark contrast to the sense of bereftness the occasion inspired
in me: a lack of grief, more than anything, just a sense of
bewilderment that Jane had grown old and vulnerable and
I was middle-aged and there was a void where a bond
should have been.

Sometimes it seems to me when I look back that things
could not have been so bleak and cold as I remember them.
Then again, I can find no evidence that they were otherwise.
So you see where all this has left me: outside most people's

frame of reference and without any illuminating context except my own. There are Jane's outlines, waiting to be filled in, if only so that she will get up off the page and make herself felt as something other than a flickering, ominous shadow in my head. Or perhaps it is already too late for that. For when I look around, everything is gone or in the past—my childhood, Ed Sullivan, Indian Walk shoes, Jane herself—and I am left to conjure with ghosts.

12

The simplest test for gauging depression that I know of—
infinitely more efficient than answering a long list of questions about how much you've been sleeping, or how little
you've been eating, or how often thoughts of suicide have
flashed across your mind—is the arrival of the first beautiful day of the year. The sort of day Dorothy Parker balefully
serenaded: "Every year, back Spring comes, with the nasty
little birds yapping their fool heads off." The sort of em-
blematic day they're always composing song lyrics about,
when the normally indifferent world nudges you, like a
persistent shoe salesman, and says: *Try me, I've got a couple
of tricks up my sleeve that will make you smile.* The kind
of day that hints at green shoots, and splashes of yellow light:
nothing autumnal or wintry in sight. It might arrive right on
schedule at the start of spring, or it might arrive radically
out-of-season, but the symptoms are always the same: the
sun is out, the skies are clear, the air is charged with the possibility of happiness, and everyone suddenly seems to be
holding hands with someone else. It takes a day like that to
make me realize that the way I feel—which is like sticking

ever closer to the walls of my home, clutching at my skin for cover, avoiding unnecessary distraction from the deadly beat of my own deadly thoughts—is not a natural or even an inevitable condition.

One of the most intolerable aspects of depression is the way it insinuates itself everywhere in your life, casting a pall not only over the present but the past and the future as well, suggesting nothing but its own inevitability. For the fact is that the quiet terror of severe depression never entirely passes once you've experienced it. It hovers behind the scenes, placated temporarily by medication and a willed effort at functioning, waiting to slither back in. It sits in the space behind your eyes, making its presence felt even in those moments when other, lighter matters are at the forefront of your mind. It tugs at your awareness, keeping you from ever being fully at ease in the present.

When I'm depressed it's hard—almost impossible—to keep track of the reality that even the most extreme depression will pass with time, or can be made to pass more quickly with the help of medication or therapy or some combination of both. It is not, for instance, "the blight man was born for," which happens to be death and is, in point of fact, unavoidable, even for those lucky people who've never had a suicidal moment. The phrase is from the poem "Spring and Fall," which was written by one of my favorite poets, the self-loathing nineteenth-century Jesuit priest Gerard Manley Hopkins. I imagine Hopkins as having been fat and white and sweaty, reeking of despair. In the sonnet "My Own Heart," he wrote: *My own heart let me more have pity on; let / Me live to my sad self hereafter kind, / Charitable.* He may, in fact, have been thin and pristine, but what I do know to be true is that he had an ongoing lover's quarrel with God and that he died in his rooms at the top of a building that was once part of University College in James Joyce's Dublin and now houses a sleek restaurant.

It is probably all but impossible from a contemporary perspective to avoid at least nibbling at the speculation that Hopkins's anguished bid for signs of divine attention—his "cries like dead letters sent / To dearest him that lives alas! away"—was a sublimation of his homoerotic urges. But what I find more interesting, and far more moving, is the poet's pre-Freudian approach to his own undeniably depressive nature, which leads him to interpose his religious calling between himself and his conviction of hopelessness; it is his lack of faith he blames for his condition, rather than his genes or his childhood.

I wake and feel the fell of dark, not day, Hopkins wrote in another poem. Lives there a depressed person who doesn't recognize this sentiment, who isn't familiar with the feeling that the end of a night's sleep is the end of recumbent escape—that to be awake is to be hauled back into a pained consciousness? All in all, the number of days that I've woken up with anything but a deep longing to burrow further under the covers, the better to embrace the vanished night, add up to pitiably few over a lifetime. What would it be like as an adult to open my eyes with a feeling of even mild anticipation? For many years now, the only periods of my life during which I can recall waking up with something approaching receptivity to the day ahead are those in which I have started certain energizing medications.

But even on medication, there is nothing tempting enough to make me want to rise, much less shine—not even a languorous morning at a tropical resort, where all that awaits me is a prettily set breakfast accompanied by the sound of chirping birds. Not even the fact that I have always loved lying in the sun, soaking up the rays. Aside from sleep and the numbing of awareness that can occur during a certain sort of sex, only tanning provides the kind of self-obliteration that enables me to forget the blackness. It seems significant in this regard that many famous depressives, like the poets Sylvia Plath and Anne Sexton, have taken pride in the bronzed color of their skin. The ever-observant Plath noted to a young male correspondent during the summer of 1950, when she was seventeen, that she was so deeply tanned that women stopped her on the beach to ask what suntan oil she used. But the real fanatic was Sexton, who loved the sun so much that she sought out beach resorts even when she had to sit under an umbrella because of the Thorazine she was taking.

I can remember waking up in an elegant hotel in Rincon, on the western end of Puerto Rico, for instance, where there were petals floating in a bowl on the bathroom sink and nothing but the sunshine and the ocean to fill my days, with a familiar sense of dread. I'm not sure what I was dread-ing, although I suppose I could have found reasons scattered about. I could, for instance, have pinned it to the piercing dissatisfaction with my body that would inevitably follow upon my pulling on a bathing suit, or the fact that I felt in-creasingly claustrophobic in the company of the man I was with. But there are always reasons, if you look hard enough; there is always a telltale cloud inside the silver lining. The point, of course, is not to look.

Hopkins's "Spring and Fall" comes with a dedication, "To a Young Child," and is a rumination on the awareness of self that is accompanied by the consciousness of mortality—both being part of a specifically human endowment. The poem begins: "Margaret, are you grieving, / Over Goldengrove unleaving?" Hopkins liked to put his own original touch on the language, stringing words together willy-nilly (he had a particular fondness for hyphenated arrangements, such as "dapple-dawn-drawn" and "blue-bleak") and scattering punctuation marks as he saw fit. I used to like to recite these lines out loud when I first read them; their sad music made me feel eloquently mournful, as if I were speaking on behalf of all the anonymous sufferers from depression. Sometimes I substituted my own name, just for the effect, like trying on someone else's coat: "Daphne, are you grieving, / Over Goldengrove unleaving?"

No one has ever asked me anything remotely as formal and gentle and just plain *comprehending* as this when bleakness overtakes me. They are more likely to say casual, disbelieving things like, "It can't be so bad," or gruff ones like, "Come on, try and pull yourself together." When I was young and despondent, they dispensed with even the brusque kindness of those remarks. "There she goes again," one or the other of my brothers would announce, rolling his eyes, when I would start on one of my crying jags. It would begin as a neighing sound through my nose, as though I were a filly coming 'round the bend, and proceed from there to something louder and weepier. Sometimes, when I wonder why this blackness got started so early and why it has stayed around for so long, it seems to me that it would have helped to look on myself as a kind of Margaret grieving for the end that awaits us all—to have that sort of elegiac perspective. As it was, I grieved over everything indiscriminately and no one ever inquired into it. "You like to be sad," my mother frequently said to me, with her usual Germanic lack of sentiment. As though it were a choice. Hopkins would have understood, I am sure of it.

I envy Hopkins his faith, complexly negotiated as it

was, and have often wished my own Jewish upbringing had
provided more of a religious anchor; I imagine a belief in
God must come with a dazzling sense of purpose. Somewhere along the way, however, I substituted a more tentative
and secular faith in the power of art to uphold and console.
I think I share with Hopkins not only a delight in words but
an underlying conviction that language can transmute personal pain into a shared grief about what living in the world
entails.

"Spring and Fall" ends starkly—"It is the plight man
was born for, / It is Margaret you mourn for"—and I suppose the poem can be read as an exploration of the sober-
ing idea that all paradises are lost paradises, and that to be
born is to be expelled from the Garden. It cannot be said to
be about depression—but of course, to someone who is
depressed, everything is about depression. And, too, the
implicit bereftness of Margaret made me feel less alone.
Although I recognize that people who aren't depressed are
not automatically superficial or inauthentic—terminally
perky, like morning newscasters—in my heart of hearts I
believe they are deluded. For some of us, the sadness running
under the skin of things begins as a trickle and ends up a
hemorrhage, staining everything.

Then a beautiful day comes along and throws the issue
back in your lap.

13

My mother was a victim of history, of catastrophic world events, in a way none of her children had been, and some responsive chord in her had hardened early on to any but the most compelling of disasters. For complicated reasons having to do with her father's political allegiance, she could not go to university in Palestine and was instead sent back to Europe in 1938 to attend a women's teaching seminary in Chernowitz, which is now in Ukraine; she got back to Palestine by the skin of her teeth. She also lost a clutch of close relatives in the concentration camps, including a grandmother, two uncles, and a favorite widowed aunt together with all but one of her five children.

I learned about the Holocaust when I was too young to understand its implications except personally: as a murderous hatred aimed at me. I remember looking at an album of photographs, taken by Nazis for their own documentation, depicting Jews having their beards cut off and being made to wash the streets on their hands and knees. My mother had acquired this album on one of her trips to Europe with my father; it was only much later that I wondered uneasily why she had thought to show it to me at such an impressionable age, before I could make sense of it.

I was equally unable to make sense of something else my mother did in this connection, which was to casually draw tiny swastikas on the inside of my arm with a ballpoint pen, starting when I was about eleven or twelve. This strange ritual, which first took place one evening when I was sitting next to her desk in the upstairs hallway, going over homework, was never introduced or explained, and eventually ceased as suddenly as it had begun. My mother drew the swastikas methodically and neatly, one after another, a daisy chain of swastikas. I remember watching with fascination, my heart beating wildly, although I couldn't bring myself to ask what she meant by it. I'm sure she would have made some kind of ghoulish joke if I had questioned her, playing on my childish fears, as was her way: "Oh, you know, I was one of them in my youth. Don't you know I'm a secret Nazi?" When I was young and unhappy she would tell me to think of the concentration camps and nothing would seem so bad by comparison. Rather than a useful perspective, the extreme tactic simply instilled guilt in me for being unhappy in the first place.

Did my mother suffer from survivor's guilt of a specialized, previously undocumented sort? On some unarticulated level it was clear she had been traumatized as a sixteen-year-old by having to leave her beloved Frankfurt—with its marvelous zoo and the hills just outside the city, called the Feldberg, where she used to hike with her family—and, of course, by the discovery of what the Nazis had been up to. But on another level she seemed eerily cool-hearted about the whole thing, almost as though she identified with the aggressors.

This was something I wondered about even more after she showed me a short story, one of a group she had written after she came to New York in 1949 and signed up for a famous writing class taught by Martha Foley at Columbia. She had been serious about writing in English (her third language, after German and Hebrew) and had been considered talented enough to be taken on by an agent named John Schaffner, who represented Ray Bradbury and Craig Claiborne. The story in question was called "To Be One of Them," and told of a young Jewish girl who attends a Nazi rally and is transfixed by the impassioned oratory. The story was powerful but disturbing, and had more than a grain of autobiography in it, since my mother had actually been to just such a rally before her family left Frankfurt for good in 1936.

One of the things that struck me most about it, though, was the bravery it took to see beyond the usual strictures into the enemy's allure. It was like her, to take a different position than the one you would have expected her to take. As a mother, her unpredictability may have been problematic, but her subversive imagination—her impulsively denouncing herself as the Wicked Witch of the West, for instance, sparing me the trouble of having to draw her attention to her badness—was an aspect of her that I admired. Still, there was no doubt that the theatrics and sadism of the Germans excited her in some peculiar way.

What I also realized fairly early on was that Jane, although a tyrant in her own right, both feared and worshipped my mother, giving me an early lesson in the power of sadomasochistic attachment. My mother only once in a while broke out of her cool remove to offer Jane crumbs of approval that were all the more gratefully accepted for being so infrequent. More worrisome was my mother's endgame: Was Jane, certainly in many ways her "creature," also her instrument, exercising stringent discipline in her stead? Or had my mother refused to come to terms with the level of violence in her own household—insidious and actual—by the simple act of pretending not to know about it?

Years later, my mother admitted that she considered Jane to have been one of her "mistakes," explaining, with a dazzling degree of indifference to our welfare, that she had deliberately chosen someone we wouldn't grow attached to so we wouldn't end up preferring Jane to her as she had preferred Helena—the warmhearted woman who looked after her and her four siblings—to her own mother. I don't know if she accurately sized Jane up when she first met her, but she had certainly succeeded in ensuring her own preeminence in our affections by picking a caretaker who offered no competition. Still and all, I wondered: Whose side was my mother on? Mine or Jane's? The Jews' or the Nazis'? Why was she so fascinated by cruelty, the glint of metal, in herself and others? And above all: How could I make her love me?

14

Perhaps because my mother's admiration was reserved for a kind of intellectual facility that didn't show any sweat, I never fully imbibed, during those so-called formative years, the lesson of consistent application—of "chair glue," as the current idiom goes, or *sitzfleisch*, as the pungent Yiddish has it. It's a lesson Jews and Asians are supposed to be particularly good at instilling in their children, one that involves unceasing effort and the deferral of immediate gratification for long-range goals. It usually requires a steady parental presence offering coaching and reinforcement, and there wasn't that kind of presence for me or my siblings. I went through Jewish day school in a helter-skelter style, ignoring what I wasn't good at—math and science and who said what to whom in the Bible—and focusing on the subjects I liked: English and history, Hebrew and Talmud. (I liked the loop-the-loop reasoning of Talmud so much, those digressions that ingeniously led back to the main point, that I continued to study it with a private teacher after I finished high school.)

Although I was capable of demonstrating intense interest

in a variety of subjects, I tended to pull back from too much absorption in any one thing—lest I lose sight of the flickering, mutating essence that stood in for a more integrated self. I never understood how people made it through years of law school and medical school, grinding on and on, how their furies didn't upend them along the way. Which isn't to say that I don't have my own kind of tenacity—I can read for hours on end, and when I am involved in my writing I don't notice the passage of time—but that it is fitful and given to moods. I blame this on my inherent darkness, my inability to envision the day after today, but I must also admit to a certain faltering supply of will, self-discipline, call it what you like—that nub of stamina without which nothing major is accomplished. No wonder I fell upon Cyril Connolly's 1938 book *Enemies of Promise*, that ur-document of unfulfilled creative talent, with such avidity when I came upon it in my twenties, recognizing the outlines of my own dilemma in its exploration of foiled potential. "Somewhere in the facts I have recorded lurk the causes of that sloth by which I have been disabled . . ."

All the same, from childhood on I had been a voracious reader, desperate to escape my surroundings, and I look back on my summers in Atlantic Beach as one long, impassioned immersion in books. While other girls my age hung out at the beach, comparing tans and flirting with the cute lifeguards, I would lie in the garden in one of the tattered deck chairs with the webbing hanging out—my mother could never be bothered to replace them—and lose myself in reading.

My fare included modernist novels (Christina Stead, Elizabeth Bowen, Henry Green); fat biographies (Lytton Strachey, Diane Arbus, Edie Sedgwick); and shapely memoirs by everyone from Virginia Woolf's niece, Angela Garnett, whose *Deceived with Kindness* put a different spin on Bloomsbury than the one I had known, to a title I loved, *Tears Before Bedtime*, by a kittenish English writer named Barbara Skelton, whose husbands included Cyril Connolly and the publisher George Weidenfeld, and whose legion of lovers numbered among them King Farouk. I can still remember the ping of amazement I felt upon discovering Henry James, the way he wove the sinuous movements of his characters' interior consciousness into the elaborate orchestrations of his plots. For a while, my own life "hung fire," to borrow one of James's signature expressions, as I imagined myself into the life of Isabel Archer, standing on the verge of a splendid future but about to make a huge misstep—to be bedazzled by the wrong man, a girl after my own misled heart.

Then again, my sexual identity had been a conflicted issue almost from the start. It began with my precocious worrying that I was a lesbian, attendant upon my discovery of the word when I was ten, because I longed to sleep next to my mother in my father's place, and also because of the sense I had that men, like my father, were a closed-off territory. Added to this was my persistent fear that I was insufficiently (by which I meant imperfectly) "feminine," despite all evidence to the contrary. True, I got my period late enough (I was almost sixteen) to make me wonder whether I was going to get it at all, but when I finally did, my figure developed at an alarming rate, endowing me with large breasts that were all the more conspicuous because of my narrow hips.

Big boobs or not, there were other circumstantial developments—a few errant hairs around my belly button, and unruly eyebrows that grew together in the middle—that were somehow enough to persuade me that I wasn't truly, genetically female. I addressed my fear of being unattractively hirsute by undergoing the painful ministrations of an electrologist named Madame Geva, who worked out of a tiny, overheated room on Lexington Avenue, and left me with too wide a space between my eyebrows when she was done.

So it was that, decades before gender issues and queer theory became culturally fashionable, I would spend hour after hour in a bored therapist's office discussing my conviction that I was meant to be male. I suppose matters weren't helped by my mother's relative lack of interest in or cultivation of typically feminine concerns; as my sisters and then I came of mirror-assessing age, we never discussed clothes or hair or makeup or, god knows, our anxieties about our attractiveness to the opposite sex. Then again, these topics never seemed important to my sisters in the way they were to me, in part because they went to an all-girls' Jewish high school, whereas I stayed on at the coed yeshiva day school they had both left after eighth grade. It was crucial to me to be attractive to boys—to cover my bases, so to speak—even if I wasn't sure I was a bona fide girl. As if to compensate for the lack of attention feminine concerns were given in our household, I became an avid reader of *Seventeen* and *Glamour*, carefully noting down the skin and beauty products that I planned to acquire, beginning a lifelong habit of collecting far more lipsticks (as opposed to my mother's spartan reliance on one or two) and eye shadows than I could ever make use of.

My mother's decidedly masculine edge further confused matters. She was completely without coquetry or softness, or, indeed, conventional female allure. She had the sort of strong-featured good looks that are described as "handsome" rather than beautiful, and this aspect of her became more explicit when she wore certain clothes, in particular a black leather trench coat she favored that made her look like a member of the Gestapo. (A renowned shrink my eldest sister saw once described my mother as a "phallic" woman, a description that seemed more categorical than explanatory.)

Another, more psychological substratum contributed to my sense of feminine inadequacy, which was that I secretly believed I didn't have a sufficiently girlish brain. For one thing, I never laughed at remarks boys made that were meant to be funny but weren't, the way other girls routinely did to flatter them. For another, I sensed that I was too critical-minded for a girl, my thoughts angular and penetrating rather than round and accommodating, the way I thought they should be. It seemed to me that the whole point of thinking about something was to probe ever more deeply rather than to gracefully accept some less-than-satisfying statement offered up by someone else. I went so far as to imagine that I was a hermaphrodite, someone born with a dual set of sexual organs. Who knew but that there wasn't a tiny penis nestled inside my vagina, glinting with untapped power? I must admit that the feeling that there is something innately aggressive, even penile, about intellectual endeavor has never left me.

·

When I think of those years, I think of the dreariness of Sunday afternoons, following the enforced inactivity of Shabbos, when my sisters and I used to walk over to Serendipity, the boutique-cum-café on East Sixtieth Street, for hot chocolate and lavish amounts of real whipped cream after the occasional movie. These outings, let me hasten to add, sound cozier than they really were. For one thing, my two sisters and I didn't get along that well—at least, I didn't get along that well with either of them—and we saw fewer movies than I would have liked, thanks to my mother's unshakable belief that less was more, in all things but books. For another, when I look back on those Sunday afternoons, I have an overwhelming sense of loneliness. It was as though the loneliness had wrapped itself around my bones, as though it were something palpable that I would be able to touch, if only it weren't so evasive—like a shadow, moving forward or backward whenever I did.

In the years I'm referring to, when I was in my teens and twenties, the neighborhood around Serendipity hadn't yet been colonized with quite the same fervor it would be in the late seventies and eighties. It would take another decade before the store's hybrid atmosphere, with its combination of funky merchandise for sale in the front and its menu of retro-chic comfort food (chili, foot-long hot dogs, and outrageously fattening desserts) in the back or up the stairs, would acquire genuine tourist-in-the-Big-Apple, standing-room-only cachet. In the days when I used to go there with my sisters, Serendipity was frequented mostly by Upper East Side locals and a smattering of especially savvy foreigners staying at the Plaza or other nearby hotels. Then, too, Bloomingdale's, which was just across the way, hadn't yet opened its doors to Sunday shoppers. So the neighborhood might legitimately be described as being relatively unpopulated.

And yet it is also entirely possible that none of what I describe is true; maybe these subtle sociological shifts I have painstakingly observed in the attempt to persuade myself that there is some objective reality to my memories are not only questionable but beside the point. The real, factually unverifiable point being that in my mind, that stretch of Sixtieth Street between Third and Second Avenues where Serendipity was located has a permanent Edward Hopper-esque desolation to it. The block is always deserted and it is always four-thirty or five o'clock on a gray Sunday afternoon sometime in February. Or, again, was this sense-memory simply a projection of my own state—I the one who felt gray and deserted, my bleakness spread across the neighborhood like some form of tear gas?

It was at Serendipity that my mother bought me a Virginia Woolf doll for one of my birthdays, which she had read about one morning in *The New York Times* over her usual languid breakfast. The doll was artistically rendered out of cloth rather than plastic, a work of craftsmanship rather than a toy. She wore a knitted maroon cardigan over a gray wool skirt and had enchanting miniature letters tucked into a sweater pocket addressed to her c/o The Hogarth Press in a scratchy, authentic-looking handwriting. I took the gift to be a recognition—even an affirmation—of my passionate identification with this writer. Given my own intense fantasies of suicide, however, there was a part of me that wondered whether the gift also hinted at my mother's perverse sense of humor. Was she suggesting that my end would mimic Virginia's? I would sometimes take the letters out and slip a small stone or two into the doll's pocket instead, testing the waters only to then retrieve her from harm.

·

Meanwhile, behind the fancy address and the white-gloved doormen, things were falling apart. For one thing, none of us could get away, leave home, get on with it. Time would tell that it wasn't just me who had been left with a hole; we were all too full of holes, some more Swiss-cheesed than others, to make the transition into the outside world. We were all stuck to my mother, as if by glue, unable to stand tall without her; it was as though being away from her placed us in positions of unforeseeable peril. I was merely the canary in the coal mine, warning of things to come. I watched as my three older siblings went off, one by one, for what seemed to be an obligatory post-high-school year in Israel and ended up, one by one, in some kind of situation of high distress that required medical or psychiatric care.

One sister, returning midway through her year at an Israeli university, was unable to leave my mother's orbit when she arrived home except when she went to her psychiatrist. Another sister seemed irreparably weakened by her year in Israel, as though some vital fluid had been drained out of her; she, too, started frequenting a therapist. I could see that it was dangerous to leave, precisely because there were so many of us. There was always the chance no one would notice, much less care, that you were gone—that someone else would fill your place the moment you vacated it.

How else to explain this: When my older brother Ezra was in a deadly car accident in Israel (the boy sitting next to him was killed), neither of my parents saw fit to visit him for weeks—make that months—on end. After finishing high school at the same Jewish day school I attended, my brother had been forced over his protests to go to a yeshiva in Jerusalem instead of starting at Columbia, because my mother thought him lily-livered about religious observances. The accident occurred the day he arrived, when a cab he was in collided with an oncoming truck. Neither my mother nor my father bestirred themselves to board the next plane despite the fact that he was in a coma, needed skin grafts, was linked up to all sorts of machines for an extensive period of time, and would overall undergo five surgeries. This, too, despite the fact that Israel was not a distant, exotic destination but a place my parents regularly visited, where each of them had close family. Instead they depended on phone calls from various relatives who stepped in where my parents failed to.

I looked on and felt scared for my brother, for myself. How could it be that my parents didn't rush to his side—at least one of them? Wasn't that what normal, caring parents did when one of their children got injured? My brother, who was left-handed, had suffered severe burns on his left arm and could no longer use his left hand to write. Instead of picking up and going to see him, my mother was determined to show him that where there was a will there was a way: she wrote him a letter using her left hand, despite the fact that she was a righty. If she could do it, she pointed out, he could as well.

I looked on and couldn't figure it out: Was it simple indifference? Some Germanic form of tough love? What I'm trying to say, I guess, is that there was something monstrous and unaccountable going on for which there was no name. I can't remember ever discussing the aftermath of the accident with my siblings, mostly because my mother had done such a successful job of dividing and conquering that our strongest allegiance was to her rather than to one another. Far safer, I thought, never to even attempt to leave, to stick close to home, so my parents would remember I existed.

In this respect, I remember being dumbfounded by my sister Debra's decision to marry, at the relatively young age of twenty-one. The boy in question was finishing up Harvard Law School and wrote her long letters in a rigid print. (I analyzed his penmanship closely for signs of deviance, having inherited a rudimentary interest in graphology from my mother.) Her wedding was at the Pierre Hotel and she wore the plainest gown I have ever seen, a white dress of such unembellished simplicity that it resembled a nightgown.

To begin with, I had noticed none of what I took to be the telltale signs of romantic involvement, the blushing indications of love-struckness that might have alerted me to my sister's momentous next step. She barely talked about her husband-to-be and the most amorous act I had ever seen the two of them indulge in was holding hands. But what really stymied me was the fact that she was able to attach herself to and set up a household with someone other than our mother. Debra struck me as even less separated than I was; I, at least, put up a semblance of a fight, tried to counter my mother's overwhelming influence by dyeing my hair blond or bandying about threats to take up lesbianism. My sister, on the other hand, seemed to lend herself to my mother's imprint like a form of human clay, ready to be molded. I couldn't figure out how so habitually tentative a creature had gathered up the spirit—the courage, really— to choose a mate and solemnly walk down the aisle with my parents on either side toward a flower-bedecked *chuppah* before an expectant audience. Surely she had been the recipient of the same undermining messages as I (*You're not that important; You're helpless and a bit of a nebbish; Don't compete with me*), and had suffered the same steady erosion of self-worth.

As it turned out, my sister seemed even more connected to my mother after she married than she had been before, turning to her for the last word on everything having to do with setting up a home, from interior décor to what cutlery to buy. Friday afternoons Iva the cook would send over a complete Shabbos meal to my sister and brother-in-law's apartment on the West Side in a graduated series of pots and pans, ensuring them a Friday night dinner exactly the same as ours. Coming from another family, this might have seemed like an over-involved but essentially nurturing gesture. Coming from my mother, it seemed to stamp my sister as but a faint replica of her own strong self, incapable of overseeing her own domestic arrangements.

15

As far as my own hazy vision of a future was concerned, the only thing I was sure of was my passion for literature. I had been writing and reading poetry from the age of ten, and loved declaiming lines from John Masefield's "Sea Fever" or Robert Frost's "The Road Not Taken" to whomever would listen. It was something that spoke to both my love of language and my sense that there were feelings that language couldn't get at directly. I began publishing my poetry while at Barnard and went on to win the college's annual poetry award in my senior year. Nonetheless, when I was accepted into Columbia's MFA program in writing, it took me all of a day to decide it wasn't for me.

I went instead to Columbia's graduate school in English (I had applied simultaneously to both programs), where I became enamored of Samuel Johnson, Mrs. Thrale, and James Boswell and devoured the nineteenth-century essayists, but eventually dropped out after taking the written test but before completing my master's thesis. It was to have been an examination of the influence of Thomas Hardy's poetry on Philip Larkin's development as a poet. Larkin was not yet on everyone's radar screen but he had fascinated me, in all his crabbiness and unexpected leaps of empathy, ever since I had come upon a poem of his in M. L. Rosenthal's anthology of modern poetry in my first year of college. The poem was "Deceptions," about the aftermath of the rape of a young woman, and I was immediately struck by his use of vivid and unexpected imagery: "All the unhurried day /" the poem begins, "Your mind lay open like a drawer of knives . . ." (These were the same lines that Margaret Thatcher, whom Larkin greatly admired, quoted to him when they met and he challenged her to recite something from one of his poems.) I had done an enormous amount of work on the thesis, filling notebooks with quotes from scholarly sources as well as my own thoughts, but in the end I couldn't summon up the determination to bring it all together.

I was at heart a fairly academic type, fascinated by the close reading of texts and by following up stray leads spotted in footnotes. And yet it was somehow impossible for me to envision myself as being two things at once—as both studious, say, and attractive to men. For me it was either/or; I could be one thing or the other, but I couldn't be an abundant Sylvia Plath type, possessed of blond hair, long legs, *and* talent to burn. It was a version of the men-don't-make-passes-at-girls-who-wear-glasses axiom (and, indeed, my mother disliked me and my sisters in glasses), but taken up a notch. In the end my leaving graduate school had to do with my fleeing an image of myself as a plain-Jane sort, a Charlotte Brontë or George Eliot, stuck permanently in the stacks like a fly in amber. It was an image that bore little resemblance to my own physical reality, but seemed contrived expressly to torture myself into a paralyzing ambivalence about who or what I might become.

What did appeal to me, from the start, was writing to a shorter length, which the episodic nature of reviewing provided; it was a natural step to go from reviewing books and movies for the *Barnard Bulletin* and the *Columbia Daily Spectator* to writing about them for more professional publications, like *The New Republic* and *The New York Times Book Review*. For one thing, these assignments didn't require the sort of sustained effort I found difficult to muster. But perhaps more significantly, they didn't call upon the overriding sense of purpose—the conviction that I was, above all else, a writer—that more ambitious projects would have demanded.

And yet, within these confines, I was remarkably industrious. I subscribed to *Publishers Weekly* and tirelessly sent out query letters to editors, suggesting myself as the perfect reviewer for this or that forthcoming book. I was wary of aligning myself to a particular political position after my early experience at *Commentary*, where I had published several book pieces right after graduating Barnard but then failed to sound a sufficiently alarmist note about the post-sixties culture in a review of the movie *Looking for Mr. Goodbar*. This experience, along with a calamitous attempt at writing a book review for *The Nation*, in which I delivered an opinion about the psychology of a member of the Weather Underground directly at odds with the publication's agenda, had only strengthened my sense that I didn't want to be a spokesperson for either the ideological Right or Left. Other than that, I was willing to review most anything—new novels, biographies, literary studies—and kept myself open to being influenced and shaped by persuasive argument. I also began publishing short stories in *Mademoiselle* and *Encounter*, a British magazine originally funded by the CIA. Even as

I inched my way forward, though, publishing madly and striking up friendships with editors, part of me remained stuck in the long-ago past, with the eight-year-old who kept vigil by the hospital elevator lest her mother fail to visit.

In my early twenties I started writing a book column twice a month for a small highbrow magazine called *The New Leader*, which required me to wade through mountains of books and offer up crisp, knowing assessments that ran to about twenty-five hundred words and paid $50 each. The work often seemed both onerous and thankless, since I didn't know anyone who read the magazine and felt as though I might as well have been sending out messages in a bottle. But I enjoyed crafting the column, especially when I was midway into it and could see an end in sight, and liked going into the magazine's offices to go over my copy. The editor, Mike Kolatch, was a rough-and-ready sort who wasn't inclined to treat writers with kid gloves, but he also lavished a kind of care and attention on my prose that was nothing short of thrilling.

My pieces and stories attracted the notice of a literary agent named Harriet Wasserman, who represented a small group of distinguished writers, including Reynolds Price, Alice McDermott, and Saul Bellow, and who now offered to take me on as a client. I was still halfheartedly enrolled at Columbia and living with two roommates in a railroad apartment on 106th Street one hot August when Harriet invited me to accompany her for a weekend visit to Bellow's summer house in Vermont. Although I wasn't a slavish Bellow fan of the Martin Amis/Christopher Hitchens sort, I had loved *Herzog* and his epistolary effusions, and I was excited to be asked along.

Bellow was on his own—his fourth wife, a mathematician,

was off in the Schwarzwald—and I felt a little like Tuptim in *The King and I*, who is brought to the King to satisfy his roving eye. Harriet waited hand and foot on her most important client, literally sitting before Bellow and holding open hard-bound copies of "The Silver Dish," a short story of his that had appeared in *The New Yorker* and had now been published in a limited edition, for him to autograph. Bellow turned his considerable charm on me, going so far as to share his secret recipe for tuna fish, which included a dollop of ketchup, and playing his favorite classical records for my cultural edification. But I found myself resistant to his need for—rather, insistence on—adulation, and kept escaping the psychologically sweltering atmosphere of the house for long walks by myself.

By the weekend's end Bellow seemed puzzled, almost hurt, and I in turn felt that I had failed to live up to my part of the bargain, whatever it was supposed to have been. Shortly before I left, we were standing in his garden when he suddenly turned to me and said: "Be kinder to the male gender." I kissed him good-bye on the cheek and got into Harriet's rented car, where I immediately burst out crying. Despite all his show of masculine ego, I had suddenly felt Bellow's vulnerability. That, and the fact of my own frightened, armored response to his wish to be fussed over, overwhelmed me with sadness.

During this same period, I attended a dinner party given on Martha's Vineyard by Diana Trilling, the widow of the critic and teacher Lionel Trilling and a formidable critic in her own right. Diana was then in her early seventies; she was a vigorous hostess and excellent cook who had slightly bulging, hyperthyroidic eyes and a habit of pronouncing upon people and society in a way that brooked no disagreement.

She had begun airing her outspoken views as a fiction reviewer for *The Nation* in the 1940s, where she deemed Saul Bellow "talented and clever" but his *Dangling Man* "not the kind of novel I like," and judged Vladimir Nabokov's *Bend Sinister* as having had "by my count . . . four successful moments." Diana went on to write essays on the counterculture, included in a collection called *We Must March My Darlings*, although there would always be those among the backstabbing, self-enamored tribe known as the New York intellectuals, like Mary McCarthy and Hannah Arendt, who regarded her effort to obtain cultural eminence with suspicion and thought she did better at cooking than cogitating.

As I came to know her better, I discovered that beneath her highbrow stance, Diana also had an endearingly robust appreciation of the less exalted aspects of life, such as diets and movie stars and good gossip; this side of her can be seen in her 1981 book, *Mrs. Harris*, about the seamy murder trial of Jean Harris, a former headmistress who had killed her faithless lover, Herman Tarnower, also known as the Scarsdale Diet Doctor. Diana and I would eventually develop a close if complicated friendship—she would become something of a mentor and over the years we would spend Thanksgivings and share many long late-night conversations together—but on that first occasion I found her mostly intimidating, someone who crackled with energy on all fronts.

I was in my mid-twenties that summer of 1979, slim and tanned, with a fetching Jean Seberg haircut and a head full of Roland Barthes and esoteric film theory. I was staying with my friend Leon Wieseltier at the Vineyard home of the historian Daniel Bell and his wife, Pearl, although I was careful to disabuse onlookers of the notion that Leon and I were

lovers—we weren't—by insisting on a room to myself. I remember Diana was particularly nonplussed by our sleeping
arrangements; in her plummy voice, with its slightly British-
ified accent, she expressed a mixture of amusement and
dismay that my relationship with Leon was not sexual in
nature.

At Diana's dinner, I met William Phillips, co-editor of
Partisan Review, a publication the name of which rings an
ever-fainter bell but which occupied a position of cultural
prominence in the mid-twentieth century. Phillips had a kind
of laconic, shrewd intelligence and I think he initially sized
me up as brimming with possibility, someone who had begun
to make a name for herself as a writer at an impressively
young age. I would go on to publish poetry and a couple of
essays in *Partisan Review*, but after a while I would agree to
write a piece only to stagger off with a clutch of new novels
that suggested a trend toward, or away from, Realism, or
Minimalism, without much intention of actually producing
anything. True, I was unclear, once again, who actually read
the magazine and the pay was dishearteningly minimal. But
what really stopped me was the underlying sense of futility
that plagued me whatever I did—the thought of making all
that effort, like finally getting to a standing position in the
playpen, without anyone to applaud me at the end of it. Phillips knew none of this, but he saw what he saw: "You're scattered like dust," he told me. He said it affectionately—I don't
think he ever quite lost his faith in my native ability—but it
echoed like a death knell.

16

It is early winter 2012. At a dinner party I go to, the subject of antidepressants comes up and an excoriating critique of them that had appeared months earlier is quoted approvingly by several of the people present. The piece in question is a two-part attack in *The New York Review of Books*, written by Marcia Angell, a former editor-in-chief of the *New England Journal of Medicine*. It had cited the usual evidence for the prosecution, including the claim, based on clinical trials submitted to the Food and Drug Administration in the late 1980s and 1990s by companies seeking approval for new drugs, that antidepressants were only 25 percent more effective than placebos.

As I listen to the conversation I sense an unspoken investment in holding depression up to censure, as though it were still, after all these years, a fraudulent bundle of symptoms, an inflated case of malingering that everyone suffers from but that only a select, self-indulgent few choose to make a big deal about. No wonder people keep it a secret, especially people who are celebrated in some way, like the fashion designer Alexander McQueen, and have something to lose by revealing that they do battle with what continues to be treated as a suspect malady, *Prozac Nation* notwithstanding. I have often wondered whether it is depression's very failure to fit into a neat, easily recognizable category that contributes to the ongoing stigma that attaches to it. It never ceases to surprise me the way it brings out the partisan in people, leading them to diehard positions, to swear for or against it as a real disease, for or against medication. One of the guests speaks up weakly for his own regimen of Paxil but I say nothing, unwilling on this particular occasion to enter the fray.

Although I have been on antidepressants for three and a half decades, I continue to feel defensive about them, as though I were the scientific version of a fashion victim. I think protectively of my own panoply of multihued pills: pale pink and taupe, apricot and carnelian red, with a dash of light blue, a sophisticated amalgam of serotonin- and dopamine-tweaking agents (Effexor and Wellbutrin) along with a small dose of an antipsychotic (Abilify), which also works on neuro-receptors, as well as some uppers (Vyvanse, Dexedrine), which release dopamine into the brain to get my mood rolling in the right direction. Even as I faithfully took my pills I couldn't help wondering: Was I medicating a bad childhood or a chemical irregularity? And did it matter what the cause was if the drugs helped keep me going, steered me away from the thoughts of suicide that had haunted me ever since I was a young girl?

Then again, there are many factors that make depression and the chemical treatment for it uniquely vulnerable to questioning in a way that schizophrenia, for instance, is not. Depression is viewed as being on a continuum with normal sadness or unhappiness—"Everyone," an actress I interviewed once told me, "is a little depressed"—so there is far more latitude in not viewing it as a true pathological condition. Because its symptoms don't involve seeing green Martians or hearing robotic commands, it is easier to disguise—and harder for other people to detect. On top of which, not everyone who is seriously depressed is a depressive type per se, walking around with a hangdog expression, a shuffling gait, and an air of great suffering. I have hurled all the charm and wits I have at my disposal against my proclivity to depression, such that it would be difficult for even close friends of mine to detect how low I am at any given time. I can be near-catatonic, paralyzed by misery, an hour before I go out to dinner and still manage to hold up my end of the conversation with gusto. It's only after I get home and am stuck inside my own head again that I begin to sink. And it's only when I begin to sink that I remember why I am on antidepressants to begin with, which is that they seem to keep me from hitting rock bottom, sliding a floor under me so that my downward trajectory goes so far and no farther.

Still and all, here is a piece of heretical personal truth: despite the fact that I have been on antidepressants for much of my adult life, I have never been entirely convinced that there is something seriously amiss with my brain chemistry. (I have never been entirely convinced that depression is a "disease" as such, either, but more on that later.) I say this in part because I don't believe that it all comes down to genetics in any case—only 50 percent of our temperament can be traced back to our heredity—and I am enough of a believer in the effects of early experience to attribute a great deal of my chronic depression to an emotionally traumatic childhood.

I also recognize, however, that you can talk yourself blue in the face in a therapist's office about crucial failures of love or nurturance with little effect on the inner blackness you carry around with you. As a result, you might be pointed in the direction of medication, as I was by Dr. Alpert, the psychiatrist with a red beard and an intense gaze who explained to me when I was an anguished person in my early twenties, talking longingly of suicide, that my depression was an entity in and of itself, regardless of its root cause, and needed to be treated as such. Meaning that even if my original brain chemistry was fine, somewhere along the way it had been altered by my environment, so that I now needed this same brain chemistry to be re-jiggered once again.

Parnate was the first of a long succession of pills I was put on, after Dr. Alpert succeeded in convincing me over several sessions that even if it was my lousy childhood that had made me want to die in the present, these feelings had taken on a chemical life of their own. Dr. Alpert has been dead for decades, but I have never forgotten that what clinched the deal for me—made me willing, that is, to at least give medication a try—was his comparing my emotional state to an ulcer. "You can't speak to an ulcer," he said. "You can't reason with it. First you cure the ulcer, then you go on to talk about the way you feel."

Still, it was hard for me to agree to try medication for something that seemed so intrinsic to who I was—not something *out there*, like having a case of measles, but the state of mind in which I lived, so to speak, however negatively. This was back in the 1970s, before Prozac arrived and changed everything, when mood medication was still associated with bored housewives and *Valley of the Dolls* psychodrama, and psychoanalysis was still in fashion. But I had already put in fifteen-odd years in psychiatrists' offices by the time I saw Dr. Alpert and I was tired, unbelievably tired, of wanting to kill myself.

The theoretical view of depression on which most anti-depressants are based is that something is amiss with the biochemical system—that not enough of one kind of neuro-transmitter, or too much of another kind of neurotransmit-ter, is being released into the synaptic spaces in the brain. Parnate is one of a small group of antidepressants technically referred to as MAO inhibitors, which includes Marplan and Nardil as well. These pills have a sturdy, albeit unglamor-ous, reputation, but they come with a major drawback in the form of the dietary restrictions they entail—no red wine, hard cheese, pastrami, dark chocolate, or soy sauce—which one is free to ignore at the risk of provoking a poten-tially lethal hypertensive reaction. That first exposure to Parnate was something of a revelation: I was able to get up in the morning without feeling as though I were being torn, limb by limb, from bed, and I could entertain unhappy thoughts without getting stuck in a stranglehold of despair.

I have been taking one or another variety of antidepres-sants ever since, keeping apace on a personal level with the larger changes in the thinking about psychotropic medica-tion. This included being a guinea pig for the aforementioned Prozac, a serotonin reuptake inhibitor, in my late twenties before it was FDA-approved, at a point when Parnate no longer seemed to be effective. I was writing *Enchantment*, my highly autobiographical first novel, and involved with the man I would eventually marry, and by all rights I should not have felt as blue as I did. I was put on an unthinkably high dose of Prozac (eighty milligrams), and in a matter of weeks it had me so wired that I needed a sedating antidepressant—Desyrel—in order to fall asleep at night.

This particular combination of drugs ended up causing

a severe case of urinary retention—paralyzing my urethral sphincter muscle so that I could no longer pee on my own—and for six weeks one hot summer I had to catheterize myself several times a day. I also wore a plastic bag to catch urine that was connected to a Foley catheter and taped high up on my thigh, which made for an attractive sight when I went swimming. (Snapshots of me looking slim and tanned in a bathing suit with the unwieldy bag and its bright yellow liquid contents actually exist.)

For a while it appeared that my situation couldn't be reversed. My mother, as was her habit when it came to medical problems, acted weirdly nonchalant, as though the possibility of my remaining on a catheter for the rest of my life weren't worth bothering about. It was only due to the concerned intervention of my fatherly employer that I consulted a series of urologists, one of whom was completely stymied and another of whom blithely suggested that I learn to accommodate myself to life on a catheter—"Just go into the ladies' room in Saks Fifth Avenue and put it in," he advised in a strong New York accent. I finally found a doctor who experimented with various medications and succeeded in getting me to urinate on my own again. The whole situation was a hazardous one, inducing many a grim thought, but if this malfunction didn't put me off medication forever, I suppose nothing will.

Many years later, I continue to look upon my meds with a wary eye, and what should by now have become a reflexive gesture, part of my daily routine, is an action still weighted with unease and ambivalence. For one thing, no one, not even the psychopharmacologists who dispense them, studying their intake jottings and considering the odds, seems clear as to how these drugs work when they work or what damage they might inflict on their way to doing good. (In my case, I have a sky-high liver count, which is partially attributable to my meds.) If any of them worked conclusively, the researchers at Pfizer and Lilly and Merck wouldn't keep trying to find a better, newer, more lucrative drug, like Heinz's 57 varieties. So for now we are stuck with what comes down to a refined form of guesswork—a selection of some thirty-odd pills that affect neural pathways—dopamine, serotonin-reuptake and noreprinephrine levels and what-have-you—in not completely understood ways. There are, of course, new treatments for depression being developed all the time, including the use of the onetime party drug ketamine, as well as electrical implants that provide deep brain stimulation, DBT (dialectical behavioral therapy), and new forms of CBT (cognitive behavioral therapy). Not to overlook ECT, or shock therapy, which I have always been afraid to try but which my psychopharmacologist insists is "the most effective antidepressant we have," adding with a triumphant flourish, "It reboots the system." Then again, when I press him, he admits: "We don't know how it works . . . It's like hitting the brain with a sledgehammer."

As for the repercussions, the possible side effects of various medications, these are shunted to the side until such time as they must be dealt with. I have wondered variously over the more than three decades I've been on them whether I might one day keel over from some errant brain function, or suddenly start slurring my words. Then, too, there is a sense that I have ceded part of my autonomy in exchange for some incalculable relief from the burden of self—*my* self, such as it is. I fight against this perception by arbitrarily not taking my pills for a day or two at a time, or taking one and not the others in a forlorn effort to prove myself independent of their sway. On a number of occasions I've even gone off drugs altogether, sometimes at the suggestion of a shrink, sure that they are causing me irreparable harm in the form of weight gain, incessant fatigue, or memory blips. But, invariably, the effect has been unfortunate; I sink perilously downward before finding my way back to them again.

In the here-and-now, loaded up on drugs as I am—Effexor (450 milligrams), Wellbutrin (300 milligrams), Abilify (5 milligrams), Dexedrine (30 milligrams), not to overlook the medication I take at night, Klonopin and Restoril and on occasion trazodone—I'm not sure what else there is to be done to stave off what seems to be another bout of potentially immobilizing depression coming my way, flexing its muscle once again, lest I think it gone forever. On my desk sits one of those artificial light-boxes you're meant to use for twenty minutes every day to help battle SAD (seasonal affective disorder) and brighten your mood, which I avail myself of erratically, as I do everything. I've put it on today, hoping by flooding my brain with fake sunshine it will be fooled into thinking I am lying on a beach, but the hour is all wrong—afternoon instead of morning—and the warmth is faint, reminding me of the sun's heat not at all.

Lately I've also added something new to my regimen: an electrical device called the Fischer Wallace Stimulator that comes packaged in a sleek black leather pouch, like a Prada makeup bag. It consists of two round yellow sponges you soak in water and place inside earphone-type things that are wired to a gizmo that resembles a television remote; you then slide the sponges under a stretchy headband that holds them in place over your temples. After you click on the device, a pinprick of green light begins pulsing on and off, followed by a blinking yellow light, which sends a low current into your brain; twenty minutes later, there's a slight ping and the device turns itself off. I was apprehensive at first and kept thinking of it as a mini session of shock therapy, but it actually feels entirely benign. The device is supposed to help with all sorts of problems, like anxiety and mood and sleep, but at moments like these it's hard to believe that anything would help short of a new brain or at the least a different childhood, so that I wouldn't find myself in these straits to begin with.

Today, for example, I began to give in, the first step in an incrementally eroding process I recognize from other times. I slept away the morning, right through my midday therapy session, and rolled out of bed at two in the afternoon, hating myself for it. The apartment seemed hollow and shadowy, but even as I thought this I recognized the perception as a projection of my mood; it was the same apartment it had been yesterday, an apartment other people find warm and welcoming, an apartment I have lavished attention on. How everything goes askew when depression sets in, mislaid plans and all. I want to kill myself again because everything seems hopeless and loaded with pain everywhere I turn. Most of all I am tired of myself and my battles. All my choices seem wrong and now it's too late to undo most— any—of them.

First there was the confinement of my childhood, like an incessantly replayed loop of film, and now there is my adulthood, which seems like a prison of a different kind. Nothing makes sense to me. Everything seems permeated with meaninglessness, from the people filling their grocery carts at Fairway to the magazines I get in the mail. I've lost track of what used to keep me going, what made me agree to meet a friend for dinner at the Mexican restaurant on

Hudson Street or how I am capable of taking an almost childish delight in the search for a new shade of lipstick. I could go on and explain further but the truth is that no one is interested in why you want to kill yourself, no one really believes that you will, until you've already done it, and then it becomes morbidly intriguing to try and map it backward. I think of the British fashion editor and stylist Isabella Blow, who apparently talked about killing herself forever, boring her stylish friends in their designer duds, only to surprise them all by eventually going through with it.

Yesterday in therapy I described my life as "horrific," which I realize is subjective and self-dramatizing. I know I lead a privileged existence, I know there are people hanging on by a thread in Haiti and the Congo and elsewhere across the globe, I know, I know, I know. There are earthquakes and plane crashes and famines and droughts and terrorist attacks everywhere. But I still can't get out of being me, a desperado from way back, an eight-year-old who cried so much they stuck me in a hospital for observation, a person who doesn't know how to feel good in the present. In the background Leonard Cohen sings "Ain't No Cure for Love" in his growly, jaded voice. Make that "Ain't No Cure for Life," I think to myself, and call it a day.

17

I am lying naked in bed with a man who is making me feel good, in a box-like apartment somewhere east of Third Avenue in the Eighties—the kind of apartment an aspirational lawyer might rent for himself in the late 1970s. I am twenty-five, still fiercely self-conscious about my large breasts, and still a technical virgin. I have been sexually intimate with men for a few years now, since my early twenties, kissing and groping, on rare occasions shedding myself of clothes, feeling the touch of skin against skin, but I have held on to my virginity as though it were a medal—or, perhaps, a spoil of war—worth keeping against all incursions.

I recognize that my attachment to my virginity at this relatively late age has something to do with my Orthodox upbringing but it has even more to do with my attachment to my mother, some irrational sense of safekeeping I assign to her. Do I imagine myself to be my mother's lover, not able to give myself fully to someone else for fear of "betraying" her? The thought isn't fully formed, yet I feel it pressing against me in an inchoate fashion, rendering me resistant to men. For a while I worry there is something wrong with me in this area as in so many others, some piece of female anatomy that is incorrectly formed, making it impossible for a man to enter me.

And then finally on a night in late spring, so late it is almost morning, I yield to the careful, persistent ministrations of this particular man, and the deed is done. I am exhausted and he is even more so; we have climbed Mount Everest together and now look down on ourselves, spread against the messy sheets, triumphant. The next morning as I walk back to my apartment I stop at a phone booth to call my mother, who has recently told me to stop acting like the Virgin Mary, and deliver the news.

I bring my mother everything, inappropriately, all the details of my sexual life; it is a natural extension of my belief that I belong to her. "Mazel tov," she says now, on the other end of the line, her messages confusing as always. I had expected a different kind of response—more heated, somehow, not so la-di-da. Why isn't she making more of this, asking more questions? She is the Keeper of Modern Orthodoxy, a lighter of Friday night candles, but she is also selectively open-minded when she chooses. Unless she's something else, something less enlightened and appealing, something more perverse. She is—dare I think it even now?—a voyeur in disguise, peeking through the keyhole as a man plays with my nipples, then leans over to kiss me. We are involved in a virtual three-way; I bring her places she would not go on her own and in return I have her with me, always.

•

Those were the years my body spoke for itself, although I walked around in relative ignorance of my own nubile allure. Or it might be truer to say that I walked around in studied obliviousness of my own effect, unable to put together the me that was attractive—the me that came with high cheekbones, long legs, and almond-shaped "bedroom eyes," as someone once described them—with the me that was unacceptable, the me that was ashamed of shitting, that was stuck forever back in childhood with Jane commenting on the stink in the bathroom after one of us went.

The fall after I graduated college I worked in *The New Yorker* typing pool, consisting of a select group of young women who could tap out text at the rate of ninety words per minute; during the lunch hour we took turns sitting at the receptionist's desk on the eighteenth floor. In the summer months, I wore T-shirts and cotton pants, never anything more revealing, but years later one of the editors there told me that he and his colleague used to take a detour expressly to check me out. It is impossible for me to conceive of myself in this light, as a showcase of female sex appeal, and I often wonder if I would have acted differently if I had known my own value in that arena. Surely I would have flirted with some of the handsome cartoonists as my friend J. did, perhaps even ended up in bed with one or more of them only to have my heart broken.

As it was, I acted like a startled fawn around men, shy beyond telling until such time as I felt comfortable enough to let fly with my biting observations and undoting, ungirlfriend-like behavior. My breasts never failed to elicit male attention, whether from my young nephews, who ogled them unabashedly when we were in the pool together, or from Anatole Broyard, the *New York Times* book critic who taught a writing class at the New School, which I attended in my early twenties. Although I regularly disguised my chest by wearing large, man-tailored shirts and other androgynous fashions, Broyard once referred to me in class as a "Jewish Sophia Loren." I must have been pleased on some level to be compared to the buxom actress but another part of me felt like an imposter. (I would eventually have a brief affair with Broyard, as did several other women in the class. I remember his agile, scentless body and his recalcitrant penis, and how we talked companionably afterward in a small bed in an Upper East Side apartment he borrowed from a friend for just such trysts.)

The reality was that I didn't feel like a girl, or whatever it was I imagined girls were supposed to feel like to themselves, and my breasts were a symptom of that discrepancy. They seemed to belong to someone else, a brassier kind of creature than myself, and I would eventually, after much hesitation, have them surgically reduced in my early forties, from a double D to a small C, a decision I have pondered the wisdom of to this day. Part of me wonders whether I reduced them as a sort of penance—so as not to be in competition with other women, beginning with my mother and my sisters.

The almost complete lack of fatherly attention didn't help my confidence, either, from a man who saw me in passing every day of my childhood but never seemed to take me in. I have memories of myself as a little girl trying to sit on my father's lap and sliding off, like water. At some point I stopped trying to attach myself to him in a demonstrably affectionate way and resigned myself to being the pliant object of his odd gestures, like the one in which he would take my index finger and place it inside one of his nostrils, primed to pick his snot. I never knew what to make of this, how to read it for its underlying message. Was it a sign of love or, as seemed more likely, of contempt? Did it suggest a com-

forting familiarity or a debased objectification, with me reduced to a stand-in for his own finger?

These considerations, needless to say, would only occur
to me years later and they still remain incompletely processed,
despite all my efforts to examine them. (Even today, observing a father being tender with a daughter on a playground
or in the supermarket can put me in an off mood for hours,
reminding me of an absence that will never be filled.) What
I do recognize is that I have both tremendous yearnings and
an almost equivalent amount of animus toward men, which
together render me a bad candidate for successful hetero-
sexual romance.

•

The man I lose my virginity to is bearded and casually funny,
both pluses in my book. He acts more like a boyfriend than
any man I've known, helping me assemble bookcases from
Conran's in my subterranean little apartment way over east
on Seventy-ninth Street—a gesture I find endearingly and
competently male and one that I can imagine none of my
three klutzy brothers managing. We have an impassioned
time in bed, so much so that he deems it wise to invest in a
pair of pajamas so that we won't be up all night.

All the same, our relationship lurches rather than sails
forward. The truth is that I don't know how to act around
a man, what to do with my own near-rabid interest. I have
tended toward an obsessional style in love from the moment
I became sexually involved. Although I am riddled with
doubts about anyone I actually date, I am paradoxically unable to move on with any ease if a relationship doesn't work
out. I am always bereft, convinced that I have lost the one
person who not only understands me in all my complexities

but accepts me in all my neurotic behavior. Like the Orthodox medical student (bearded, again), who had praised my
body as "Amazonian" when we took our clothes off one
night on my parents' living room floor, only to then go off
to Israel and get engaged to a first cousin. I still shudder to
think of the ornately entreating notes I wrote him, trying to
lure him back.

Always, I am afraid I will be found out for what I know
myself to be: an abject creature, waiting, with legs wide
open. I act one way—sharp and gleaming—but inside I am
Bobbie, the aching character Ann-Margaret plays in *Car-
nal Knowledge*, yearning for more of her man, feeding on
lovesickness. Perhaps in unconscious response to this tendency in myself—or perhaps because the master/slave dynamic is encoded in my neurons, something I've absorbed
from watching the interactions between my mother and
Jane, something I've experienced myself at the hands of my
mother, who is forever hardening her heart, like Pharaoh
against the Israelites—I am drawn inexorably to starting
fights, to upping the ante. I am excited by displays of hostility, by the chasms they open up in the smooth flow of intimacy, and by the opportunities for dramatic reconciliations
they bring with them.

So it is that in between our ardent lovemaking, which is
better than any antidepressant medication I know of, I bait
the bearded lawyer, poke at his vulnerabilities, make fun of
what I insist are his irrevocably suburban ways (wearing a
gold necklace under his shirts, owning three different ski
outfits, hanging out with his male friends watching football
games). Instead of rising to the bait as I hope he will—one
argument after another leading to torrid sessions of makeup-
sex, an endless stop-start trail—he is at first puzzled and
then increasingly annoyed by my tactics.

One Saturday evening, as we are barreling our way down Second Avenue to dinner, I criticize him for some failure of sensibility and he brings the affair to a precipitous end by demanding that I get out of his car. I can recall with the sort of pained immediacy that I associate with only the most traumatic events phoning him for several nights in a row and proceeding to play Linda Ronstadt singing "Heart Like a Wheel" into the earphone, saying nothing but trusting that the lyrics will speak for me. I eventually inveigle one of my brothers into calling him up to explain that my acid tongue has always gotten the better of me but didn't mean anything. Needless to say, my now-ex-boyfriend listens politely to my brother's salesman spiel but remains unpersuaded.

After that, my taste irrevocably darkened. Instead of backing off when I sniffed a seductive misogynist, I went straight for the flame. I picked men who were drawn to my body but distrusted everything else about me, from my Park Avenue background to my bookishness. One of them, an expert in sexual maneuvers that left me breathless, drove out with me to Atlantic Beach one day in early summer when no one was there and proceeded to swim naked in the swimming pool, as if to leave his mark.

Years later, when I am involved with a man—another lawyer—with whom I finally play out my long-standing interest in sadomasochism, I show my mother the bite marks I have all over my body, deep purple-green bruises on my breasts, arms, and stomach. It is a Friday night, after Shabbos dinner; she is lying in her bed, in one of her short-sleeved cotton nightgowns, reading the latest issue of *The New Yorker*, and I want her to be disturbed by what I have undergone— spring to my defense, shed tears for what I have become— but she refuses, as always, to come through on my behalf. "I hope you enjoyed it," she says dryly. I feel defenseless and unprotected, the girl whose head Jane banged now grown into a woman who seeks out pain in the name of pleasure, a costly trade-off of my own devising. The circle closes around me; there is no way out, no friendly onlooker standing on the sidelines, shouting, trying to warn me off.

18

I was in my late twenties, working at *McCall's* as a writer of what was called service copy for features on fashion, beauty, and food ("Ground meat again? That old staple of the dinner table . . ."), as well as the occasional piece on subjects such as love addiction and what your voice said about you, when I received a message out of the blue that someone named William Jovanovich had called. It turned out that Diana Trilling had shown Jovanovich, a book publisher, a sheaf of my reviews for *The New Leader* and *The New Republic* as well as the two short stories I had published, and they had piqued his interest. I had been feeling understimulated at *McCall's* and was putting my energies into an emotionally warped but sexually fevered love affair when I wasn't batting away the despair that continued to plague me. I remember feeling wrung out on the day I was scheduled to meet Jovanovich, and that I had to make a herculean effort to put on something presentable and apply a bit of makeup. I knew it was important to make a good impression, but I also felt that Jovanovich would see through my efforts to charm him to the mess of anxieties that lurked within.

I don't know what kind of man I was envisioning, but Jovanovich wasn't at all what I was expecting. He was tall and handsome—he looked a bit like a smarter William Holden—with clear blue eyes that didn't miss a thing, and a rancher's rolling way of walking. I couldn't place him, but almost despite myself I felt an immediate rapport.

In a discussion over a champagne lunch at Le Périgord, on East Fifty-second street—Jovanovich's favorite French restaurant—he quizzed me as to what kind of novel I had in mind to write. I wasn't sure I had in mind any kind of novel, but I said it was to be about a sexual obsession. How many characters would be involved? he wanted to know. Three, I said, but two of them were me. He liked the answer and we struck a deal. I left my job writing copy for *McCall's* with the book advance Jovanovich gave me ($20,000, more than I was making annually at *McCall's*) and set off to try and write a novel.

Three years and many misspent days later, I published *Enchantment* with Harcourt Brace Jovanovich, at the age of thirty-one. The book came garlanded with endorsements from writers I admired to whom I'd suggested galleys be sent on a whim, with no expectation of their actually weighing in: Walker Percy, Frederick Exley, Stanley Elkin. There was also an ambivalent quote from Mary McCarthy, one of Jovanovich's authors, expressing astonishment at the novel's "lack of shame," although she did concede that "the book fascinates one by its openness." In the end, the sexual obsession peg had dwindled down to one scene late in the novel and the main drama revolved around my relationship with my mother and my inability to separate from her.

In many ways the book reenacted my habit of self-sabotage, placing the blame for my feeling of having been unloved on my insatiability rather than on my mother's incapacity. All the same, it caused a small stir in the incestuous Orthodox Jewish community from which I came, in part because my family was a fairly prominent one and in part because the book appeared to spill the beans with an almost embarrassing candor. In truth, I was torn between exposing my family and protecting it, and left out as much as I put in; in this sense the book was collusive, albeit unconsciously so. In the larger literary world, the reviews were mostly glowing and saw beyond the lighthearted aspects of *Enchantment* to its pained reality, but I will never forget the one in the Sunday *Book Review* that referred to the novel as a "strange, disembodied suicide." The reviewer was Southern and the world I was invoking must have seemed totally alien to her; all the same I wondered uneasily if she knew more than the other reviewers, if she had managed to read past my attempt to shape a compelling fictional narrative into the stark truth of my inner reality.

Jovanovich entered my life like a whirlwind, a godsend, a guru, a father figure—those terms and many others would all apply. He was a self-made man, a first-generation American born of a Montenegrin coal-miner father and a Polish mother; after attending the University of Colorado, he had gone to Harvard on a scholarship and studied literature and philosophy. He had begun at Harcourt, Brace & World as a textbook salesman and advanced rapidly to running the company, eventually tacking his name onto the original one and expanding its holdings to include SeaWorld, the marine theme park. When I met him he was in his early sixties, imbued with limitless energy, wide-ranging curiosity, and extraordinary powers of concentration. He read voraciously in literature and politics, and had befriended some of the more intellectually muscular writers he published and personally edited, like Hannah Arendt, Mary McCarthy, and Diana Trilling.

Although the word "brilliant" is bandied around readily in general discourse, Bill Jovanovich is one of the few people I have met who strikes me as genuinely worthy of the term. I remember sitting next to him on the camel-leather seats of the corporate plane as we flew to his summer house in La Malbaie, Canada, feeling buoyed by the mere fact of his presence. He was explaining some esoteric company strategy, his light blue eyes ablaze with excitement at the germination of a new project. He told me once that he would have liked to become an architect, but I'm not sure any one profession could have held him.

I was more than a little in love with Bill—and he, I suppose, with me. In his presence, I felt both alluring and whip-smart; one quality no longer contradicted the other. Despite the romantic undertones—he wrote me long letters in slanting India ink offering all sorts of advice, on everything from the right hotel to stay at in London (Brown's) to the right way to treat book publishing (like Bloomingdale's: go in, get what you need, and leave)—and notwithstanding the rumors that circulated within the gossipy publishing network, our relationship remained virtuously chaste. I remember once talking to him in the swimming pool at his home in Canada and wondering for a moment what it would be like to kiss him, really kiss him, not just a peck on the cheek. But my fantasies remained just that, fantasies. I gradually got to know his family, becoming friends with his gracious Southern wife, Martha, who shared with me her recipe for crab cakes, and staying with their daughter, Martha, Jr., in her London apartment.

After I handed in my novel I went to work as an editor at HBJ, acquiring books directly with Bill instead of having to run them by the editorial and marketing staff. He had a fax machine and a Wang word processor installed at the rose-colored vinyl desk in my bedroom, well before I or anyone else had heard of these devices, so that I could work from home, as he knew I preferred to do. In a typically extravagant gesture, he also flew me to SeaWorld to be kissed by baby Shamu, the original orca whale born in captivity. I remember being scared out of my wits as, in front of an excited audience, I climbed a small stepladder that put me in the vicinity of Shamu's snout; when I touched her skin it felt impermeable, like the hood of a car.

And so began one of the most productive periods of my life. Several years earlier, Bill had infamously fired most of HBJ's New York staff in a single day, which went down in publishing history as Black Tuesday, and abruptly moved the company's publishing division to San Diego, which is where he had decided to live after leaving New York. He kept himself removed from the hurly-burly of publishing, which earned him no small degree of enmity from agents and other editors; he was seen as arrogant and whimsical, both of which perceptions had some truth to them. For me, though, he was supremely confidence-inspiring, affirming me both as a woman and as an intellectual, and allowing me to inhabit both aspects simultaneously. He was always willing to stop everything to read the proposals I passed along that required a quick turnaround and he also provided me with the financial wherewithal to acquire "big" books that were out of reach for many of my peers at other houses. With Bill behind me, urging me on, I went about carving out a place for myself in the insular world of book publishing.

Soon enough I learned how to hold my own at auctions, where the object was to get the book away from other interested editors without overbidding on it. Bill and I were both lovers of the movies; I quickly swept up biographies of Gig Young and Cary Grant, the latter detailing Grant's early homosexual affair with Randolph Scott. Bill was also independent-minded, enabling me to buy one of the first books written about AIDS—a riveting memoir called *Borrowed Time*, by Paul Monette—when other publishers were still wary of the subject. I began to have a vision of the sort of list I wanted to build, a mixture of the literary and the commercial, the quirky and the mainstream, with an emphasis on good writing. I realized quickly enough that the sort of nuanced, psychological novel that went under the rubric of "literary" fiction was a hard sell and although I continued to acquire novels and short stories that appealed to me, I was increasingly drawn to buying nonfiction, whether a swashbuckling history of Nike, a biography of the writer John Kennedy Toole, or a tale of drugs and mayhem in Hollywood featuring a show-business promoter named Roy Radin.

My schedule became increasingly hectic; I flew to London and Frankfurt to meet with foreign publishers; to L.A. to meet with Motown honcho Gordy Berry; and to Washington, D.C., to meet with former Ronald Reagan staffer Donald Regan. I was also making over six figures, far more than I ever could have imagined just a few years before, and employing two assistants as I tirelessly wooed leery agents, who doubted Bill's commitment to book publishing, over expensive lunches and dinners. It was a vertiginous transformation, one that I found difficult to fully absorb. It didn't help that my mother regularly mocked my swift rise, raising her eyebrows in disbelief whenever Bill sent a company car to pick me up. *Just who did I think I was?* Then I brought in the house's first bestseller in a number of years—Regan's *For the Record* (ghosted by the talented Charles McCarry)—for which I oversaw the editing, marketing, and publicity. The book landed a front-page article in *The New York Times* on the day of its publication, and not long afterward I was made a vice president and associate publisher of the company.

But if Bill was like a good parent—perhaps the first I'd ever had—he had come very late to the party. I continued to harbor a desperately unhappy and besieged counter self, which went undercover during the daylight hours when I had to function but reasserted itself at night and on the weekends. I might be possessed of enough intellect and poise to hold my own with music moguls and former Secretaries of the Treasury, but right under the surface I was held together with safety pins and bravura, still unable to get up in the morning or to fall asleep without drugs, still chronically constipated, still dependent on my mother to define where I began and she left off.

Then again, for a person as racked by ambivalence and indecision as I was, the steps to full-fledged adulthood were destined to be faltering ones, no matter what it looked like from the outside in. I had watched as my older siblings tried to take flight only to end up crashing back to earth in worse shape than when they left. With their examples before me, I knew better than to attempt a full escape into the wider world; it was bound to fail. I mean, you could go through the motions of independence—go to college, have a boyfriend, get a job, eventually even marry and have a child—as long as you knew where your true allegiance lay. And that was to my mother, of course, the beginning and the end of everything. And to the family, the original family, the six of us and the two of them, bound by misery everlasting.

This conviction didn't translate into anything you could see, of course; it wasn't as though I stood around, clearly shackled. To other people it might look as though I were a free agent, someone who could choose where she wanted to go and who she wanted to be. And, indeed, as the years went by, outsiders saw me as something of a "rebel": the one who didn't remain Orthodox; the one who wrote a novel that was treated as a lightly fictionalized memoir, so identifiable were all the characters; the one who married a man whose knowledge of Jewishness was so limited, he might as well have been a goy; the one who got divorced; the one who wrote candid pieces about her sexual peccadilloes and her family's attitude toward money.

Looking back now, I can see that I was the child my mother had designated to work out her unspoken conflicts with the life she had chosen: one which set marriage and children and religious observance above other interests. She had rebelled in her own way, after all, leaving the impecunious circumstances of her family's life in Jerusalem for New York and dropping some of the observances her own mother had kept—such as covering her hair with a *sheitel*, or wig, after marrying, and abstaining from wearing pants. She opened the door to the outside world a crack, but with the implicit assumption that I understood the implacable and unreasonable crux of the situation: *there was no getting away.*

Talk about a double bind! Part of me recognized that it was an irrational and dangerously airless way to live, especially since I had never liked being in my family's orbit to begin with. And yet this insight, honed and chiseled in one therapist's office after another—that my only hope lay in escaping under the net and slipping out of my mother's hold—didn't stand a chance when it came to actually going up against the feeling of lostness that was induced in me at the idea of breaking free. Who and what were waiting for me on the other side? No one and nothing, as far as I could make out, just a vast and indifferent universe, got up in the guise of a welcome mat. Such thoughts accompanied me everywhere, more or less overwhelming depending upon the day. Sometimes very little was needed to send me spiraling downward; so it was that, despite a booming career, I slipped from a functional depression to a state of paralysis in my early thirties, and ended up at Payne Whitney, the psychiatric clinic of New York Hospital.

My stay, which lasted only four days, was precipitated, at least in part, by my having broken off my engagement to Michael, whom I had been seeing on and off for six years, minutes before we were to spend a week in Mexico together. My mother had organized a small dinner party to celebrate our engagement; she had done it with her usual style, the table beautifully set, the long white tapers flickering. But within days of the engagement I felt the same uneasiness that would assail me after we got married, and this uneasiness mushroomed into a state of dread that flattened me completely.

I had been harboring a fantasy of psychiatric hospitals and what they might offer ever since I read F. Scott Fitzgerald's *Tender Is the Night* at the age of sixteen or seventeen; I was particularly taken with the idea of Dr. Dohmler's vine-covered sanatorium in Zurich, "the first modern clinic for mental illness." Its cultivated multilingual clientele and

French windows that opened onto "a blue sea of sky" seemed a perfect backdrop for the romance that develops between the newly minted psychiatrist, Dick Diver, and the lovely young patient, Nicole. Further encouraged by movies like *Now, Voyager* and *David and Lisa* and books like *I Never Promised You a Rose Garden*, I began shaping a vision of psychiatric hospitals as soothing, hushed places that embodied some magical fusion of therapeutic sophistication and cradle comforts. From what I understood, you could regress there to a degree of immobility that would, paradoxically, allow you to blossom into emotional health. You might even fall in love with some other privileged, tormented person and acquire some sexual experience while you were at it.

The reality was dizzyingly dismal. I was scared at Payne Whitney, which seemed more like a holding cell for drug addicts and other assorted miscreants than a benevolent place in which to get well. I made frantic calls from the phone booths on the unit, which retained a sickeningly pungent smell: a mixture of stale urine, chewing gum, and cigarette-infused air. To calm myself down, I scribbled my observations in a loose-leaf notebook, trying to follow Henry James's advice that a writer should be a person "on whom nothing is lost," and use my stay as grist for the mill. I transcribed overheard remarks, such as one made by a painfully thin girl who floated disconsolately around the unit like a modern-day Ophelia: "I'm addicted to ice cubes. I just need to chew on them. Maybe for the vitamins." And I hoarded my own perceptions: "2 thumbtacks in my room," I studiously noted. "Could you thumbtack yourself to death?" I espied one romantic prospect on the unit, a young guy with a beard who struck me as sullen and mysterious—no doubt because he was wearing a body cast and was rumored to have jumped out the window. But by the time I had worked up the nerve to approach him, his room was empty.

I got out of the hospital after less than a week, in time to have one of my periodic lunches with Bill Jovanovich. I felt tentative about seeing him—would he be able to detect that I had recently been whiling the hours away in a loony bin?—but after the first glass of Dom Pérignon my anxieties dissolved. We talked with the same intensity with which we had always conducted our conversations, against the muted, expertly orchestrated background of Le Périgord, with its clinking of crystal and china, and the arrival on silver trolleys of shimmering dessert soufflés that had to be specially ordered and were presented as though to the sound of trumpets. Although only a few days before I had been hobbled by panic, for a moment under Bill's all-protective wing I felt almost invincible.

19

I never got it together to make the sort of wedding album that people used to make (and for all I know still make), with "X and Y's Wedding" embossed in gold lettering on a leather cover, followed by the date. I still have, all these years later, a box of photos on a shelf in a closet that I was supposed to go through and choose from for precisely such a book, which had been paid for ahead of time by my mother. I kept postponing the task of looking through the photos and deciding which to include; something about having to study those posed images of celebration—all the dressed-up grown-ups and children—made me feel profoundly sad just to contemplate. Maybe it had to do with the discrepancy between the elegant look of the affair, which had taken place in my parents' apartment, and my chaotic experience of being a bride, outfitted in full bridal regalia bought in a mad rush at Kleinfeld's, the famous bridal emporium. At any rate, before the photos were chosen for the wedding album, Michael and I got divorced.

•

I had been utterly apprehensive about getting married; it was something I knew I was supposed to embrace even though I wasn't at all ready for it, not even at the antique age of thirty-four. The truth was I wasn't ready to do anything that involved leaving my mother in such an official, wholesale fashion, and the decision to marry had been made not in a blurry, love-struck moment with my husband-to-be, but under far stranger circumstances. Less than a month before the wedding, Dr. E., the female therapist I was seeing at the time, scheduled a session for my mother and myself, at which the three of us discussed the probability of a marriage between Michael and me working out as though we were placing odds at a betting parlor.

You would have thought that the fact that I had broken off our engagement only months earlier didn't augur well for our future, but no matter. My mother opined to Dr. E.—a young and inexperienced blond WASP analyst who was clearly no match for this embattled-but-entwined Jewish mother-daughter duo—that I was "loyal." "That's one thing you can say about Daphne," my mother repeated in her heavy German accent. "She's very loyal." Ergo: once I got married, however much I kicked and struggled, I would stay married. This implicit line of reasoning seemed to carry the day with Dr. E. and the date was set for three weeks later, to ensure that I wouldn't have enough time to reconsider.

In addition to everything else, I remained deeply unsure of my femininity and the various roles—girlfriend, wife, mother—attendant upon it, and standing under a *chuppah* bedecked with white flowers on a late November evening before the group of about seventy people who had congregated in my parents' living room would do little to clarify matters. As the assembled guests watched me walk stiffly down the staircase in an off-white gown that added pounds to my figure and had an unbecoming bunny-like pom-pom on the back, some of them must have assumed that my hastily convened wedding was a shotgun affair. Whereas for me it was a different sort of masquerade: What was I doing there, dressed up in the costume of a bride, when I was already irrevocably linked to my mother?

My first reaction to most transitions continued to be one of desolation, which must explain why I sobbed myself silly on my wedding night as my brand-new husband looked on in disbelief from his side of the bed in our beige-on-beige room at the Regency Hotel, a few blocks away from my parents' apartment. He had purchased a pair of black silk jockey shorts in honor of the occasion, a gesture I found both touching and a little hokey, and which somehow made me sob even more.

•

In the girlish fantasies I entertained for my future I rarely conjured up an image of a husband but I always saw myself with lots of children—three or four, at the least. My early passion for playing with dolls mutated into an abiding interest in babies and young children, and when I became an aunt in my early twenties, I transferred my substantial reserve of maternal energies into being an exceptionally devoted one.

I adored babysitting for first my nephew and then my niece, arriving at my sister Debra and brother-in-law Lewis's apartment early to help give the children baths and get them into pajamas before their parents left for the evening. Once the front door closed after them, I settled down to the serious work of entertaining Noah and Erica, the latter still in a crib, on the way to coaxing them to sleep. Their bedroom was decorated in bright colors, red and blue and yellow, and boasted a charming night-light in the shape of a carousel that cast a cozy glow over everything. I played countless games with them, many of my own invention, before reading them a bedtime story or two, usually finishing up with *Goodnight Moon*, which neither of them could get enough of. The three of us would squash together on Noah's narrow bed, like castaways about to set off on some great voyage, while I read. At some point, when Erica's eyelids began to flutter, I would pick her up and put her in her crib. Then I would lie back down next to Noah and continue discussing which food we would elect to eat all the time if there was only one food item left in the world. Would it be rice with gravy? Or spaghetti? Or perhaps chocolate?

After my nephew had gone silent and all I heard was his soft, even breathing, I continued to lie there, caught in a tangle of thoughts, unwilling to leave the dark room for the lit-up apartment on the other side of the door. If I concentrated hard enough, I could split myself into two, peel the years off one part of me and imagine myself as a well-looked-after child, lovingly tended to by the adult half of me. It was a slightly surreal exercise in re-parenting, one that went well beyond the discussions of healing neglected and wounded "inner" children that I would read about in the therapeutic literature by John Bradshaw and his ilk in the years to come. I felt for a moment as though I were my own "good enough" mother, seeing to needs that hadn't been attended to when they should have been.

I identified strongly with young children, seeing myself as a responsive, would-be adult in their midst who understood their joys and sorrows with harrowing intimacy.

(Years later, it made perfect sense to me when someone told me that one's views on abortion depended on whether you identified with the mother or the child. Although I theoretically subscribed to the correct liberal views on abortion, I sympathized with those who saw it as murderous, and couldn't imagine ever having one myself.) In later years, as my other siblings married and had children of their own, I became the go-to aunt at family gatherings during the summers at our house in Atlantic Beach. I liked heading down the block to the ocean with a small gang of excited kids and building sand castles or making cakes for an imaginary bakery, just as I liked organizing a game of my own freewheeling concoction called "Boarding School."

This last was a bizarre but infinitely adaptable mixture of *A Little Princess*, *Oliver Twist*, and the musical *Annie*, which my nieces and nephews vied to take part in. You had to be orphaned or have at least one physically mangled parent to attend the school; then, once you were accepted by me, the school's tyrannical headmistress, you had to sign on for a series of backbreaking daily chores as well as a choice of demanding studies. I was forever barking out orders and there was always a child who felt overlooked or that he or she had accepted the wrong role. But the game had its own twisted logic and there was something about all the melodramatic harshness and mistreatment that my nephews and nieces found strangely satisfying. (Many years later I would write a profile for *The New York Times Magazine* about Daniel Handler, the author of the Lemony Snicket children's book series, and thought I recognized in the ghoulish happenings that characterize these books some of the same spirit that informed "Boarding School.")

All this interaction and maternal role-playing ideally

should have prepared me for becoming a mother myself. Certainly it was something I had thought about for many years, far more than I had ever thought about becoming a wife. I loved the vision of myself holding a baby at my hip, careless but prideful. Such fantasies made it possible for me to imagine that I might reach this life passage without too much angst, too much painful trafficking with my demons. But that was to underestimate their power, not to mention the black haze that stalked my every move, lying cunningly in wait until an opportune moment presented itself.

•

I became pregnant—for the first time in my life, at the age of thirty-five—on my honeymoon in Hawaii, at a Maui resort that seemed disconcertingly built to host thousands of people rather than couples bent on intimacy. It was the only night during our embattled honeymoon on which Michael and I consecrated our once-impassioned amatory union by having sex. I had been inattentive about birth control for years, in part because I had been told by a gynecologist that I would have trouble getting pregnant on my own (I had been diagnosed in my mid-twenties with polycystic ovaries, a hormonal imbalance that led to irregular periods and potentially compromised fertility), and in part abetted by the rationalization that I wanted to have a child more than I wanted to be with any particular man and therefore didn't need to use contraception. Apparently my psyche—or, perhaps, my hormones—needed the legal sanction of marriage to enable the reproductive process.

As it was, I had begun to feel trapped by marriage almost from the moment I entered its portals. I felt as though all my other identities—as a writer, book editor, aunt, friend, daughter—had been vanquished by this one single act, reducing me to a character called a "wife," who was in turn defined by a "husband." Feminism may have come and gone, leaving other women with a greater sense that their autonomy was not necessarily hampered by the state of being married, but the minute we officially became a couple, I felt I was no longer anything but the woman wedded to Michael. Already on the way to JFK I felt panicky, as though I were inhabiting an alien being who happened to be carrying luggage that belonged to me, and that there was no way of shedding this creature and recovering my former self. Added to this, I was grief-stricken at what felt like the loss of my mother, the ceding of her primary role in my life to another person—a man, my husband, someone I wasn't sure I wanted to be with in the first place.

Looking back on it, from the vantage point of having lived without a man for more than a decade and having entertained the thought that I may not have the psychological equipment to be in a sustained and up-close relationship, I feel sorry for what my ex-husband must have gone through. I would get up in the morning in our impersonal but pretty room by the ocean and proceed to sit numbly at breakfast on the terrace with Michael, who exclaimed anew each day over the wonders of papaya. Afterward, on the long stretch of beach, I hunkered down in a chair, reading a mirthless hard-backed tome on the narcissistic personality by a psychiatrist named James Masterson, while Michael cavorted with the waves. He went to look at coral reefs and other local spots on his own, like a vacationing widower, while I remained engrossed in my book.

I recognized that I wasn't acting wifely but felt helpless to do otherwise. I raised my face to the sun, imbibing my beloved rays, and wondered, once again, what was wrong with me. Perhaps I was meant to live on a commune, lose my problematic self in the service of the larger good as I worked side by side with other women in a hot kitchen, all of us dressed in faded, nun-like clothes. Perhaps I was meant to make my way through the world on my own—live more on the edge, like Amelia Earhart, or bear a child as a single mother and write radical manifestos. Or perhaps I wasn't cut out for heterosexuality to begin with, there was always that possibility: Was I concealing a deep Sapphic urge out of fear that I wouldn't fit in with family or friends? Given my singular attachment to my mother and lack of paternal connection, it would have made perfect sense for me to become a lesbian—except for the crucial fact that I had never felt sexual desire for a woman.

Meanwhile, Michael inquired if I'd like to accompany him on a whale-watching expedition, which was the last thing I wanted to do. The most exertion I could manage was to take walks and the occasional swim. In truth, I felt psychologically so precarious that I imagined myself disintegrating whenever I looked into the bathroom mirror—as if my face were about to fragment into pieces in front of my eyes in my own personal version of a horror movie. I couldn't figure out what I was doing on this laid-back island, with its many T-shirt and surfboard shops, and with this man permanently installed at my side. In addition to being in a quasi-dissociative state, I was suddenly besieged by guilt for abandoning the religious observances of my childhood. I hadn't been Orthodox for more than a decade now, but I had dipped in and out of the context of Orthodox Judaism as I pleased, trekking frequently to my parents' for Friday night dinners, occasionally showing up in shul on Saturday mornings, and imagining that I might return to its confines one day with an equally faithless but all the same religiously knowledgeable mate by my side. Now here I was, married to a man who—aside from having a mother who liked to make ethnic dishes, like brisket and kasha—was minimally conversant with Jewishness and had none of my nostalgia for all that had been left behind.

•

After our ten days away, I returned to the city tanned, despondent—and, unbeknownst to me, carrying a child. Although I should have been thrilled to discover this fact, especially since I had doubted my ability to get pregnant in the first place, I instantly felt trapped by the future barreling its way toward me. How was I going to deal with being a mother when I was still locked in an ancient war dance with my own mother, still looking for confirmation of her love? And what about the father of this child, who just happened to be my husband, who was part and parcel of this claustrophobic arrangement called marriage that I had impetuously stepped into after years of vacillation? Where did he fit in? Nothing seemed clear, except that life was hurtling ahead, with or without my cooperation.

20

I read recently of a study that, utilizing PET scans, has identified a potential biomarker in the brain that can predict whether a depressed patient will respond better to psychotherapy or antidepressant medication. This sounds like a step forward and no doubt there will come a time when brain scans will be able to create 3-D images of the landscape of despair. But in the interim I plug up my psychic holes with large quantities of both therapy and medication, hoping one will stick where the other fails. I imagine the inside of my head as scarred and bloody from the battles that have been waged there. I can't tell anymore whether it's my chemistry acting up or the ancient griefs I carry with me rearing up in response to a present provocation, the old nature/nurture conundrum: I only know it hurts to have to go on.

I have spent more than four decades and gobs of money in psychiatrists' offices, exhuming my memories in an effort to understand their pernicious effect on me; indeed, I could be said to be a one-person boon to the faltering therapeutic industry. Do I have trouble with *object constancy*—with holding on to other people, keeping them in mind when they are not in front of me instead of letting them drop over the edge—because my mother regularly let me fall off her radar? Am I skittish about the thrust and pull of intimate relationships because there was no one to rely on *except* my inconstant mother? Then, too, was it inevitable, given my nonexistent relationship with my distant and often terrifying father, that I would end up fearing men as much as I was attracted to them? Inevitable that I would get married to a man I was fiercely ambivalent about, and equally inevitable that I would get divorced? Could I have been anything other than lonely as an adult, given how lonely I felt as a child?

To this day, I don't know what I feel about the whole therapeutic enterprise, whether I would have been better off never delving into the wreckage. I don't really believe so; in many ways I think therapy has saved my life, offering me a means of understanding myself and the family I came from. It is because of the shrinks I've seen, all of them, the talented and the not-so-talented, that I can say, with the poet John Berryman, in the first of his *Eleven Addresses to the Lord*: "I am still here, severely damaged, but functioning." All the same, the business of self-disclosure remains a curious and slippery one, despite many years of practicing it; there is always so much one is tempted to sidestep, if only in the interests of preserving an already deflated sense of dignity—so many crevices of shame and regret and pure, undiluted guilt that seem hazardous to pry into. Do you admit to your long-ago bout of shoplifting in Sephora that reveals you for the petty criminal you are underneath your show of moral exemplitude? Or the inexcusably cruel remarks you hurled at your daughter in a fit of ire? Is the relief of confessing to your sins in an officially nonjudgmental atmosphere worth the writhing inner discomfort that accompanies it?

The curious thing is that, although both my parents are dead, I feel breathless with anxiety when I talk about the past in a session even now. I am hardly able to finish my sentences or provide telling details, although you'd think the ongoing narrative of my story, pieced together as it's been over the years, would flow easily by this time. Why am I still protective of those who did me ill, so afraid to render a final verdict? Is it masochistic or self-preserving—or a bit of both? Then again, what can you do with the knowledge that there was something ineffably wrong with your family, the only family on offer?

I think of an eminent shrink, one of a growing cast, I consulted in my mid-twenties when I was skittering toward another depression. He had an office at Payne Whitney and was known for his rapier intelligence. I believe he had met with my parents about one of my siblings before I saw him, but in any case he leaned over at the end of the hour and said, calmly and decisively: "You know, both your parents are crazy." I felt a stab of sorrow upon hearing these words—for myself, stuck with crazy parents, and for my parents, who didn't know they were being written off as crazy by this psychiatric eminence. I realized as soon as I heard it that I would repeat his verdict to my mother, if only because I told her everything, and that in the process of relaying his words to her they would lose their power. My mother would surely dismiss them, as she dismissed everything she didn't want to look at, with the strange-sounding German word for nonsense. *Quatsch!*, she would say, putting an end to the matter.

While I am on the subject of psychotherapy, I shouldn't overlook the crucial matter of the listening Other, the therapist him- or herself. In my many years of therapy I have never developed a set of criteria by which to assess the skill of a given practitioner, the way you would assess a dentist or a plumber. I tend to attach to the latest therapist more easily than would make sense, given my generally vigilant critical powers, and then at some point he or she will reveal some insurmountable failure—a tendency to speak in homilies or an inability to retain a piece of information I consider crucial—and I move on. And yet, although my faith in the curative potential of therapy has taken many knocks over the years, I persevere, convinced of the power of my unconscious life to misdirect me, to keep me stuck in the captivity of my childhood. It is, admittedly, a slow and incremental process, not to mention an expensive one, this attempt to untangle the threads of one's interior life in forty-five- or fifty-minute sessions several times a week, week after week, month after month. I understand how other people can look at it as a folly—as a waste of time and money, lacking in concrete results—but for me it has been invaluable.

21

It is late on a Saturday morning in October and I am lying in one of two twin beds pushed together in my brothers' old bedroom, unable to move because of the din in my head, the rush of violently tinged thoughts that keep coming at me. My hair is unwashed and I am wearing a crumpled nightgown, as though I were in an ongoing state of recuperation. I am thirty-five years old and suffering from postpartum depression, although no one has seen fit to articulate this diagnosis as of yet. My mother has come in to say hello on her way to shul, acting as though all is well. She knows otherwise, knows that I am thinking obsessively about drowning my weeks-old daughter in the bathtub— the same one where Jane used to give me wordless baths— because I have told her as much.

Part of me loves Zoë and everything about her, from the smells of baby powder and diaper rash ointment that cling to her after she has been washed, to the way she flaps her chubby legs in the air when she is happy. My daughter is very cute-looking, with a ruff of red-blond hair that stands up like a rooster's comb, a rosebud mouth, and an easy disposition. She is not given, like some other babies, to wailing noisily until her face turns red; when she cries she does so gently, ingratiatingly, as if not to disturb the universe.

But I also feel hemmed in by her, overwhelmed by the constant presence of such a needy being. And right underneath this feeling, I feel enormous rage at my own unabated neediness, my sense of having been starved of the nutrients I myself needed in order to grow into a confident adult. Surely there is not room enough for both of us in this world: How can I protect her if I am still searching for a lap to crawl into? Surely she'd be better off if she'd never been born. I envision cradling Zoë's tiny body in my arms and pushing her head under the bathwater, how trusting she would be—I am the same person, after all, who nurses her when she's hungry—and how quickly it would all be over. I am aware that it would be a terrible, "sick" thing to do. No one would sympathize with me, I am aware of that as well. I would be viewed as monstrous, no matter the condition that led me to do it, as Medea incarnate. I would be carted off to a prison or a psychiatric hospital for the rest of my life. Nothing would be the same ever again.

Postpartum depression remains largely hidden in our culture, like other kinds of severe depression—and is, to this day, barely given its due as a legitimate clinical condition, although the recently issued recommendation by a government task force for all mothers-to-be to get screened for depression before and after giving birth is certainly a step in the right direction. Mothers who kill their children in such a state—Andrea Yates, for instance, who drowned her five children on a June morning in 2001, after suffering repeated bouts of psychotic postpartum depression—are often seen as nothing more than criminals, unworthy of empathy, deserving of only the most dire condemnation. I was

asked to write about Yates for *Talk*, a magazine started by
Tina Brown after she left *The New Yorker*; the magazine
went under before I could write the piece but not before I
had researched it. Yates's hospital records and other documents helped me to understand more of her case, revealing
the intense pressure put on her by her strange religious convictions and her husband to continue having more children.
Both the evidence of her acute psychological suffering and
the danger pregnancy posed to herself and others are there
in black-and-white, yet these factors were all but ignored in
the original rush to judgment.

Right after I gave birth, I moved back into my parents'
apartment together with Michael, Zoë, and a baby nurse
named Maria, who had been hired to help me through the
transition to motherhood. Maria was an elderly spinster of
German extraction and infinite Christian faith who had def-
inite ideas—indeed, a thoroughgoing methodology—about
how best to get infants to sleep without too much fretting.
Her approach involved tucking Zoë up into a tight bundle,
placing her on her stomach—always her stomach!—in a corner of the white wicker cradle that had been passed on from
one grandchild to another, and went on from there to a great
deal of rocking and patting on the back. Maria was also a
big believer in the power of the pacifier, although its use was
already looked down upon, together with that of playpens
and walkers, in the current ideology of enlightened child
care. I watched Zoë suck on her pacifier contentedly and
imagined that she was learning how to provide solace for
herself—a psychic process that is described by child developmental theorists as "self-soothing"—through finding consolation in that rubbery, invincible nipple. It was something, or
so it seemed to me, that I had never learned to do.

I was still working in book publishing—my recent

promotion to associate publisher had come with a new raft of responsibilities—and had negotiated two book deals while I was in the hospital, within a day of Zoë's arrival. My own one-bedroom on the West Side was a bit tight for all of us but I think the real reason I moved back into my parents' apartment for what was originally planned as a two-week stay (and ended up lasting three times as long) was because I couldn't resist my mother's offer to make a nursery for Zoë—and, by extension, to take care of me. She set up the cradle and a makeshift changing table in the small room off the boys' bedroom and bought some Carter's polyester onesies at the neighborhood Woolworth's to kick-start my daughter's wardrobe.

I cried rivers when I saw the onesies—not out of gratitude, but because I had hoped my mother would suddenly become expansive and buy my daughter a proper layette, featuring a baby blanket and matching outfits of softest cotton and touches of pink, the kind they sold at the posh children's clothing stores that had begun cropping up on the Upper East Side in the latter half of the eighties, in keeping with the vast amounts of new hedge-fund money. But that was to mischaracterize my mother as an affluent and indulgent grandmother, when she saw herself in another spirit altogether—as a tough-minded matriarch who didn't believe in spoiling anyone, not even infants. She steadily refused to rise to auspicious occasions with auspicious gifts; years later, when Zoë turned twelve, the significant age of a bat mitzvah, and might have expected a strand of pearls or a silver bracelet, similar to the gifts her friends received at their bat mitzvahs, my mother gave her a Timex alarm clock. Love or money, money or love, my mother scrimped on both, had always done so, and at some point I had begun confusing the two. Those Carter's onesies felt like a mortal blow because they suggested a larger withholding, a refusal to respond with unstinting maternal largesse to anything about me, not even the birth of my child.

Michael, Zoë, and I eventually moved back across town to my one-bedroom, urged on by Maria, who came right out and told me in her guttural accent, that my parents' apartment had "bad vibes." (This was particularly independent-minded of her, seeing that her wages were paid by my mother.) I think she was appalled by the lack of interest expressed by my parents in their new grandchild, but I don't think that's all she was referring to. There was some crucial deficiency she was picking up on that went beyond simple inattentiveness, some hardened form of indifference—call it a calcification of the heart or a failure of the bonds of affection—that must have stood out from the usual deviations in family interactions she would have witnessed in her line of work. It was the aberration at the heart of our family, the ties that bound in all the wrong ways and none of the right ones. It was what had made me inconsolable with sorrow as a young girl and rendered me inconsolable now.

•

Shortly after we got married, before we left on our honeymoon, I received a phone call from my mother asking that Michael and I come to my parents' on an upcoming evening, with no explanation given. The four of us met in my father's study, which signaled that it was an official occasion. After a few minutes of perfunctory chitchat—neither of my parents were good at warming up a conversation—my father said that he had asked us here because now that we were married we must surely be thinking of providing for the next generation. He didn't use the phrase "starting a family" because that kind of benign pastoral tone wouldn't have been like him. He went on to say that he wanted to help us with the purchase of an apartment, as he had done for my siblings, but he had one stipulation: I was to agree to sign a contract that I would keep kosher in our new abode. I was the only one of my siblings who hadn't remained observant—something my father knew implicitly if not explicitly, from my mother if not from me—and this was one way of correcting the situation, of bringing me into line.

I listened to all this in a state of dazed alarm, not having had any indication that my father's habit of control was so ingrained that he was planning to oversee my marital conduct. I looked at my mother, who sat next to me on the couch, and who had uncharacteristically said nothing. Feeling as though I had been thrown under a bulldozer, I sat in silence for a minute and then came out with the trembling assertion that I didn't believe in it. By "it" I meant the whole institution of religion, but I didn't want to be too specific for fear of insulting my father. I needn't have worried either way; he was already enraged that I had dared to state my article of nonbelief as though it carried any weight with him. "I don't give a shit," he shouted, with the emphasis on the word "shit," "what you believe in." His face had gone red and the spit flew out of his mouth. I felt that the sheer force of his fury would blow me to pieces. Michael, meanwhile, maintained a diplomatic—or terrified—silence. Before things could get any worse, he and I got up to leave.

Outside, as we walked along Park Avenue, I felt my heart banging loudly against my chest. I suggested that the two of us should try and make it on our own, without benefit of a parental infusion of money. For a minute I had an image of us as a feisty young couple taking on the city; we would be like Robert Redford and Jane Fonda in *Barefoot in the Park*, finding the comedy in making do, flying free of the family. Michael gave his wobbly assent but I could tell his heart wasn't in spurning my father's offer for higher principles. I'm not sure my own heart was in it, but it seemed important to me to at least pretend to be above such power-broker tactics.

About a week later I received a note from my mother on her light blue stationery saying that she didn't agree with my father's approach and was sorry it had happened the way it did. The issue of my signing a contract was never brought up again and shortly after Zoë was born we moved from my one-bedroom to a three-bedroom off Lexington Avenue; the apartment boasted an imposing entry that gave the impression of leading on to a much larger apartment than it actually did. This aspect was enough to impress my mother, no matter that, once past the living room, the apartment collapsed into a dining nook and a cluster of bedrooms one on top of the other. I took the closet-like third bedroom as my office and tried to like the apartment more than I did. Every time my mother visited she would look around the foyer approvingly and say, "It makes such a good impression"— whether to convince herself or me that I had made the right choice, I was never sure.

22

By the time I was back on my own turf—Zoë must have been about six weeks old—my depression had deepened. I didn't go into my office at HBJ but continued to work as best I could from home, although I was officially on maternity leave. I had acquired and edited a book that meant a lot to me, about the eerily symbiotic relationship that existed between John Lennon and Yoko Ono, written by a former live-in assistant. The publishing house was excited about the book's prospects and I talked frequently on the phone with the head of publicity about our marketing plans for it, which included a large first printing. Once in a while I ventured out to a restaurant near my apartment and met an agent for lunch, feigning enthusiasm for some project or other, smiling past the despair that gripped me, wondering if my eyes looked as sad as I felt.

Most days, though, I shuffled around my apartment in a nightgown until it was time to go to my therapy appointment. Or I arranged to meet my closest friend, Susan, whose daughter was nine months older than Zoë, and walk with her in Central Park, two mothers out with strollers.

These excursions usually ended with me sitting on a bench in tears, explaining to Susan that I couldn't go on anymore. The antidepressants I was on seemed to do little other than make me feel logy, sapping me of what scant energy I had left. I found myself thinking less about killing Zoë and more about killing myself. Sometimes, when Maria, who had agreed to stay on longer than planned, was out with Zoë, I would take a big knife out from one of the kitchen drawers and stare at it, willing myself to plunge it into my chest.

It was right around this time that the book about John Lennon that I was so committed to was abruptly canceled, without any discussion, after Yoko Ono sent a cease-and-desist letter from her lawyers to the recently appointed new publisher, who happened to be Bill Jovanovich's son. This change had happened abruptly, with no prior notice given to me by Bill to the effect that he was stepping down. Peter had some of his father's arrogance but little of his charm, and he and I had an uneasy relationship. Peter was corporate above all else and I think he both admired and resented my ascent in the company and in his father's affections. When he called to tell me that he had killed the book because of Yoko Ono's letter, I said without pausing to reflect, "I don't work for you, I work for your father." This was clearly no longer true, but even if it were, it was a provocative and undiplomatic thing to say. Within minutes of this phone call I was unceremoniously fired from my job at HBJ, my office kept under surveillance by two security guards lest I try and enter it, my high-flying career over and done with. I never set foot in the office again.

I felt as though I had been punched in the stomach; my professional identity was shattered, and with it my fledgling sense of being more than a damaged child. In the coming weeks I found it impossible to accept that Bill, who had so much faith in my abilities and whom I had felt far closer to than my own father, didn't come to my rescue. I faxed him a letter telling him how important he and the company were to me but never heard back from him. (Years later, he wrote me a letter complimenting me on a piece of my writing he had read, and attempting to take things up where we had left off. I regret to say I never answered it, putting off doing so until it was too late.)

·

When Zoë was six months old, I left her in Michael and our housekeeper's care, and went into a hospital in West-chester. The hospital was recommended by a psychiatrist I had consulted with at my mother's urging, a cultured Aus-trian named Peter Neubauer who tried to engage me about my literary career and seemed dismayed by my inability to do anything but shed tears in his office. My depression had taken an ever stronger hold since my termination at HBJ, and by the time I entered the hospital I had nearly stopped eating and was barely speaking.

This time around, the hospital had a misleadingly lyri-cal name, which made it sound more like a spa than a psy-chiatric institution. It was an hour north of the city and I was driven there by Conrad, my father's driver, on a week-day afternoon, accompanied by my sister Debra, who hap-pened to be in from Israel. We talked little on the ride up; I was lost in my thoughts and, even had I been able to form the words, didn't want to discuss how anxious the idea of going into another hospital was making me. The psychiatrist who ran the hospital was overseeing my care and seemed disconcertingly jubilant to see me. I said a weepy good-bye to my sister and then was checked into the unit I had been assigned to, where "sharps"—anything that might be assessed as a danger to myself or others, such as nail scissors or glass containers—were taken from my luggage. I was weighed, like an express package, on a scale in the nurse's office. I still remember my weight (138 pounds, which was a steep decline from my post-pregnancy weight of 180) and how strange I felt being away from Zoë. I had become very attached to her, despite my depression, and wondered whether she would notice that I wasn't there to kiss her good night and sing her "Numi, Numi," the Hebrew lullaby my mother had sung to me.

At first, the hospital seemed like a summer camp, with rustic cottages, green lawns, and a pleasant cafeteria. The staff was gung-ho about a type of therapy called Psychodrama, in which you punched pillows and pretended they were the father or the spouse or lover you were angry at or hurt by, while the other members of the group made encouraging noises. But, this vigilantly supportive atmosphere notwithstanding, I soon decided that the facility was run, quite matter-of-factly, as a business—that the fit took care of the unfit not only out of compassion but also the coolest of profit-making instincts. With the exception of myself, the hair-spray-drinking wife of a prominent politician, and a man who sang in the chorus of the Metropolitan Opera, most of the patients in my cottage worked at blue-collar jobs for companies that provided excellent medical coverage for psychiatric illnesses—places like IBM and Con Edison. It seemed to me that these patients stayed out their allotted time whether it was indicated or not, and were discharged promptly on the day their insurance ran out, even if they had talked about killing themselves the day before.

I remained at the hospital for five or six weeks, during

which period my mother visited once, regally carrying a gift of a T-shirt that was printed with the concert hall that bore my family's name thanks to my father's philanthropy. I was taken aback that this was what she had chosen to bring me—did she really imagine I'd walk around a mental institution wearing a T-shirt that said "Merkin Concert Hall"?—as if to remind me of how far I had fallen from the lofty heights that once were mine to claim. In another person's hands it might have been a cute gesture, but coming from my mother it seemed punitive more than anything else. Although my doctor had indicated a wish to meet with her, she declined his request.

Meanwhile, my father called once a week on the pay phone in the unit kitchen and we talked briefly; he asked if I found the place to my liking, as if it were a hotel. After the first week or so, when it was determined that I could go off the grounds, I started taking short outings with fellow patients to the bakeries and coffee shops that dotted the pleasant upstate village in which the hospital was located. Once in a while we were taken in a van to a movie and I felt as if I were on the other side of a mirror, part of an exotic group of "aliens" being observed by "normals."

On weekends, Michael would come up with Zoë in a baby carrier, together with Susan and her one-year-old daughter, Emily. He would go to some effort to dress Zoë in her most charming stretchies or overalls and sweaters, which I had carefully chosen at an Upper West Side store called Monkeys & Bears, but there was usually a button missing on the sweater or a hole somewhere in the fabric of the stretchie. These tiny details made me feel unreasonably sad, as though Zoë's well-being were being neglected in a more essential way during my absence. I would hold her on my lap as we talked, more hesitantly than usual. I loved the feel of her warm, wiggling body and the way her round brown eyes, under delicately arched eyebrows, followed everything. I tried to ward off the gusts of guilt that came at me for being away at this crucial period in Zoë's development. "Hello, noodle," I would say over and over again, kissing the top of her head or her velvety cheek. "Your mommy misses you a lot. Do you know that?"

After these visits I would return to the unit, with its faux-homey look, in a black mood, feeling more dislocated than usual. I couldn't figure out how I had ended up at this institution, playing endless card games with an obese lesbian who was on permanent disability for reasons I couldn't quite fathom and who had taken a distinct liking to me. Indeed, she told me that I could be a lesbian star, if only I cared to follow this line of romantic allegiance. I also had long conversations with my roommate, a tall and efficient-seeming woman who was planning to move to Israel when she got out. She didn't strike me as particularly depressed and seemed to have checked into the hospital as a respite from her ordinary life, with a well-organized bag of toiletries in tow.

It occurred to me yet again that not everyone saw psychiatric hospitals in the same magnified light as I did—as a hoped-for rescue or, alternately, as a last-ditch escape hatch to climb into, with accompanying feelings of shame and self-loathing, when all else had failed. In spite of the ubiquity of depression as a term in general conversation, I was fully aware of the cultural opprobrium that still attached itself to mental illness, and the even greater stigma that came with admitting that you had become so unhinged that you could no longer function. Indeed, it made sense to me that there were people who killed themselves rather than face the social and professional consequences of hospitalization. In her memoir *An Unquiet Mind*, the psychiatrist Kay Redfield Jamison recalls her panic at the thought of entering a hospital, even when she was at her most suicidal: "I was horrified at the thought of being locked up; being away from familiar surroundings; having to attend group therapy meetings; and having to put up with all of the indignities and invasions of privacy that go into being on a psychiatric ward . . . Mostly, however, I was concerned that if it became public knowledge that I had been hospitalized, my clinical work and privileges at best would be suspended; at worst, they would be revoked on a permanent basis."

When I wasn't lying on my narrow bed, anxiously staring at the ceiling, or pummeling pillows in Psychodrama, I sat in the smoky "lounge," playing board games or talking with other patients about their lives. The director of the hospital who doubled as my therapist had a hearty way about him and seemed prepared to sweep away all the vestiges of my former life, including Michael. "He's not up to you," he would proclaim. "You deserve something better." I didn't know what he was basing his opinion on, since he didn't know my husband other than to nod hello to him in passing when he came up to visit with Zoë, and I didn't quite know what to make of him and his convictions in general—that my parents were noxious and cheap, that I was meant for a bright, writerly future—although I continued to see him for a time after I left the hospital.

I emerged from the place with some stuffed animals that I had been given as going-away gifts; a batch of odd new friends—including the obese lesbian—with whom I had been told by the unit staff I wasn't supposed to remain in touch (but did); a taste for Crystal Light, a chemical-ridden drink that was served in the cafeteria; and a newly unde-luded sense of the institutional world.

Although I felt very tentative about leaving, something must have been internally renegotiated over those weeks in a subterranean way—beneath my ability to recognize it. Perhaps it was no more than my realizing that there was no rescue on offer, no amount of Psychodrama that would re-store my job at HBJ or fix my marriage—never mind fix my parents. I came home and gradually resumed my life where I had left it off, enjoyed playing with Zoë, and got back in touch with friends I hadn't spoken to in months. After some time I even started writing again, taking on as-signments with an enthusiasm I thought I had permanently misplaced, occasionally mining my own experience for material; a piece I wrote for *The New York Times*' "Hers" column about losing a scarf in a taxi became a stand-in for all losses, big and small, sung and unsung.

23

Within four years, despite my efforts to keep afloat, I was back in the hospital. I had been working as a freelance writer, writing pieces about the voyeurism inherent in watching movies and my resistance to attending my college reunion, as well as the book reviews that paid next-to-nothing but drew on a writerly side of me that I liked, discerning but fair-minded, erudite but not snobby. All the same, without an office to go to or an allegiance with a particular magazine, I felt professionally unmoored. I was on handfuls of prescribed pills that left me woozy and dry-mouthed but didn't seem to penetrate the severe depressive episode that had been steadfastly circling me for months, cutting off my air, sealing all exists. I felt unsteady in my being and caught up once again in long-ago grievances and privations.

I also felt propelled to get out of my marriage even as I realized I had never really given it a chance, never accepted Michael on his own terms instead of borrowed ones—modes of assessment that I had inherited from my parents but that didn't necessarily reflect who I was, much less suit Michael. The very qualities I had once been drawn to—his artistic bent of mind and ease with the physical world, what

I thought of as a kind of masculine fluency—now seemed of questionable value to the life we lived.

It didn't help that my parents had continued to view Michael as a foreign entity, a garrulous hippie imported from the terra incognita of California, or that he was unhappy and undervalued in his work, or that both of my in-laws were problematic in their own ways. Michael's mother, who had married his father twice and left him the second time when Michael was a year and a half, was a self-made woman possessed of great resourcefulness—eventually managing a lingerie store in Los Angeles. But she was also a stubborn and dominating creature who exerted her claims on her only child with all her might. Michael's much-married father, meanwhile, was a moderately successful Wall Streeter who had taken Michael into his business with as little graciousness and generosity as possible, paying him poorly and treating him like a personal handyman rather than a broker-in-the-making.

In addition to which Michael and I continued to fight, as we had from the moment she was born, over who was to be Zoë's primary parent, who possessed the know-how and emotional wherewithal to best look after her. Michael, who had two daughters from his first marriage, thought he was ideally suited to supervise every aspect of Zoë's care, from her diet (he insisted on feeding her broccoli every night as soon as she was old enough to digest it) to her toilet-training. I wasn't used to so much fatherly involvement and felt that my role was being usurped. But the bigger truth was that I had never stepped into the present with Michael, never really seen us as a grown-up couple, the parents of a child conceived between us. Despite the passage of time I remained, to paraphrase a line from one of my favorite writers, the novelist Malcolm Lowry, "a small girl chased by furies."

In the weeks before I entered the hospital, the usual

symptoms struck: I became paralyzed by anxiety, unable once again to get up and function, or read, or eat. At some point I packed a few items of clothing and moved back into my parents' apartment, mostly to escape the scrutiny of others, leaving my daughter in the care of my husband and Desi, our elderly Jamaican housekeeper. I didn't want witnesses to my radical deterioration, especially Zoë. When she was brought to visit me by Michael or Desi, she was her usual chatty self, eager to talk about everything from the illustrations on the backs of cereal boxes to the cute little boy on the television show *Barney & Friends*. It was crucial to me that she not sense that anything was wrong, yet the possibility that she had no idea of how I felt also pained me, making me feel far away from her.

I wanted to pick her up and hold her in my arms, inhale her freshly shampooed hair—hair the color of burnt sugar that regularly elicited admiring comments from women who paid high amounts to skilled professionals to mimic its nuanced caramel tones—until it blocked out the angry whirring in my head. But I lacked the energy to answer her nonstop questions or to invent one of our usual jolly games. "Let's pwetend," she'd say to me, at which I could only smile weakly. How could I keep up a fount of maternal enthusiasm when all I wanted was to lie down forever?

At this point, I was afraid of going outside, and spent most of my time sleeping. I shed ten pounds in as many days—which would have delighted me under any other circumstances, but felt irrelevant now. When I did venture from my bed to see my shrink, someone had to accompany me lest I lose my way—or never get started. Once again, I had been ruminating obsessively about killing myself, conducting a running internal debate on the preferability of one method over another. Jumping seemed the most satisfactory as a statement of my rage—splashy and decisive—but it was also the most scary, and potentially painful; pills were too female and too iffy; slitting my wrists seemed poetic, but, again, I wasn't sure how foolproof it was. I had finally hit upon walking into oncoming traffic as the best tactic; it might look accidental, and my daughter, who still slept with a night-light, would be spared the ordeal of grappling with the reality of my suicide as she grew up. On one or two occasions, when I insisted on going out by myself, I experimented with crossing the street on a red light against the oncoming traffic. An irate driver, who screeched to a halt within inches of hitting me, yelled, "Hey lady, are you nuts?"

I checked into the hospital, which was in midtown Manhattan, on the same day that I met for a consultation with a psychiatrist who had been recommended for his expert diagnostic skills. His office was in the hospital, where he was head of the inpatient depression unit. My mother, who had brought me in a cab, waited in an ugly reception area with aqua-colored plastic modular seating. The doctor wore a white coat, unlike other psychiatrists I had known, which gave him an extra air of authority. All the same, he seemed like a logical man, and I tried to get him to see things my way. I spoke haltingly, my voice dropping to a lower register than usual, mostly about why it was crucial that I kill myself. I didn't care anymore what caused my depression, I said, who or what was to blame. I felt exhausted by the effort to explain what seemed self-evident: there wasn't anything left to do *but* kill myself. It was a siren call I had been ignoring for too long and the time had come to heed it. I was prepared to be dead, I announced matter-of-factly.

The doctor, who sat behind a desk, asked me what I

wanted to accomplish—whom I wanted to get back at—and
I answered that I was doing it for myself. I simply wanted out,
I explained. He mentioned my daughter, and I said she'd be
better off without me. He assured me that I wouldn't always feel this way, and I answered that I couldn't remember
ever having felt any differently. It was at that point that he
suggested, quite casually, that it might be a good idea for
me to come into the hospital. I shook my head, but I felt a
surge of relief. Somewhere inside me I knew that he knew I
had come here because I could no longer remain on the outside, "moving from pain to pain," as Styron put it. Later that
afternoon, after sitting in the hospital cafeteria with my
mother, saying little except to ask her repeatedly whether
she was sure it was a good idea that I go in and what people
would think of me, I went back up to the doctor's office
and he escorted me into the unit.

24

Once inside, I felt strangely safe. I remember feeling most protected against my despair when I watched TV late at night with several other insomniacs. I had been prescribed sleeping pills, as had almost all the other patients, but I resisted the pills' effect (or, more likely, was inured to it after years of taking sleep medication), the better to enjoy those cozy hours when the unit was cast in darkness except for the nurses' station and the flickering, multicolored nimbus of the television.

I would sit in my robe and watch the eleven o'clock news, in which all the catastrophes and crises seemed to take on an almost anthropological cast, so far removed were they from the constricted life of the universe I now inhabited. After the news, the group of us would go on watching a movie or talk show, usually chosen with little disagreement. When the talk-show audience laughed, we laughed along with it. It was like staying on at the zoo after closing time, and not only finding yourself stuck in a cage with other strange creatures but discovering that you actually liked being there. I wasn't lonely, for one thing, which I often was at home. Although I wasn't living among friends, exactly, no one around me appeared

to feel much more hopeful than I did, which was a form of
company.

When I look back on the time I spent on 11 West—an
unlocked ward with about twenty beds, occupying half of
a floor—I think first and foremost of the sound of a Ping-
Pong ball being volleyed back and forth, an endless game
played in a small, still space, under the watchful glare of
fluorescent lights and a hospital aide or two. The competi-
tive spirit was surprising, given that most of the players were
heavily sedated. I used to play quite a bit with Bruce, a
patient in his mid-thirties who was tranquilized into a half
stupor, and who wore the same stained crewneck sweater
and dragging trousers for days on end. He was one of the
few men among a mostly female patient population, which
made me wonder: Where were all the depressed men? Drowning their sadness in alcohol, seeking diversion by going on
homicidal sprees? At some point, I discovered that Bruce
was the cousin of a friend of mine from childhood—a girl I
first met on the bus going to sleepaway camp, who wore her
hair in two looped braids on either side of her face. I thought
I could detect something of my friend in Bruce, a slight
querulousness, which made me warm to him, despite the
fact that he was hard to warm to.

The two of us were well matched at Ping-Pong, and we
played in steady volleys, both of us concentrating on getting the little white ball over the net so that it could be sent
spinning once again, making that satisfying *pok* sound when
it met the rubber paddle. I enjoyed those sessions and I sometimes entertained a vision of Bruce and myself, spruced up
in matching boy-and-girl outfits, like Mickey Rooney and
Judy Garland, playing in tournaments across the land. Ping-
Pong could be played at almost any time, but it was played

with greatest fervor after dinner, when people in the outside world were going to cocktail parties or meeting in restaurants or helping their children with homework.

Dinner on the unit was served at the nursery hour of
five-thirty. Trays of food were delivered on two steel trolleys, which were parked outside the large, windowed space
that functioned as the dining room and general meeting
place. You picked up your tray (meals were selected at breakfast on the previous day, via flimsy paper menus that made
everything sound more appetizing than it actually was) and
carried it into the room, where you looked for an opening
in the straggly lineup of patients, who sat across from each
other at two long, narrow tables, like monks. The whole
meal took about fifteen minutes, tops. During my first few
days, I wondered why people didn't linger, since it was a
relatively normal social opportunity in the midst of an abnormal social environment. But there was some intangible
pressure to hurry, to replace the trays on the trolleys as quickly
as possible—perhaps so that the aides could be done with
their day.

There was a TV at one end of the room and a pay phone
at the other; the phone would ring in the midst of whatever
wobbly efforts at conversation were being made and invariably disrupt them. Whoever answered the phone would act
visibly annoyed, as though he or she had been called away
from important business, and then leave the receiver to dan-
gle forlornly until the person for whom the call was meant
picked it up. Sometimes ten or more minutes would pass as
one of the elderly patients, retrieved from down the hall,
shuffled with excruciating slowness over to the phone. But
it was mostly the same two or three girls in their late teens
or twenties who kept getting calls, as though they had won

Miss Congeniality awards in the outside world and carried their charmed aura with them into the hospital.

The other detail I remember vividly is the astringent, not unpleasant smell of the detergent that was used to swab down the floors daily. Workers in gray service uniforms would suddenly appear with big aluminum buckets and stringy, gray-haired mops; when they left, the beige linoleum shone with an incongruous brilliance. The wastebaskets were also emptied every day, and the communal bathtub and shower kept clean, if not spotless. It sometimes seemed to me that an inverse relationship existed between the high standard of institutional maintenance and the quality of patient care; no one, it appeared, paid such loving attention to any of us. Although in theory you were in the hospital because you needed more emotional bolstering than was available on the outside, in practice the prevailing atmosphere, under the routinized monitoring, was one of benign neglect: *We'll leave you alone if you leave us alone.*

The hardest part of the day was the early morning. I always woke up—in my narrow bed, which I made up with hospital linens consisting of a single unyielding pillow, worn cotton sheets that were oddly comforting to the touch, and two paper-thin blankets—feeling bleak, wishing for nothing more than to go back to sleep. But unlike my life at home, where I also woke up feeling bleak, life here did not require me to put on a face to greet the world. After all, wasn't I in the hospital precisely because I had given up on the tiresome chore of self-presentation, of feigning a cheerful countenance, an onward-and-upward energy I didn't feel? Other people were out there, striving, hustling, competing, winning. You were in here, having temporarily retreated from the battle, attending to your wounds. True, patients were supposed to dress for breakfast, but after a few days I realized that no one made much of a fuss if you didn't, so I began appearing in a terry robe and slippers along with the other laggards.

I was usually one of the last to pick up my breakfast from the trolley standing in the hall. No plush bedside service here, as described by Sylvia Plath in *The Bell Jar*. No blue china decorated with white daisies, either, or scalloped glass shells filled with orange marmalade—merely an individual box of cornflakes or a plate of overcooked scrambled eggs. Clearly, I had been born too late: with the advent of managed care, drastically shortened hospital stays, and increased pressure to medicate rather than listen, private psychiatric hospitals, like so many other things in life, weren't what they used to be. The glamour days of nuthouses, when wealthy patients—"thoroughbred mental cases," as the poet Robert Lowell described them—strolled across two hundred acres of manicured grounds at McLean Hospital in Massachusetts, a site chosen for its beauty by Frederick Law Olmsted, were a thing of the past.

"Time hangs heavy in the hospital," Styron wrote in *Darkness Visible*. For me it wasn't so much that time hung heavy as that it began to take on a different, less imperative dimension, to recede into the background. For the curious thing about life on the unit was that, even after breakfast, the day never really started up. The hours passed, and at some point it became lunchtime and then the afternoon, and soon enough it was five-thirty. There were various interruptions, of course—the chief ones being your therapy session and the dispensation of "meds," when a queue would form at the nurses' station while each pill was laboriously freed from its individual plastic wrapping and dropped into

a tiny paper cup—but mostly you were at leisure to peram-
bulate in your own mind, peeking in at various nooks and
crannies. You could sit around, or lie on your bed, and muse
upon the basic question that you'd never been able to answer
satisfactorily: Did you want to live or die?

Indeed, from a certain perspective, entering a psychiatric hospital could be viewed as an implicit challenge to the
status quo—an affront to the defensive maneuvers, the self-
protective habits, of those who managed to soldier on. What
was so special, so delicate, about you, that you couldn't
bear up? (In Jane Kenyon's poem "Having It Out with Melancholy," a friend suggests, "You wouldn't be so depressed
if you really believed in God." I guiltily wondered from
time to time whether I would be less depressed if I had
stuck to the rules of my faith and remained Orthodox.)

I remember picking up a glossy magazine one day and
paging through its breathless coverage of anyone with a
claim on the spotlight. It seemed inconceivable that I, not so
long ago, had written for such magazines myself, had been
courted over expensive lunches by editors eager for my work.
For a moment, I felt panicked. Did anyone—not just at the
red-hot cultural center, but anyone—care that I had with-
drawn from the fray? Would people mourn me if I never
returned, never took up my place again? On the other hand,
perhaps withdrawal was the nobler choice: if my soul—
my psyche, my neurochemistry, whatever it was that had
foundered—was in need of mending, it comforted me to
think that maybe there was something flinty and superficial
about those who continued to rise at the shrill call of their
ambition.

In the end, I left the unit late one morning after the ten-
thirty staff meeting, with a suitcase and two shopping bags

filled with my accumulated possessions. I had stayed about three weeks, and although I don't think I was in dramatically better shape at the end of them, I do know that I felt a growing aversion to being in the hospital, and that the psychiatrist who had initially urged me to check in was now urging me to go home. Part of me was afraid that if I didn't leave I might become like Lillian, a patient on the unit who both frightened and fascinated me, like the proverbial bag lady who portends the future you fear for yourself.

Lillian appeared to be in her mid-sixties or early seventies and had been in the hospital so long that she was something of a self-appointed mascot. She had come up and introduced herself, offering to show me around on the second day of my stay, as though she were the director of a spa, pointing out the amenities I might have overlooked. I noticed that the staff and other patients treated her with a kind of long-suffering patience, which did little to curb her sociability. I could see that she felt secure within the cloistered atmosphere of the unit—that she liked being taken care of, even in a peremptory and impersonal manner. I found myself wondering uneasily about her: Was it possible to be so fiercely needy, so passive on your own behalf, that you would want to tarry forever? That you would want to make the unit, with its harsh fluorescent lights and endless expanses of waxed linoleum, its tasteless food and unchanging days, your home?

As it happened, during the second week of my stay, unbeknownst to me, arrangements were under way for Lillian to finally leave the hospital. She met constantly with her therapist and the unit's social worker. With the rest of us, she talked about her fears of leaving every chance she got, especially during meals. Lillian was scheduled to go to a group home in the Bronx, and she worried about everything. Who would see to it that she took her medications? What if she didn't get along with the other residents? Was the neighborhood safe?

On the day of her departure, she hugged and kissed everyone good-bye, taking special pains with the nurses and aides, whom she insisted on regarding as intimates. After she left, the unit seemed somehow less cohesive; I found myself missing her presence. She called me on the pay phone several times, fretting about being stuck in a place she didn't like. I promised I would try to visit after I got out, but I never did. Once in a while I still think about her, the way you'd think of someone in a dire dream, calling out for help while you scramble your way to safety.

My mother came to pick me up, acting exaggeratedly jovial, as if to override my ambivalence about my departure. The truth was I didn't feel quite ready. Then again, I'm not sure that you ever feel ready to check out of a psychiatric hospital. It isn't easy to resume your life, the same old life you wanted to throw away less than a month earlier, with nothing substantially changed except the intensity of your desperation. Ideally, at some point during your stay, you come to the realization that you have other choices besides dying—that you can decide to live with your demons, if not without them. But finally the decision to check out requires an exertion of will—or, at least, a suspension of disbelief.

As I stood by the slow-moving elevators with my mother, my heart thudding wildly, I told myself that things would be all right, although it wasn't the slightest bit clear to me that they would be. What was clear to me was that the nurturing womb I had been searching for in a clinical setting simply wasn't out there. I was beginning to understand, however tentatively, that my quest for a new and improved childhood was so futile that it was tantamount to a wish to die—to stop the world and get off. The time for absolute caretaking was past, and if I hadn't gotten it thirty years earlier, I wasn't going to get it now, no matter how implacably I insisted on it.

25

It is the second winter storm of the season, and newscasters are having a field day, excitedly predicting how many inches or feet will fall before the weekend. Flakes of snow fall at a slant, as though a child's hand had drawn them, turning to gray mush as soon as they hit the street. Thursday used to be my favorite day as a child, with only one more day of school before the weekend, and meatballs and spaghetti for dinner. Now I find it an ominous harbinger of the weekend to come, when I flounder without the tiny bit of structure the weekdays provide, turn ever more inside myself despite the effort to stave off melancholia and immobility by making plans. How many plans can a person make before they become an empty exercise: another brunch, another movie, another conversation going over the same old territory? And, more to the point, why aren't such plans enough for me? Why don't these diversions satisfy? Why am I so inconsolable?

Long ago, Dr. C., one of my many shrinks, told me that my childhood had left a hole in me, a hole that could never be filled. It's the sort of hole that people turn to drugs for—or religion, or reality TV—to numb the ache. In another life, with a different background, this same therapist told me, I would have become a heroin addict. I feel the instinctive truth of this statement, this longing for oblivion at whatever cost, the next infusion of relief. Some part of me has never caught on to the idea of a future, doesn't know how to plan, has too few reserves of self-discipline to call upon, feels undone by having to fill out an application, is terrible at follow-through.

Marijuana, the drug of choice of my peers, has never done much for me—in fact has more of a negative effect than anything else, tending to make me paranoid and disoriented. I was much more drawn to Quaaludes, in the days when they were still around, the way they numbed the edges of things. Pity they took them off the market. Then there is nitrous oxide, laughing gas, which kind of lulls you. And Ecstasy, the few times I tried it, made me feel that everything was all right; even more to the point, that *I* was all right: Whatever had made me so unhappy? I would have gone on taking it except for the fact that this same Dr. C., who was generally tolerant about my fiddling with recreational drugs, specifically warned me off Ecstasy, saying that it burned holes in the brain.

Friday night looms, no longer heralding the beginning of Shabbos as it once did, signaling the cessation of work and imposing a twenty-four-hour interval of sanctified rest—or, at least, inactivity. It has been decades since I observed Shabbos, but I am still nostalgic for the way it marked off the close of the secular week and ushered in a different, more suspended dimension. Although I don't consider myself an especially spiritual person (I don't, in truth, even like the word "spiritual," with its suggestion of a chaste otherworldliness), I don't think I have ever fully come to terms with the dropping of Jewish rituals—the rituals that ordered my growing up—from my life. For all my having abandoned them, I continue to feel a strong sense of Jewish identity and have never been drawn to passing myself off as other than decidedly of the Hebraic persuasion. I remember when I worked in *The New Yorker* typing pool in the late seventies how surprised I was by the undercover nature of the staff's Jewishness. I was still living at home and explained that I had to leave early on Fridays—which caused something of, if not quite a scandal, certainly a stir, as if I were a creature freshly emerged from the bush.

Of late I have taken to wondering whether in giving up the Orthodoxy of my childhood I have also given up on the potential solace of community. I say "potential" because I never remotely felt a sense of community growing up. This was in part because the Fifth Avenue Synagogue, the formal, discreetly affluent shul on the Upper East Side my family went to, was very much my parents' stage (although my brothers had more connection to it than I or my sisters did), and in part because there were very few other Orthodox families residing in our Upper East Side neighborhood in those years.

Then, too, I've never really allowed myself to think of community in a positive light, as other than a form of censorious group-think, speaking out against betrayers of the faith, lambasting Philip Roth and other purveyors of less than exemplary Jewish characters or traits. And yet I believe there is something to be gotten from associating with people on exclusively tribal grounds, a kind of strength that is derived from the knowledge that there are folks you can rely on to show up for state occasions—births and deaths, particularly—beyond the ties of friendship. People who will pay a shiva visit, even if the hour or location is inconvenient, simply because you are one of them.

These days I go to shul only on Rosh Hashanah and Yom Kippur, mostly at the synagogue on the Upper West Side that my sister and brother-in-law attend. I like the solemnity of these two holidays and find myself strangely soothed by the obsequiousness of some of the prayers, especially those that slavishly praise God and ask for his forgiveness for all manner of hypothetical wrongdoing. *Ashamnu, bagadnu.* There is something tonic about the discourse of penitence, something elemental that does away with shades of gray. Everything is in stark black-and-white: You live or you die. You're saved or you're doomed. You've held to the straight and narrow or you've diverged—lied, stolen, gossiped, betrayed someone's faith in you. My depression evaporates under such conditions, gives way to a feeling of relief that our fate is not in our hands, whatever we do.

I understand what the psychologist Bruno Bettelheim had in mind when he argued in a controversial essay that being in a concentration camp was, for him, curiously cathartic, allowing him to come down unambivalently on the side of life. (He was briefly in both Dachau and Buchenwald, in the early days, before conditions became lethal.) He went so far as to tell a French journalist that his year in the camps was the only time in his life when he did not have thoughts of suicide.

On weekdays I am supposedly working—and indeed, from the outside in, I look like a person with something to do. I write or take stabs at writing; I answer emails, stare into space, get up and root around the fridge. My part-time assistant James comes in, furthering my veneer of productivity. He fields calls, creates an exemplary filing system that I make little use of, critiques my prose, pays bills, calls other people's assistants and sets up interviews, or requests review copies of books, or overdue payment for articles I've

published. James is a luxury but I have come to see him as
a necessity. He helps me stay organized, something I have
trouble doing on my own. He also helps keep the distractions
at bay. I live in distractions: they are where I want to be, away
from the main event, the habitation of my consciousness. It
turns out that James is not free of depression, either, and on
certain days he comes in and lies on my bed instead of working; other days he stumbles in at two in the afternoon, groggy
and out-of-it from a bout of late-night partying. Sometimes
we discuss each others' darknesses, but gingerly, like two ele-
phants sidling up to each other, testing each other out, warily
seeking companionship in our misery.

At night I often stay up watching *Chopped*, a late-night
cooking show, featuring competing chefs and baskets of exotic ingredients, like quail eggs and kumquats. It is one of
several food-themed shows I watch, my favorite being *Din-
ers, Drive-ins, and Dives*, which features a chubby, fast-
talking host with choppy bleached-blond hair named Guy
Fieri. He careens across the country in a red convertible seeking out homey establishments where cheerful people gather
and chow down on enormous platters of chicken wings, mile-
high burgers, or tacos filled with pulled pork. These shows
induce a deep sense of tranquillity in me, of things being all
right in the world; I love watching the infinite number of
small steps, of chopping and scraping and pouring, that go
into the preparation of meals, the gradual buildup leading
to the final presentation.

Although I have what passes for a highly developed
palate—I can often figure out what ingredient is missing in a
dish, or what might give it just the needed boost—I have
always felt intimidated by the act of cooking itself. When
my daughter was little I had her convinced that the making

of scrambled eggs was a high art, involving a judicious use of milk, a calibrated tweak of salt and pepper, followed by careful stirring, to which only a select few were privy. She would sit on a stool and watch me make eggs with wide eyes, alert to every step, and then eat them with gusto, each and every time. I would have liked to become a cookie-baking mother for her, unlike my own—a Donna Reed of a mother, reliably wearing a checked apron and carrying a wooden spoon with bits of chocolate-chip cookie dough sticking to it—but that was not in the cards. Instead, I was cast as the mother in *Gilmore Girls*, a fun but skittish companion who had mastered a few simple dishes, like tuna fish and spaghetti and meatballs, and served them up with a flourish as though they were culinary masterpieces.

As the days pass, I feel less and less up to the requirements of my life, which at the moment include teaching my course "The Art of Reading" at the 92nd Street Y. (Reading list: *To the Lighthouse*, *The Good Soldier*, *The Moviegoer*, *Play It as It Lays*.) So I head over to my mother's apartment on a Wednesday evening, thinking it will do me good to be in her presence. These days, since she's been widowed, she is more available to me, more overtly supportive of my efforts to write and teach. Being back in the place I grew up in also allows me a slightly distanced angle on my own situation; there is something comforting to me, now that I am no longer confined by its strictures, in the very fact that everything is still as it was when I last lived there.

I am reading *Play It as It Lays* for the third or fourth time, identifying wildly with the anomie-ridden Maria (pronounced "Mari-ah," as in Mariah Carey) Wyeth. I take careful notes, underlining phrases I especially like, as is my habit, and scribbling questions and thoughts I intend to bring to class. "A perfect, deadly little book," I write. And: "Is she [meaning Maria] a type? Or a particular problem?" And again: "Her [meaning Didion's] tone—a uniquely distanced sort of intimacy—comes closer and then moves away. Influenced a lot of deadpan prose, from Ann Beattie to Deborah Eisenberg. Suited to a certain kind of inchoate emotional pain."

Can you be Maria Wyeth, a laconic thirty-one-year-old divorcee who cruises the freeways of Los Angeles to escape her pain, and an astute observer of Maria Wyeth at the same time?

That is my dilemma in a nutshell.

26

During the spring break of her junior year in high school, I decided to take Zoë to Sedona, having won a five-day stay at a resort there in a Barnard fund-raising raffle. Usually such a trip would have seemed too fraught, given the anticipatory unease I experience when going anywhere outside of my usual circumscribed orbit, but my mother had been diagnosed with lung cancer several months earlier, and I was suddenly desperate to get away.

The cancer came seemingly out of the blue. She hadn't been a smoker, although both her father and husband were, and it had been assumed that what would eventually get her was her heart condition. But somewhere along the way, about two years before her stage 4 diagnosis, a shadow on her lung had been picked up on an X-ray and then promptly overlooked by the doctor she insisted on continuing to see.

The vigil around her had already begun; my sister Debra had flown in from Israel, and arrangements were in place for one of the six of us to be with her nightly, with the burden falling on the daughters, as it tends to at such times. I had been gripped by terror when my mother had informed me of her fatal illness—sounding bizarrely cheerful, in her perverse way—but I also felt a belated urge to get out from under her, to grab hold of my own life, as I had never succeeded in doing when she was well. Thus the perhaps questionable decision to take up the Arizona offer.

The first night we arrived in Sedona my mood collapsed in on me for any number of reasons, ranging from the disappointing quality of the hotel's toiletries to the gnawing feeling of guilt I had for going away when my mother was so ill, however flawed a mother she might have been. The truth was I had been feeling shaky even before we left New York, having barely begun to absorb the reality of her impending death. Added to this was the fact that I always felt fragile when I left home base, unsure of who I was and how to navigate strange territory. My daughter and I had squabbled about something on the flight from New York and were now studiously not talking to each other, which didn't help matters. I found myself weeping madly in the locked bathroom as the fake fireplace flickered in our room, overcome by despair. Everything seemed wrong about me and my life: my failure to remarry, my failure to learn to drive, my failure to produce another book. Not to mention my failures as a mother, which included exposing Zoë to my suicidal leanings at crucial moments in her young existence. Although I recognize that depression is not contagious, like the measles, I have always feared that my susceptibility will somehow "rub off" on her—that she might pattern her responses to life's inevitable difficulties after my own.

One evening when she was a little girl, no more than six or seven, Zoë announced after I had become annoyed with her about something that she was taking a kitchen knife to bed in order to kill herself. I remember that she was wearing her favorite pair of pajamas, imprinted with pink bows, and how incongruous such a declaration seemed, coming from someone whose bedtime was 7:30. I rushed after her into her bedroom, panic-stricken, and pried away the knife. I attempted to soothe her, and read to her until she fell asleep. She never repeated this gesture or anything like it, but I feel intensely guilty about it to this day, since I can only assume that she modeled her behavior on some distraught conversation she had overheard between my mother and me in which I threatened to kill myself. As Zoë has grown, it has become harder to shield her from my periods of acute despair; at the worst points, she has observed me sink into virtual immobility and wordlessness. No wonder she didn't seem excited about the prospect of going to college like the rest of her friends; she probably figured that I'd crack up if she left home.

Our stay in Sedona was marked by a lot of rainy weather and a vast degree of lethargy—so vast that Zoë and I never managed to explore the scenic surroundings the resort was famous for, although we glimpsed its impressive red rocks from our window. I hired a local guide to take us to look at Native American sites, and on the one clear day of our visit I booked us a helicopter ride over the Grand Canyon, which we flew down into, its steep sides looming above us, making me feel pleasurably lost in its immenseness. I remember having a conversation with our pilot about the Mormons in Colorado City, with whom he had dealings. I had recently been reading up on Mormon life for a piece I wrote for *Slate* about the HBO series *Big Love*—I accused the show's writers of making polygamy seem more tedious than troubling, like "one long harem nightmare"—and had been toying with the idea of trying to gain access and report on Mormon

culture directly. That was the energetic, life-affirming side
of me, which put in an appearance whenever I became truly
absorbed by something, taken out of my own battering
consciousness.

Most of the time, however, I sat around in a terry robe
in the resort's famed spa, feeling overweight and unfit, drinking flavored water and nibbling raw vegetables between appointments while Zoë sporadically did her homework. I
tried out a smorgasbord of massages and for a moment seriously considered moving to Sedona to continue having
bodywork done by a lovely woman whom my daughter and
I took to be, based on a passing remark, a close relative of
the writer John Steinbeck. This woman told me that someone important to me was very ill and that I had a lot of
painful experiences in my past to put behind me. She was
right on both accounts, which immediately made me want
to assign her a starring role in my life.

Otherwise the time dragged: I spent an inordinate amount
of it studying cutesie items in the gift shop after dinner,
carefully examining slogan-bearing mugs and T-shirts, and
CDs containing the sort of ethnic, woodsy music I never
listened to, as well as a variety of beautifully tooled leather
belts with hammered silver buckles made by native tribes-
people, although I never wore belts. In between I fought off
fiercely judgmental thoughts, wondering why I didn't respond to the seductions of nature more enthusiastically—
was I simply too self-absorbed to appreciate the raw beauty
around me?—and why we had come here in the first place.

The last night of our stay I decided to make reservations
at the resort's fancy restaurant instead of our eating at the
coffee shop, as we had been doing. My daughter and I were
back to being friends and we lingered over a multicourse

dinner, featuring Fred Flintstone–sized slabs of meat served by a beaming waiter. I let Zoë order a glass of wine along with me and we talked in the almost-empty restaurant like a couple of many years' standing, sharing tidbits about our day and what we had observed during our visit. At one point Zoë impassionedly lectured me about the plight of the uprooted tribes we had been hearing about; I nodded my head in agreement, struck as I always was by her empathic spirit. I glanced out through the floor-to-ceiling windows that circled the restaurant to the darkness outside and suddenly felt pleasantly stranded, cut off from the usual currents of my life and all the ties that bound me. I suddenly wondered whether I should go away more, wander the world like the poet Arthur Rimbaud, stop looking for an anchor, when the thing to do was to set myself purposefully adrift . . .

Meanwhile, New York and my dying mother were waiting to reclaim me, and soon enough all I would have left to remind me of our trip were the trio of tiny clay pots that I had picked up in the resort's gift shop and placed on my bedroom bookshelf. They were variously colored in turquoise, sienna, and burnt umber, and all three of them contained a small amount of sand in which was buried a miniature plastic figurine that looked something between a horse and a dog. I could no longer remember which Native American rite these pots alluded to, although I thought it had something to do with commemorating death. In any case, I liked the playful yet concrete spirit of loss they conveyed, so different from my own immersion in long-ago memories and timeworn conflicts—not to mention my own fleeing in the face of imminent loss.

How would I make do without my mother? Much as I resented her, I also looked to her to share my every thought, even my thoughts of killing her. Not least, she had always been the person I wrote to and for, from the moment I had first slipped notes under her bedroom door—the one I counted on to appreciate a silky turn of phrase or apt piece of wording. How would I go on living in a world in which she was no longer only a phone call away? This unspoken question had haunted me throughout the trip, leading me to call and check in on her condition every evening, tying me to her as surely as if I had stayed home and hovered around her, vying with my two sisters as to which one of us was the best daughter.

27

"Can't you do something with your hair?"

It was the first thing my mother said to me when I came to visit her at Sloan Kettering the summer she died. She was in a private room on a VIP floor, a room large enough to contain a couch and coffee table, decorated to look like a hotel suite, at some astronomic daily rate. (Although my mother liked to think of herself as an unpampered woman who had remained unaffected by her husband's affluence—the sort of person whom salespeople in the neighborhood mistook for the housekeeper rather than the mistress of the house, with a car and driver at her disposal—it was clear that anything less than the finest in accommodations would have angered her.) You would think her illness, the palpable imminence of death, would throw her off her footing, her compulsive fault-finding. Who cared what my hair looked like? Wasn't the point our being together in the time that was still available to us?

Then again, my mother hadn't really liked my hair since it had inexplicably changed texture in the years after I became pregnant with Zoë, slowly becoming curlier and less

silky, inclining toward outright frizziness during the high
humidity of summer. Unlike most women I knew, I had never
mastered the art of styling it on my own with either a blow
dryer or some other handy appliance, like a curling or flat
iron; as a result I wore it in its natural air-dried state, shaping it with the help of some pricey glop into what I hoped
would be taken for an artfully mussed nonstyle. My hair—
my youthful hair—had been one of the few things about
me that my mother had seen fit to unequivocally admire. It
had hung shiny and straight, "like a curtain," as she used to
say, and when I was about five or six she had stopped having
it hacked off and it was allowed to grow to shoulder-length.
(My opinion was not consulted on these matters.) Jane
would glumly and harshly brush my hair into pigtails and
sometimes, for Shabbos or other special occasions, tie rib-
bons around them.

I arrived at my mother's hospital room laden with videos
and books, the latest Philip Roth and a recently translated
novel about Parisian life under the Nazis, *Suite Française*,
written by Irène Némirovsky, a French Jew whose conver-
sion to Catholicism and high literary standing couldn't save
her from the death camps. Although my mother had always
been a rapt reader of contemporary fiction, including the
kind of light fare she referred to as *"shmerkers"* (either a
Germanism or a linguistic invention of her own, like the
term *"Artfremd,"* which she insisted was a word Hitler had
used about the Jews, attesting to their essential alienness,
that I could never find any trace of), it was the videos she
was really interested in. In between her hospital stays, as her
illness had progressed and she felt ever weaker, my mother
had taken to sitting at home in a pale leather Barcalounger-
type chair in the room that adjoined hers—what used to be

known as the "girls' room"—and settling into hours of watching films, sometimes two back-to-back.

It was there that I watched *Don't Look Now* with her one evening. She was wearing one of her long velour robes and white leather slippers, although she always got dressed during the day, and there was a glass of tea by her side. She smelled faintly of Vitabath; during my childhood she had favored a delicate perfume called Antilope by Weil—a scent that I associated, somewhat incongruously, with wildlife. *Don't Look Now* was one of my favorite movies; it is about a married couple who are grieving the accidental death of their daughter and take a trip to Venice, where they encounter two sisters, one of whom is a psychic.

Rewatching it for the first time in more than two decades, I was as shaken by its eerie, half erotic and half violent atmosphere as I had been years earlier. My mother looked deeply absorbed and I wondered what she thought of the extended sex scene with Julie Christie and Donald Sutherland, the uncut version that seemed so real because it reputedly had not been a case of two actors pretending to have sex but actually *having* it. My mother had always prided herself on being sexually unshockable; I remember a conversation about masturbation we had had a few years before she got sick, and how surprised I had been with her ease in talking about the subject. How was it possible that I, born in freewheeling America, was more sexually inhibited than my Old World, European mother?

I sat next to her and occasionally put my hand on her freckled one, but otherwise there was just the chuffing sound of the air conditioner and the faint hum of the city behind closed windows. I wondered how lonely my mother felt now that her end was in sight; her loneliness was something I

had often wondered about over the years, stuck as she was
with my unexpressive father. Although she was capable of
icy coldness, she also could be thrillingly, unexpectedly warm.
I especially liked her rare hugs, the way she'd hold her arms
out and clasp me to her chest when I arrived at her apartment for a visit, as though I had just returned from the Pelo-
ponnesian Wars. There was so much I still wanted to say to
my mother, so much I hadn't yet said ("I never felt you really
loved me") or hadn't said often enough for maximal effect
("I wish you'd been a better mother")—my hope always being
that she would finally take in these dark truths and apolo-
gize for the gravity of her failings, after which a magical
reconciliation would take place. We'd fall into each other's
arms weeping and I'd finally understand that I was a beloved daughter, after all. My lifelong melancholy would be
cured, the endless bewilderment—why had her strange indifference continued on into the next generation, making
her the least doting of grandmothers?—would finally be
undone.

My mother, however, was intent on inhabiting whatever
drama was unfolding on the TV screen before us and clearly
not willing to engage on a Wordsworthian, thoughts-too-
deep-for-tears level of conversation. Admittedly, it *was* a
form of connection, sitting there with her in silent contem-
plation of a film, but it also made me realize ever more acutely
that time was running out and that there was a limit to how
much intimacy she wanted in the time that was left. I think
she felt safe from harm, cocooned from the reality of dying
and all the feelings it stirred up in her—more anger than
sorrow, for sure—as long as she could escape into a movie.

It was frightening at moments how angry she seemed,
as though she alone in the universe had been selected to

die. It was almost as though she felt that, once again, her children had been given an unfair advantage; once it had been the endowment of money, now it was the endowment of life itself. I think she also felt unjustly cheated out of the new beginning she had been given in the wake of my father's death seven years earlier. She was enjoying herself without him, like a retirement she had earned after many years of working, and she had been looking forward to more years of the same. Watching her come more fully into her own had made me wonder about her marriage and the compromises it had required. One of my mother's closest friends insisted that my parents had been deeply in love—to the exclusion of everyone else, including their children. Still, I remembered her telling me in passing that she had once sought out the help of a therapist, but stopped going after one or two consultations; she thought that if she had continued to see him she would have left her marriage. She said it in her usual no-big-deal way, but I was struck by the seismic implications of the anecdote.

My mother had always prided herself on her stoicism, on the lack of fuss with which she met discomfort and pain. This attribute was a legacy from her childhood days, when she went on long hikes during the summer in the German countryside with her brothers and beloved father and never complained of growing tired. I remember that once, years earlier, in the course of helping my sister Debra move a cabinet, the cabinet had fallen on her, leaving an enormous and disfiguring bruise on her nose. I suspected that her nose was broken, but although she mentioned that it hurt, she never consulted a doctor about it.

It became evident that my mother had planned to approach the matter of her impending death in a similar vein.

We learned that she had made some sort of pact with her internist, a palliative care expert, stipulating that she was not to be kept alive through chemotherapy and experimental drugs if she was diagnosed with a fatal condition. (Disconcertingly, this internist was the same person who she believed had overlooked the first shadow of her cancer several years earlier.) This resolution did not hold up, however, when the reality of being mortally ill hit her. In the end she opted to try as many treatments as were available, switching from Mount Sinai Hospital, where her doctor was based, to Sloan Kettering to take advantage of the latest medical care. All the while, she continued to maintain a tight and increasingly irritable control over her household and daily arrangements, snapping at the housekeeper and writing out menus for Friday night dinner and Shabbos lunch in an ever fainter hand.

On one rare occasion in the hospital when she seemed inclined to reflect on things, my mother told me that no one ever wanted to discuss the reality of dying with her. She referred to a close friend whose visits she resented precisely because this friend wanted to talk about her own ailments— her heart trouble and fading vision—rather than focus on the issue at hand, which was my mother, dying. I decided to take the bull by the horns and asked my mother how she conceived of death. She answered immediately—it was clearly something she had given long thought to—that death was like the year 1918, which was the year before she was born.

Her answer took me by surprise, the chilly clean slate of it, the implicit acceptance of self-extinction. The world before one's birth was clearly similar to the world after one's death in this single respect, if no other: it presupposed one's nonexistence, was supremely unruffled by it. The consideration of my mother's inconsequence to the universe at large, to any but her immediate family, made me feel terribly sad. How could such a powerful figure wash up on the same final shore as everyone else? It was like watching King Lear staggering across the heath, reduced to rags and rage. I wanted to protect my mother from an awareness of her own cosmological insignificance, she who had cast such a looming shadow over me and my siblings, but I realized it was too late and I'm not sure, in any case, if this poignant and self-evident truth bothered her as much as it disturbed me.

Although she was a fairly advanced narcissist, with all the self-centeredness that went with that kind of personality, she was also uncannily unsentimental—not given to massaging certain kinds of painful facts, about herself or her children. I thought of T. S. Eliot's famous comment about humankind not being able to bear very much reality and was struck how it didn't apply to my mother, for better and worse. For all her adherence to religious observance, for instance, she wasn't one to feign piety, not even at the end, when many deracinated Jews become more spiritually inclined, for safekeeping in the hereafter. My mother didn't want to be visited by a rabbi in her last days, nor did I ever see her pick up a book of Tehillim, the liturgical psalms that the sick and dying often turn to for consolation. When I asked her why she had remained Orthodox when she so clearly wasn't a believer, she answered simply and unapologetically: "For the order." The one exception to this clarity was my father, whom I was convinced she saw through a lens smeared with Vaseline, the better to blur the uglier angles.

I try to prepare myself, to think of my mother as dead, buried in a plain pine coffin in keeping with the Orthodox tradition, and the very effort feels like an assault, leaving

me wobbly on my legs. I can't imagine myself, much less
the world, without her. I think of Marcel Proust, who briefly
considered killing himself after his beloved Maman died.
In the truest sense, I have never left her, and it is hard to
believe I won't be rewarded for my loyalty with her eternal
(if inconstant) presence. It is all but inconceivable that I will
be left to grapple with my life alone, without her to delin-
eate its contours. The desolation of this prospect is overwhelming and I try to counter it with other scenarios—the
possibility that I might feel a sense of relief, for instance,
or liberation. Ours is a relationship stippled with as much
hatred as love, after all, setting the tone that went on to
mark many of my relationships with men, so surely there
will be some psychological gain to be wrested from her
death.

Or so I tell myself. Why, then, do I have such a difficult
time imagining myself as anything but hobbled by grief?
Has nothing changed in all the years that have passed since
I wrote my transparently autobiographical novel about her
effect on me, in which I observed: "Without my mother, who
will cut up the world into bite-size pieces for me?" Or, going
back a decade earlier, to the poem I wrote about her in my
college writing class, called "The Uncut Cord": "You've got
me covered / like bark on a tree: / You have got me covered
/ head to toe. / Everything I do / speaks of you." I had given
her my best perceptions, my best lines.

How is it that I was able to recognize the situation—the
dire psychological entanglement of it, like a mother-daughter
amour fou—and yet do so little about it, despite that recognition, and despite the intervention of an army of psychiatrists? Could it all come down to the fact that my mother
was so blazingly powerful and everyone else so weak? The

odds, if nothing else, dictated that someone among the professionals whose offices I frequented with my harrowing narrative would have stepped forward, flexed his or her muscles, and proved a worthy adversary. I have no doubt that most of them tried, in their way. But nothing took. I didn't want a parental stand-in or substitute, I wanted my mother, in all her elusive and mercurial glory.

•

After going in and out of the hospital for various treatments, my mother came home for the last time with tubes that had been painfully inserted in either side of her chest so that she wouldn't drown in her own liquids. In early July, I had flown to Europe for several days on a writing assignment and returned on a Monday evening. Although she had gone to see the latest film at the Paris Theater with my sisters the day before, she struck me as inescapably different when I came into her bedroom to wish her good night. She was alert enough but seemed far away, as though she had sailed out to sea while the rest of us stayed on dry land. By Wednesday she had all but stopped speaking and eating, and on Thursday afternoon she fell facedown on the bathroom floor because she insisted on not being accompanied. After that there was no engaging her. On Friday evening her doctor instructed us to up my mother's morphine and take her off all other medication, asserting that my mother was now "actively" dying. My youngest brother argued that it was against Jewish law to withhold liquids, but in the end we reluctantly acquiesced. A hospice nurse arrived the following afternoon.

From Wednesday evening on, I slept next to my mother in my father's bed, and the night before she died I held her in my arms and whispered to her that she would be all right. She had lost a lot of weight, and felt feathery-light; for a moment, I felt that our roles had been reversed, that she was the child and I was her mother. I kissed her cheek, inhaling her pale freckled skin, which had stayed miraculously smooth. Her jawline was as tight as a young girl's. On Saturday night, shortly before midnight, I stood together with my siblings and watched as she took her last gasp—five gasps, actually, I counted them. Her jaw dropped open and I leaned forward and closed it.

28

The second-to-last time I saw my mother was the evening before her memorial service at Fifth Avenue Synagogue, after her body had been cleaned and prepared for burial by the Jewish Burial Society, known as the Chevra Kadisha, a group of women (or men) from the synagogue who volunteer for precisely this chore. It was considered a great mitzvah to perform the tasks of the Chevra Kadisha and it was entirely in keeping with her unfazed approach to a task that others might have seen as unsettling or gruesome that my mother had been one of this select group when she was alive.

She was lying under a white sheet on a gurney in a small room at the Riverside Memorial Chapel on the Upper West Side. The only part of her body that was exposed were her feet, which looked blue and forlorn. My sister Dinny and I had been called in to tie linen booties around them, in keeping with German-Jewish burial customs, but the booties were difficult to maneuver and the woman from the Chevra Kadisha was visibly impatient with our clumsy efforts. I kept studying my mother's feet, with their very clean and short toenails, expecting them to start twitching, as though this were a fantasy scene from *Six Feet Under*, and at any moment she'd sit up and start talking to me as though nothing had happened.

I would see my mother—although she could have been anyone, all wrapped up in white linen shrouds as she was— once again at her actual burial, which took place in Jerusalem a day after the New York memorial service. That service, at Fifth Avenue Synagogue, was packed tight, with hundreds of people filling the men's section downstairs and the women's balcony. I spoke, among a small number of others, from the bimah, feeling slightly daunted in the presence of so many bearded rabbis, wondering whether my eulogy, with its reference to my mother's acceptance of my more candid writings, was too blatantly intimate in tone for such a gathering. "My mother was one of the most vivid people I've ever met," I began, my voice parched with nervousness. "She was full of contrary impulses, all of which she conveyed with equal emphaticness, which makes it the more difficult to speak about her today in her absence, which is very real but also very recent. Indeed, I'm half convinced that, despite the evidence to the contrary, she is still listening somewhere with her hypercritical ear attuned to every potential misstatement, lapse in grammar, or misperception. Daphne, I can almost hear her say, speak slowly and clearly. And remember: no one wants to hear another word about your childhood . . ."

After the service was over, the six of us went straight to the airport to board an El Al plane to Israel. (We flew business class, courtesy of my mother's estate, which was something she would have considered wasteful and excessive in her lifetime.) As was the custom in Jerusalem cemeteries, my mother's body was taken out of the coffin and lowered directly into a plot of earth next to my father's grave in a peaceful hilltop cemetery on Har HaMinuchot—the Mount of the Resting Ones. The setting was lovely and dignified, but, surrounded by Israeli relatives, many of whom I didn't know, I felt lost. I looked around for my mother, the one person with whom I could discuss my impressions of her funeral, but she was nowhere to be found. I felt her absence blow through me like a gust of wind. As inconstant a presence as she had been during her lifetime, I still counted on her to ground me. I felt a radical sense of dislocation with her gone, as though the world had spun off its axis.

Back in New York, after the shiva, I would have been happy to leave everything as it was, to preserve the apartment she died in as though it would eventually be opened up to a roped-off public, like Thomas Jefferson's house. But my siblings had different ideas, and in due order we gathered around the oval dining room table to make our claims on the contents of my mother's apartment. The dispersal of her goods was done in a lottery-like fashion, with all of us bidding against each other for a previously distributed list of items; if two of us wanted the same piece of art or furniture or decorative clock, we were meant to wrangle it out between us.

This bizarre and unlikely way of dealing with her material remains was specifically designated by my mother in her will, and in many ways it felt like her last joke on us, reducing all of us to scavengers. I was the only one without a spouse by my side and I left early, in some mixture of sorrow and fury. After everything had been sorted through and emptied out, the apartment was sold. I largely absented myself from this process, returning to the apartment only to go through the books that had been left behind and gather all the ones that either had my mother's name written in them or that I knew she had liked, in homage to our shared literary love. (I immediately dumped this collection in a storage unit, where I continue to pay a monthly fee and they continue to molder to this day.)

Somewhere along the way, my sister Dinny had taken it upon herself to go through my mother's desk drawers and throw out what she saw fit. Included among the things she threw out, she informed me after the fact, was a piece of paper on which my mother had apparently written the observation, "Daphne is just like me." I felt enraged by my sister's presumption that she was the sole decision maker as to which documents were too personal to be distributed, she who was the least close to my mother of her three daughters.

I wanted that piece of paper, not that it really explained all that much—I knew my mother had identified with me more than with my sisters—but then again, in another way, it explained everything. I wanted it as proof, then, of what I knew in my heart to be true: that she had failed to see me as I was, that I had been no more to her than the carrier of her ambitions and dreams, for better and worse—and of her own self-hatred, for that matter—with all that implied in the way of unwieldy projection. No wonder I couldn't get clear of her, no matter what I did or what I wrote or however lucidly I saw into the toxicity of the situation. We were tangled up like bedclothes, intertwined like two gold hearts on the kind of cheap necklace that might be sold at a subway kiosk to a besotted teenage couple.

29

In the first years following my mother's death, the much-longed-for sense of liberation didn't come; instead she kept putting in an appearance in my dreams, many of them unsettling. In one of them she came equipped with a penis and the two of us made love; I remember waking up with a feeling of great joy, as though my long search for completion were over. Small wonder that I continued to feel as if a big hole had been made in my life, and thought on and off of trying to join her. The trouble was I didn't believe in an afterlife (neither had she), so I figured there'd be no meeting up with her again, even if I arranged to die. Meanwhile, I was growing older and Zoë was aging out of being my boon companion.

Just the winter before we had gone to a posh resort in Turks and Caicos together, where I had used my travel writer credentials to get us a discounted rate. The resort was one of those places that specialized in the chicest sort of simplicity—everything was done up in whitewashed walls and natural fabrics—and it attracted celebrities and ordinary rich folk who were looking for ostentatious privacy. As it turned out, there was so much privacy on hand that Zoë and I sat in splendid isolation on the long stretch of glorious beach day after day, with barely another person to disturb our view of the glistening turquoise water. Even when we took ourselves to the poolside restaurant for lunch or dinner we were pretty much left to our own devices, with only two or three guests besides us in evidence. I found the lack of other people slightly disconcerting, even loneliness-inducing, and, as was usual when I first arrived anywhere, considered leaving early. But soon enough I began reveling in Zoë's uninter-rupted company and in the peaceful non-exertion of our days, spent talking and reading and taking swims in the ocean—and, for the sheer diversion of it, having intense discussions about what dishes we planned on ordering from the resort's limited menu for dinner that night.

During our long walks on the beach, we would pretend to be British or French tourists, making conversation in elaborately feigned accents and laughing hysterically at our own cleverness. Back at our beach chairs, Zoë would sit next to me under an umbrella, wearing a straw hat, her fair skin all covered up in a T-shirt and long skirt, looking like someone out of the Bloomsbury set, a younger sister of Vanessa and Virginia. I happily exposed myself to the rays of my beloved sun, hardly bothering with sunscreen, until such moment when Zoë would cry out: "Mom! You're burning to a crisp! What is *wrong* with you? Do you want to get skin cancer?" At which point I would dutifully slather on some cream or lotion, with Zoë attentively ap-plying it to the parts of my body I couldn't reach.

But now Zoë's graduation loomed, and she was more interested in spending time with her gaggle of school friends than with me. This was as it should be, I knew; still, the thought of her going off to college had me in the grip of a wordless despair. I had been on one of my downward trajectories since the beginning of the year, despite gobbling down my usual medley of pills and wearing something called an Emsam patch on my arm, which was supposed to deliver antidepressive relief transdermally. I was horrified by the inverted form of separation anxiety I was experiencing at the prospect of Zoë leaving me. How could I be so unprepared to accept, much less welcome, her inevitable transition to an independent life—a transition that I had been trying to effect unsuccessfully from my own mother up until the moment of her death? Nevertheless, the severity of my depression was impossible to ignore. I had no appetite and over a period of four or five months had dropped thirty pounds. When I was awake (the few hours that I was), I felt a kind of lethal fatigue, as if I were swimming through tar. Phone messages went unanswered, email unread.

In my inert but agitated state I could no longer concentrate enough to read—not so much as a newspaper headline—and the idea of writing was as foreign to me as downhill racing. The idea that suffering would eventually yield to creativity, probably best expressed in Edmund Wilson's "the wound and the bow" theory of literary inspiration, had always appealed to me, but from my present depleted perspective it seemed wishful rather than actual. James Baldwin's no-nonsense dismissal seemed far more to the point: "No one works better out of anguish at all; that's an incredible literary conceit."

Shortly after Zoë's high school graduation that June, I checked into an under-the-radar unit at the New York State Psychiatric Institute, hidden away in a small building on Riverside Drive and 178th Street. I had resisted for as long as I could my doctors' suggestions that I enter a hospital. It seemed safer to stay where I was, no matter how out on a ledge I felt, than to lock myself away with other desperate people in the hope that it would prove effective. Added to my usual attitude of resistance was the fact that I had written an article on my last hospitalization, fifteen years earlier, for *The New Yorker* (I had become a staff writer there in my mid-forties under Tina Brown), musing on the gap between the alternately idealized and diabolical image of mental hospitals versus the more banal bureaucratic reality. I had discussed the continued stigma attached to going public with the experience of depression, but all this had been expressed by the writer in me rather than the patient, and it seemed to me that a part of the strength of the piece had been the impression it gave that my hospital days were behind me. It would be a betrayal of my literary persona, if nothing else, to go back into a psychiatric unit.

Another factor that worked to keep me where I was, exiled in my own apartment, was the specter of shock therapy, or ECT. My therapist, Dr. K., a modern Freudian analyst whom I had been seeing for several years and who had always struck me as only vaguely persuaded of the efficacy of medication for what ailed me—he had once proposed that I consider going off all my pills just to see how I would fare, which I did, only to plummet badly—had suddenly become a cheerleader for ECT. I don't know why he grabbed on to this idea, why the sudden flip from chatting to zapping, other than for the fact that I had once thrown it out as something I might try. Then again, for the drowning, any life raft will do. ECT, which causes the brain to go into seizure, was back in fashion for treatment-resistant depression after going off the radar in the sixties and seventies in the wake of *One Flew Over the Cuckoo's Nest*. Undoubtedly I had frightened Dr. K. with my insistent talk of wanting to cut out for good. I spoke about watching myself go splat on the pavement with a kind of equanimity, a sense of a foretold conclusion.

Still, his shift from a psychoanalytical stance that focused on the subjective mind to a neurobiological position that focused on the hypothesized workings of the physical brain left me scared and distrustful. I didn't doubt that ECT helped in some instances—I knew two men, both accomplished and even celebrated, who swore by its efficacy—but I had no faith that it would help me. There was something about the application of galvanic currents (or whatever they were) to the brain that seemed fundamentally wrong to me—an epistemological mistake, a confusion of categories. I knew that the actual procedure for ECT had been modified. It was no longer administered with convulsive force, jolting patients in their straps, and, except in rare instances, was no longer administered bilaterally. And yet the cartoonish image of my head being fried, tiny shocks and whiffs of smoke coming off it as the electric current went through, still haunted me.

What I feared more than anything was the memory loss, however minor, that would inevitably come in its wake. What if ECT left me a stranger to myself, with but the vaguest of memories of my life before and immediately after the procedure? The thought of not being able to call up an event or image or conversation from the recent past seemed unbearable; it undid me. And what about my deeper past? I may have hated my life, but I valued my memories—even the unhappy ones, paradoxical as that may seem—and I was convinced that my writing depended on my ability to retrieve them. I lived for the details, and the writer I once was had made vivid use of them. I had ventured so far as to develop my own private theory that it was the ordeal of enduring the cloudy aftermath of ECT that had led Ernest Hemingway and David Foster Wallace to kill themselves. It wasn't anything one could prove, of course, but it was something I could imagine: the indignity of enforced forgetfulness coming on top of crushing despair.

In the end, no matter how much I wanted to stay put, I ran out of resistance. I spent the weekend before going into the hospital in my sister Dinny's apartment, lost in the Gothic kingdom of depression: I was unable to move from the bed in my nephew's bedroom, trapped in a cacophonous interior debate about jumping off a roof versus throwing myself in front of a car. Yet somewhere in the background were other voices—my sister's, my friends', my doctors', arguing on behalf of my sticking around. I could half hear them. I wanted to die, but at the same time I didn't want to, not completely. Suicide could wait, my sister said. Why didn't I give the hospital a chance? She relayed messages from both my doctors that they would look out for me on the unit. No one would force me to do anything, including ECT. I felt too tired to argue.

That Monday morning, I returned home and packed up two small bags. I threw in a disproportionate amount of books (disproportionate given the fact that I couldn't focus enough to read), a couple of pairs of linen pants and cotton T-shirts, my favorite night cream (although I hadn't touched it in weeks), and a framed photo of my daughter, the last with the thought of anchoring myself. It was because of my daughter, after all, that I had given voice to my "suicidal ideation," as it's called, in the first place, worrying how she would get along without me and about the irreparable harm it would cause her if I took my own life. (What had Sylvia Plath and Anne Sexton done with their guilt feelings? I wondered. Were they more ruthless than I or merely more determined?)

In return for agreeing to undergo one of several federally funded studies—which involved either switching my medication or availing myself of ECT—I would get to stay at 4 Center as long as I needed at no cost. My sister picked me up in a cab, and, as I recall, I cried the whole ride up there, watching the brown and beige Upper West Side buildings pass by with an elegiac sense of leave-taking, nursing all the while a conviction that I had stayed around the scene of my own life too long—that I was, in some unyielding sense, ex post facto.

As soon as my sister gave my name to the nurse whose head appeared in the window of the locked door to the unit and we were both let in, I knew immediately that this wasn't where I wanted to be. Nothing appeared much changed from the psychiatric setting I had been in more than a decade earlier. Everything seemed empty and silent under the harsh fluorescent lighting except for one fortyish man pacing up and down the hallway in a T-shirt and sweat pants, oblivious to what was going on around him. Underneath the kind of bald-faced clock you see in train stations were two run-down pay phones; there was something sad about the glaring outdatedness of them, especially since I associated them almost exclusively with hospitals and certain barren corners of Third Avenue. And then, in what seemed like an instant, my sister was saying good-bye, assuring me that all would turn out for the better, and I was left to fend for myself.

The familiar checking-in routines came next: My bags were taken behind the glassed-in nurses' station and subjected to the usual examination for "sharps." Cell phones were also forbidden, for reasons that seemed unclear even to the staff but had something to do with their photo-taking capability. In my intake interview, which followed next, I alternated between breaking down in tears and repeating that I wanted to go home, like a woeful child left behind at sleepaway camp. The admitting nurse was pleasant enough in a down-to-earth way but was hardly swept away by gusts of empathy for my bereft state. And yet I wanted to stay in the room and keep talking to her forever, if only to avoid going back out on the unit, with its pitifully slim collection of out-of-date magazines, groupings of ugly wooden furniture covered with teal and plum vinyl, and airless TV rooms—one overrun, the other small and desolate. Anything to avoid being me, feeling numb and desperate at the same time, thrust into a place that felt like the worst combination of raw exposure and obliterating anonymity.

I got into bed that first night, under a ratty white blanket, and tried to calm myself. I was sharing a small room across from the nurses' station with a pretty, middle-aged woman who had introduced herself before dinner—the only one to do so—with a remarkable amount of good cheer, as if we were meeting at a cocktail party. She wore Frownies— little patented face patches that were supposed to minimize wrinkles—to bed, which only furthered the impression she conveyed of an ordinary adjustment to what I saw as extraordinary circumstances. Clearly, she had a future in mind, even if I didn't—one that required her to retain a fetching youthfulness. I hadn't so much as washed my face for the past few months, but here was someone who understood the importance of keeping up appearances, even on a psychiatric unit.

The room was lit, like the rest of the place, by overhead fluorescent bulbs that didn't so much illuminate as bring things glaringly into view. It was furnished with two beds, two night tables, and two chests of drawers. In keeping with the Noah's-ark design ethos, there was also a pair of enormous trash cans: one stood near the door, casting a bleak plastic pall, and the other took up too much space in the tiny shared bathroom. The shower water came out of a flat horizontal fixture on the wall—the presence of a conventional showerhead, I soon learned, was seen as a potential inducement to hanging yourself—and the weak flow was tepid at best.

The lack of a reading light added to my growing panic; even if my depression prevented me from losing myself in a book, the absence of a light source by which to read after dark represented the end of civilization as I had known it. (It turned out that you could bring in a battery-powered reading lamp of your own, albeit with the Kafkaesque restriction that it didn't make use of glass light bulbs.) My mind went round and round the same barrage of questions, like a persistent police inspector: How did I get here? How had I allowed myself to get here? Why didn't I have the resolve to stay out? Even more to the point, why hadn't anything changed with the passage of years? It was one thing to be depressed in your twenties or thirties, when the aspect of youth gave it an undeniable poignancy, a certain tattered charm; it was another thing entirely to be depressed in middle age, when you were supposed to have come to terms with life's failings, as well as your own.

I plumped the barracks-thin pillow, pulled up the sheet and blanket around me—the entire hospital was air-conditioned to a fine chill—and curled up, inviting sleep. *There is nothing to feel so frantic about*, I tried to tell myself soothingly. *You're not a prisoner. You can ask to leave tomorrow.* I listened to my roommate's calm, even breathing and wished I were her, wished I were anyone but myself. Mostly, I wished I were a person who wasn't consumingly depressed.

I thought of Zoë, at home in her bed, probably absorbed in watching one of the many implausibly plotted series she followed on her laptop, and felt an enormous sense of loss. My complicated, endearing daughter, over on what seemed like the other side of the world, stuck with me as a mother. My chest hurt when I thought of her, the way she had tried to buoy me up as I grew implacably more lost to ordinary communication, suggesting that we go out for walks or to a movie. I wished I were back at home, in my room next to hers. After staring into the darkness for what seemed like hours, I finally got up and put on my robe, having decided that I'd overcome my sense of being a specimen on display—here comes Mental Patient No. 12—and approach the nurses' station about getting more sleeping meds.

Outside the room the light seemed blinding. Two psychiatric aides were at the desk, playing some sort of word game on a computer screen. They looked up at me impassively and waited for me to state my case. I explained that I couldn't fall asleep, my voice sounding furry with anxiety. One of them got up and went into the back to check whether the psychiatric resident who was assigned to me had approved the request for additional sleep medications. She handed me a pill in a little paper cup, and I took it with clammy hands, mumbling something about how nervous I was feeling. "You'll feel better after you get some sleep," she said. I nodded and said, "Good night," feeling dismissed. "Night," she said, casual as could be. I was no one to her, no one to myself.

30

I spent three weeks all told on 4 Center. What I remember most about my time there was the surreal quality of the "fresh air" breaks that patients were allotted four times a day, watched over by a more or less friendly aide. These "fresh air" breaks were also smoking breaks, make of that irony what you will, and they took place in a fenced-off concrete garden bordered by the West Side Highway on one side and Riverside Drive on the other. The garden was planted with patches of green and a few lonely flowers, the whole space cordoned off behind a high mesh fence. In between were two barbecue grills, bags of mulch that seemed never to be opened, empty planters, and clusters of tables and chairs. It reminded me of a picnic area without picnickers—and then, too, of a long-ago scene in the movie *Blow-Up*, where the glamorous sixties characters mime a tennis game without ball or rackets.

Toward the end of my stay I had become distantly friendly with R., another patient who was a writer, having just finished a novel before he entered the unit. He would sit by himself on a bench in his unseasonal cashmere polo, puffing on a cigarette and tapping his foot with equal intensity. On either side of him were ragtag groups of people culled from several units of the hospital, including the one I was on, which was devoted primarily to the treatment of patients with depression or eating disorders. (The anorexic girls, whom R. referred to as "the storks," were in various phases of imperceptible recovery and tended to stick together.) The garden was also home to patients from 4 South, which catered to patients from within the surrounding Washington Heights community, and 5 South, which treated patients with psychotic and substance-abuse disorders.

By the end of my second week, when I was no longer chained to the unit, one of the male nurses I had become slightly friendly with would invite me for coffee breaks to the little eatery on the sixth floor where the hospital staff repaired for their meals. These outings were always kept short—we never lingered for more than fifteen minutes at a time—and they always brought home to me how paradoxically artificial and yet supremely real the dividing line between 4 Center and the outside world was. One minute you were in the shuttered-down universe of the verifiably unwell, of people who talked about their precarious inner states as if that were all that mattered, and the next you were admitted back into ordinary life, where people were free to roam as they pleased and seemed filled with a sense of larger purpose. It could cause vertigo if you weren't careful.

As I cradled my coffee, I looked on at the medical students who flitted in and out, holding their clipboards and notebooks, with a feeling verging on awe. How had they figured out a way to live without getting bogged down in the shadows? From what source did they draw all their energy?

I couldn't imagine ever joining this world again, given how my time had become so aimlessly filled, waiting for calls to come in on the pay phone or sitting in "community meetings," in which people made forlorn requests for light-dimmers and hole-punchers and exiting patients tearfully thanked everyone on the unit for their help.

Although there was more uncharted time than not—great sluggish swaths of white space, creating an undertow of torpor—a weekly schedule was posted that gave the impression that we patients were quite the busy bees, what with therapy sessions, yoga, walks, and creative-writing groups. Friday mornings featured my favorite group, Coffee Klatch. This was run by the same amiable gym-coach-like woman who oversaw our puny efforts at exercise, and it was devoted to board games of the Trivial Pursuit variety. The real draw, though, was the promise of baked goods and freshly brewed coffee. Even with my drastically lowered appetite, I still had a sweet tooth, and I found myself craving food other than what was on offer on the hospital menu. Despite its being summer, there was barely any fresh fruit in sight except for autumnal apples and the occasional banana. There were some culinary bright moments—cream puffs were served on Father's Day, and one Tuesday the staff set up a barbecue lunch in the patients' park, where I munched on hot dogs and joined in a charades-like game called Guesstures—but the general standard was fairly low. After a while, I began requesting bottles of Ensure Plus, the liquid nutrition supplement that came in chocolate and vanilla and was a staple of the anorexics' meal plans; if you closed your eyes it could pass for a milkshake.

It wasn't only the anorexics' Ensure that I coveted. From the very first night, when sounds of conversation and laughter floated over from their group to the gloomy, near-silent table of depressives I had joined, I yearned to be one of them. Unlike our group, where everyone was finished eating within ten or fifteen minutes, they were required to remain at lunch and dinner for a full half hour, which of necessity created a more sociable atmosphere. No matter that one or two of them had been brought to the floor on stretchers, as I was later informed, or that they were victims of a cruel, hard-to-treat disease with sometimes fatal implications; they still struck me as enviable.

However heartbreakingly scrawny, they were all young (ranging from their twenties to mid-thirties) and expect-ant; they talked about boyfriends and concerned parents, worked tirelessly on their "journaling" or on art projects when they weren't participating in activities designed ex-clusively for them, including workshops on "self-esteem" and "body image." They were clearly and poignantly victims of a culture that said you were too fat if you weren't too thin and had taken this message to heart. No one could blame them for their condition or view it as a moral failure, which was what I suspected even the nurses of doing about us de-pressed patients. In the eyes of the world, they were suffering from a disease, and we were suffering from being intractably and disconsolately—and some might say self-indulgently— ourselves.

Forging friendships on the unit was a touch-and-go affair because patients came and went and the only real link was one of duress. The other restriction came with the territory: people were either comfortably settled into being on the unit, which was off-putting in one kind of way, or raring to get out, which was off-putting in yet another. I had become attached to my roommate, who was funny and somehow seemed above the fray, and I felt inordinately sad when she left, halfway into my stay, in possession of a new diagnosis and new medication.

Still, the consuming issue as far as I was concerned—the question that colored my entire stay—was whether I would undergo ECT. It was on my mind from the very beginning, if only because the first patient I had encountered when I entered the unit, pacing up and down the halls, was in the midst of getting a lengthy series of ECT treatments and insisted loudly to anyone who would listen that they were destroying his brain. And indeed, the patients I saw returning from ECT acted dazed and dislocated, as if an essential piece of themselves had been misplaced.

During the first week or so the subject lay mostly in abeyance as I was weaned off the medications I had come in on and tried to acclimatize to life on 4 Center. I met daily with the pretty young resident I had seen the first evening, mostly to discuss why I shouldn't leave right away and what other avenues of medication might be explored. She sported a diamond engagement ring and wedding band that my eye always went to first thing: I took them as painful reminders that not everyone was as full of holes as I was, that she had made sparkling choices and might indeed turn out to be one of those put-together young women who had it all—the career, the husband, the children. During our half-hour sessions I tried to borrow from her irrepressibly hopeful outlook, to see myself through her charitable eyes. I reminded myself that people found me interesting even if I had ceased to interest myself, and that the way I felt wasn't all my fault. But the reprieve was always short-lived, and within an hour of her departure I was back doing battle with the usual furies.

One day early into my second week, I was called out of a therapy session to meet with a psychiatrist who oversaw the ECT team. I still wonder whether this brief encounter was the defining one, scaring me off forever. This woman might as well have been a prison warden, for all her interpersonal skills; we had barely said two words before she announced that I was showing clear signs of being in a "neurovegetative" condition. She pointed out that I spoke slurringly and that my mind seemed to be crawling along as well, adding that I would never be able to write again if I remained in this state. Her scrutiny was merciless; I felt attacked, as if there were nothing left of me but my illness. Obviously ECT was in order, she briskly concluded. I nodded, afraid to say much lest I sound imbecilic, but in my head the alarms were going off. *No, it wasn't*, I thought. *Not yet. Back off, lady. I'm not quite the pushover you take me to be.* It was the first stirring of positive will on my own behalf in a long time, a delicate green bud that could easily be crushed, but I felt its force.

The strongest and most benign advocate for ECT was Dr. J., a research psychiatrist at the institute who had treated me three decades earlier—he was the one who had put me on Prozac before it was FDA-approved—and was instrumental in persuading me to come into 4 Center. In his formal but well-meaning way he pointed out that I lived with a level of depression that was unnecessary to endure and that my best shot for real relief was ECT. He came in to make his case once again as I was sitting at dinner on a Friday evening, pretending to nibble at a rubbery piece of chicken. The other patients had gone and my sister Dinny was visiting. I turned to her as the normally contained Dr. J. waxed almost passionate on my account, going on about the horror

of my kind of treatment-resistant depression and the glorious benefits of ECT that would surely outweigh any down-
side. I didn't believe him, much as I wished to. *Help me*, I
implored my sister without saying a word. *I don't want this.*
Tears trickled down my cheeks as if I were a mute, wordless but still able to express anguish. My sister spoke for me
as if she were an interpreter of silence. It looked like I didn't
want to undergo ECT, she said to the doctor, and my wishes
had to be respected.

31

As the weeks passed on the unit, instead of growing stronger I felt a kind of further weakening of my psychological muscle. The picayune details of my life—bills, appointments, writing deadlines—had been suspended during my last few months at home, then left behind altogether, and it began to seem inconceivable that I'd ever have the wherewithal to take them on again. The new medication I was on left me exhausted, and I took to going back to sleep after breakfast. I was tired even of being visited during the fiercely regulated visiting hours (5:30 to 8:00 on weekday evenings and 2:00 to 8:00 on weekends), of sitting in the hideous lounge and making conversation, expressing gratitude for the chocolates, smoked salmon, and quarters for the pay phone that people brought. I felt as if I were being wished bon voyage over and over again, perennially about to leave on a trip that never happened.

In the week leading up to my proposed departure, a date which I had insisted on despite a certain hesitancy on the part of the staff, I was permitted to go out on day passes as a kind of preparation for reentry, none of them particularly successful. On a broiling Saturday afternoon Zoë picked me up and we went for a walk to the nearby Starbucks on 168th and Broadway. I felt thick-headed with the new sedating medication I was on and far away from her. When Zoë left me for a few minutes in front of a bank to make a call on her cell phone, I started crying, as if something tragic had happened. I wondered uneasily what effect seeing me in this state was having on her—what she made of my being in the hospital altogether. The only other time she had visited me in a psychiatric hospital she had been too young to take it in. Did she see me as a burden that she would need to shoulder for the rest of her life? Did she view my depression as a pose, something I could shake off if I wanted to? In between we laughed at small, odd things as we always did, and it occurred to me that I wasn't as much a stranger to her as I was to myself.

With the staff's tentative agreement—they didn't think I was ready to leave but had no real reason to prevent me from doing so—I left 4 Center three weeks to the day after I arrived, my belongings piled up on a trolley for greater mobility through the annex to the exit. I left behind a pillow I had brought from home and a bamboo plant my friend Deborah had brought me that had been confiscated by a staff member for no discernible reason. It was a hot June day similar to the one I had checked in on, the heat pouring off the windows of the parked cars. Everything seemed noisy and magnified. It felt shocking to be outside, knowing I was on a permanent pass this time, that I wouldn't be returning to the unit.

I was sent home on Klonopin, an anti-anxiety drug I'd been on forever, as well as a duet of pills—Remeron and Effexor—that were referred to as "the California rocket blaster" for their presumed igniting effect. As it turned out, the combo didn't ignite for me—or at least not in the way it was supposed to. At home, I was gripped once again by thoughts of suicide and clung to my bed, afraid to go out even on a walk around the block with my daughter. When I wasn't asleep, I stared into space, lost in the terrors of the far-off past, which had become the terrors of the present. I was back with Jane, felt her as a scowling presence in the room. It was decided that I shouldn't be left alone, so my sister and my friend Susan took turns staying with me. But it was clear this arrangement was a short-term one, and by the end of the weekend, after phone calls to various doctors, it was agreed that I would go back into the hospital on Monday to try ECT.

And then, the Sunday afternoon before I planned to return to 4 Center, something shifted ever so slightly in my mind. I'm not clear to this day what was the exact cause of the change—maybe it was the fear of ECT, or maybe the depression had finally run its course and was beginning to lift—but it might have been any one of a number of factors, or some combination of them. For one thing, I had gone off the Remeron and started on a new drug, Abilify, which was an antipsychotic that had been found to facilitate antidepressant medication when taken in small doses. In my desperation I had also gone to see Dr. C., an old psychiatrist of mine—the one who had persuaded me to go into the hospital when Zoë was a little girl—who was doing research on new treatments for intractable depression and had given me some OxyContin on the sly.

The under-the-table aspect of the transaction had to do with OxyContin's reputation for being addictive and much-abused, and also because there was no official protocol for using an opiate to treat depression. So Dr. C. was going out on a limb in giving it to me, which even in my abject state touched me. As I recall, there was some theoretical basis to his doing so, having to do with the workings of the pineal gland—or maybe it was the amygdala—but in any case I didn't begin to understand Dr. C.'s explanation of why the OxyContin might work. What I did know was that it made sense to me that a pill that relieved physical pain might also relieve emotional pain: it seemed like an obvious connection that had been overlooked in the rush to deconstruct depression, or to avoid providing false "highs" as an antidote.

Dr. C. had instructed me to take two OxyContins in the morning and two in the evening, like aspirin. By early Sunday afternoon I was feeling a bit calmer, and my bedroom didn't seem like such an alien place anymore. The ghost of Jane was nowhere in sight. For a brief interval, no one was home, and I decided to get up and go outside. I stopped at the Food Emporium and studied the cereal section, as amazed at the array as if I had just emerged from the gulag. I bought some paper towels and strawberries, and then I walked home and got back into bed. It wasn't a trip to the Yucatán, but it was a start. I didn't check into the hospital the next day, or the day after that.

I spent the rest of the summer slowly reinhabiting my life, coaxing myself along. Admittedly, I would often yearn to be back in the hospital—some new hospital, that is, yet to be discovered. There was still a part of me that wondered whether the mistake wasn't, in fact, mine—whether it was simply a matter of my having chosen the wrong place, like choosing the wrong husband, and that there was still a "right" hospital waiting out there for me, overlooked until now. True, they undoubtedly didn't offer the sort of mental cleansing

I longed for, like a colonic for the psyche, flushing out all that was stale and foul inside you. Yet the fantasy of a formalized cure—one that would take place in some hushed, white-on-white setting—was like a resistant strain of psychological virus, impervious to corrective doses of reality.

Even though I returned to the idea of the hospital as a theoretical refuge when my mood sank, I lasted out the summer. Toward the end of August I went for a few days to the rented Southampton house of my friend Elizabeth. It was just her, me, and her three annoying dachshunds. I had brought a novel along, *The Gathering*, by Anne Enright, the sort of book about incomplete people and unhappy families that has always spoken to me. It was the first book to absorb me—the first I could read at all—since before I went into the hospital. I came to the last page on the third afternoon of my visit. It was about 4:30, the time of day that, by mid-August, brings with it a whiff of summer's end. I looked up into the startlingly blue sky; one of the dogs was sitting by my side, her warm body against my leg, drying me off after the swim I had recently taken. I could begin to see the curve of fall up ahead. There would be new books to read, new films to see, and new restaurants to try with friends. I envisioned myself writing again, and it didn't seem like a totally preposterous idea. I had things I wanted to say.

32

As is appropriate for someone obsessed with the past, the end of the year often has me looking nostalgically backward rather than making shiny resolutions for the year to come. Frequently this habit has been legitimized by writing up one of the dead luminaries being memorialized in *The New York Times*'s annual "The Lives They Lived" issue (also called the Death Issue by those on the inside). What do the departed figures I've written about have in common, aside from the relative noteworthiness of their passing? I suppose it could be said that they all, in their way, suffered from intermittent depression, a depression unsuccessfully kept at bay with drugs and food and drink and the analgesic of fame. The year my mother died, it was Patricia Lawford; the year before, it was Sandra Dee; before that, Marlon Brando; and before that, Linda Lovelace.

For someone like me who has a soft spot for all wounded birds, it is, in its way, the perfect assignment—a last-ditch chance to salvage these misunderstood and abused figures and make them sympathetic to the wider world—and in a mere eight hundred to one thousand words! I dove into this quixotic endeavor with haphazard zeal, reading dozens of articles and books, gathering enough information on Patricia Lawford, say, for a dissertation, hoping to find a path through what looked to be an occluded life: not precisely tragic but not soaring, either, a life that hovered mostly in the wings of larger lives. "But as is true of many powerful families," I wrote, "the house of Kennedy was as much gilded prison as swanky enclave . . . Indeed, you could ask whether Patricia, who had considerable gifts beside her patrician good looks and her dedication to the Kennedy legend, might have carved out an identity more definably her own had she been born into a family that valued its female members for something other than their procreative potential and skill at facilitating male ambition." I was speaking for the silenced part of Patricia Lawford, but undoubtedly I had other women in mind, as well—not least my own mother.

This particular December, however, a few years after my mother died, writing anything at any length is impossible. It has all come hurtling back at me. The sudden descent of the black season, the maximum darkness of it, just when you think you might be free at last, is one of its worst aspects. All the incriminating, scrambling thoughts pour back in, chasing each other, ruthless in their sniping insistence. *You're a failure. A burden. Useless. Objectionable. Your shit smells worse than other people's.* Self-extinction: the black light at the end of the tunnel of depression, a ghastly glow winking every bit as seductively as the green light at the end of Jay Gatsby's pier. *Come here and rest a while with me*, it says. *Abandon all struggle.*

Always, for me, it comes back to this question: Where do you go when you're depressed? That's the heart of the problem, isn't it? You can't disappear inside your own skin, although that would be ideal. Nor can you lie low and hole up in your room forever, like Henry James's sister, Alice. Once upon a time people went on months-long ocean voyages for just such reasons—or at least they did in movies and novels—but nowadays the only form of legitimate convalescence on offer is by way of psychiatric hospitals, which, as I've learned, come with their own horrors and limitations. I end up by seeking out the sanctuary of my bed, where I have wandering, wistful dreams in which I move to another country with a brood of children and spend my spare time gardening, an activity I have never attempted in real life. Sometimes I simply lie with my eyes closed, like a person recuperating from a grave shock.

On the day leading up to New Year's Eve, I sleep until two in the afternoon instead of four. It is dark before I know it and somehow or other I put on a dab or two of makeup, pull on clothes, affix pearl earrings, slip on festive pumps rather than my usual worn-out sneakers or loafers. For a minute earlier in the afternoon, I thought I would try to hurl myself into print once again, begin work on a profile I owe and thereby hitch my faltering wagon to the star of someone more determined, of adamantine will, calling on my skills to give shape to someone else's existence. Except that I no longer believe in these skills other than in the most theoretical of ways. My writerly self slides so easily off the page when I'm not actually hovering over the keyboard; it is a professional identity I still inhabit only fleetingly when I am feeling good, no matter how often I appear in print, and at times like these not at all.

I go to witness the fireworks in Central Park, near Seventy-second Street, thanks to A.'s invitation, after a civilized old-New-York type of dinner where I talk about

civilized concerns—children and schools and plays to see—
with a group of people I barely know. Reasons to live, as
opposed to reasons to die. Now, shortly past midnight, I
stare into the exploding bursts of color: red-white-blue,
squiggles of green, streaks of purple, balls of silver, sparks
of champagne. Zoë is standing nearby, with my friend B.,
and as I look into the fireworks I send out entreaties into
the sky. *Make me better. Make me remember this moment
of absorption in fireworks, the energy of the thing. Stop
listening for drum rolls. Pay attention to the ordinary calls
to engage, messages on your answering machine telling
you to buck up, it's not so bad—from the ex, siblings,
friends who care. Make me go forward.*

33

As I write this, it is 2011, and my mother has been dead for five years. The globe spins on and on, a tsunami devastates Japan, governments topple in far off-places, elections are held somewhere else. A woman in her seventies, a writer of delicate yet searing novels, sits perfectly still in her living room on Central Park West, CNN or Al Jazeera on in the background, unable to envision life without her husband of many years, who died over a year ago after a long illness. This woman is a good friend of mine, whose sadness I willingly enter into. "I can't believe it," she says, "I can't believe he's not here." I sympathize with her confusion in the face of the absoluteness of death, the irretrievable gone-ness of dead people.

Who's to say how long mourning should last? We live in speeded-up times but our limbic systems, where our feelings reside, operate as they always have, largely unaffected by the passage of days, months, even years. No matter that my mother's body must be dust at this point, I'm still having it out with her in my head, dodging her criticisms, her sharp-eyed and mostly disapproving scrutiny—when I'm not thinking that I can't go on living without her.

I remember a May fifteen or so years ago, when I was in my early forties and heading downward into another bad period. After my father's death, my mother had started spending months at a time in her apartment in Jerusalem. Now I fled my city for hers, looking for my mother, looking for a mother who was not my mother, looking to save myself from being caught in the eye of the storm once again. What had kicked it off this time? Some admixture of rage and loneliness, something gone wrong in the world both inside and out. I had stopped eating, pretty much stopped speaking, and the inner voice that popped up at times like these telling me to kill myself was operating at full volume once again.

I left my daughter in the care of my ex-husband and a devoted housekeeper and somehow propelled myself onto a plane. I trusted El Al to keep me safe, at least temporarily, even if I couldn't do the same on my own behalf. Upon arrival, I decided, I would either jump out a window—the window of my mother's apartment on a high floor in an apartment-hotel on King George Street, with a balcony overlooking the Old City—or I'd make her make me better. Sometimes she could make me feel better merely by admitting she'd done some things wrong, even though contrition certainly wasn't her long suit. And sometimes she could make me feel better just by being there, even now, when I was no longer a child.

I arrive in Israel in the evening and find myself unable to sleep for more than an hour or two that night, despite having gulped down enough sleeping pills to stun a horse for days. Now I am awake at 5:00 a.m., the sun not yet risen, standing over my mother's bed.

Who in God's name was she? I have spent decades

trying to put the jigsaw of her maddeningly self-contradictory personality together, but there is something intrinsically elusive about her. Why did she have so many children, especially with a husband who needed so much caretaking himself? Why wasn't she concerned about any of us in an ordinary, motherly fashion? She never worried that we weren't dressed warmly enough, for instance, or cared how we did in school. Why had no one stopped her in time, forcibly separated her from the children she failed to protect from her own predatory instinct? She has imbued me with a savagery toward myself that no external source can match.

"You blighted my life. I didn't have a chance." I tell my mother this, half yelling, half crying, lacking all dignity, crazed by some pain eating me up, by the angry dogs barking at me from inside. "You blighted my life," I repeat.

My mother has recently had a quintuple bypass but she will outlive me, I am convinced of it, coming from tough German-Jewish stock as she does. I know that the same renowned psychoanalyst who had described my mother as "phallic" had also compared her to a type of mythic bird that eats its young, but, as always, I can't see how someone else's recognition of my mother's acute destructiveness is of any help, especially after the fact. She is too tough—she's always been too tough—and in return I am too soft, a creature without inner resources, without a spine.

"You destroyed me, all of us." I am screaming at her now, in the darkness of her bedroom where we sleep next to each other, side by side on twin beds, just as she and my father once did. The light is slowly beginning to break through, bringing with it another relentlessly sunny Jerusalem day.

I feel that I have lost everything; I have gotten myself this far and now it is over. There is no future beyond now, and in the now that is forever I am useless. Worse than useless: worthless. I face my mother with my pent-up grief and rage: Why have I had to live with this darkness for so long, since I was a child, this debilitating dragon that hurls itself at me although no one can see it? It is she who has arranged it this way, she who blights me.

My mother, who is in her mid-seventies, is wearing a lightly flowered cotton nightgown that stops somewhere in the vicinity of her knees. She has gotten out of bed and stands before me with a cup of tea, telling me everything will be all right, that I've felt this way before and always come out of it. There is something strangely comforting in her recognition of the emotions that roil me even as she remains unflustered by the accusations I fling at her. Perhaps I am too easily mollified, but the fact is that she is not as unaware of my turmoil as she acts—or as I choose to believe. There is nothing she doesn't know, nothing that will undo her. Perhaps this resilience is what she offers instead of a more recognizable form of love, a stoic willingness to stand guard and see me through the depths. I feared the day when she'd be gone and I'd have no one left to catch my tears as they spilled, wild amounts coming out of me, a fountain of sorrow.

•

Meanwhile, I'm trying hard, really I am. What, you may ask, does "trying" consist of? Primarily it involves separating myself from the me that is depressed—flying above it, so to speak, like a plane that has lifted off the tarmac. Trying is going on, is forced engagement with the trivial and less trivial forces of my everyday life. I answer the phone, return emails, shower, set myself to writing a magazine piece on a new noninvasive form of plastic surgery, a facelift done without the aid of a scalpel. The minutiae of things, unless I am flat on the floor, good for nothing but hospitalization, arouse my curiosity, take me momentarily away from this ongoing, obsessive monologue: *Do I live or do I die?* (I fear I am getting old for this, in any case. "For interest passes," Philip Larkin observed in his poem "Neurotics," "Always toward the young and more insistent." It's one thing to want to do away with yourself in your twenties, when life dangles tantalizingly before you; another thing entirely to consider suicide in middle age, when life has settled in, for better and worse, and what was it you were expecting, anyway?)

Details absorb me, act like a balm on my festering psyche, details that I will then put back into circulation by writing a piece around them: it might be an article on looking for a girdle or a review of a new novel on the Lodz ghetto or a profile of Tom Stoppard or Cate Blanchett or Alice Munro for *The New York Times Magazine*, someone or something sufficiently intriguing to distract me from my own innards.

My hope being, I think, that I will concern myself with said subject long enough to put distance between me and the darkness. Just the other week, for instance, while I was talking on the phone with Diane Keaton for a story, I felt myself caught up in her excitement about the visual world, her love of everything from houses to Navajo blankets to the shapes of certain letters, the way images speak so profoundly to her. For a moment I felt her energy rub off on me; I saw myself chasing around for the perfect basket, dashing downtown for a piece of curtain fabric. For a moment, that is, I was all motion, a figure streaking across the landscape. But, of course, I hadn't moved an inch, I was sitting at my desk, in front of my computer, not about to go anywhere, not even dressed to go outside.

Speaking of which, mobility has always been a problem, of course. Getting anywhere from anywhere else. A certain kind of hopefulness that is required for active, planned movement that I lack. An embrace of the here-and-now that is stronger than the sense of unease that keeps you where you are instead of where you might be. When I worked at HBJ, I tended to put in my first appearance at my office only after a working lunch; mornings were as reliably difficult for me as they had been in my childhood, and the last thing I wanted to do was interact with other people. Years later, when I was on the staff of *The New Yorker*, with a coveted office of my own on the twentieth floor and a solicitous editor who bought me matching teal desk accessories to help cozy up the space, I went in no more than a handful of times all told, although many writers tended to hang around their offices for the sheer joy of being part of the scene. I wrote book reviews as well as personal essays and then went on to share the movie column with Anthony Lane for a time. I could have used some of the stimulating conversation that was available—there were lots of smart and well-informed people milling around who would have been happy to discuss, say, the merits of J. M. Coetzee's latest novel or Robert Altman's *The Gingerbread Man* with me—but I preferred to work from home.

I think I felt lonely in my office, which was situated between the offices of two writers who also rarely came in. But, if I were being wholly truthful about it, I'd say the barrier to my coming in had more to do with the fact that I had no

idea how to act in a situation that called for an easy ca-
maraderie with other writers. I had always felt uneasy in
a group, beginning with being one of six. Added to which
I didn't know the proper procedure—the correct mode of
behavior—for being part of this anointed collective. Was
I supposed to walk around trading artful quips with my
colleagues? Or was I supposed to be simulating writerly
productivity, bent over my computer with the door closed?
The whole scenario made me anxious beyond words.
Looking back, it now seems to me that I kept my distance
from what might have been a convivial scene because I
was afraid I'd be "found out" for the sad sack I felt myself to be, someone unable to keep up appearances. I wonder what I missed out on, the friendships I might have
forged . . .

To this day, I am amazed at the ease with which other
people step out into the world, zipping around the city by
subway or bus or cab. Or the simple expedient of walking.
I find it difficult to arrange myself in an attitude of leave-
taking, coat on, bag in hand, ready to engage. A melancholic
image of myself rises up before me, anonymously on the
street, no one thinking of me as I bear down the block, just
my obsessively dark thoughts, my endless ongoing debate—
Should I step in front of that bus now, finally now?—to
keep me company. Dealing as I do in negative anticipation,
it is hard for me to imagine that an encounter will prove
uplifting—or, more to the point, that it will pull me away
from myself.

Which is not to say that I don't continue to leave my
house for a variety of reasons—for dental appointments, to
meet friends for dinner, to see movies, to drop off dry-cleaning
or buy a container of milk—but why is it always such a

struggle, why am I always looking to huddle under my own roof? Surely it has to do with the relief of not having to pretend I feel other than I do within my own four walls, where I am free to inhabit or fight my depression as I choose. In the outside world it is all smiles and nods of agreement and pretending that I understand why one would look out for one's health in the attentive, prophylactic way upper-middle-class women do, checking for potentially cancerous moles, going for mammograms and colonoscopies, having one's hormone levels evaluated.

And still I live on, take my meds, fight with my daughter, watch dopey TV shows, struggle with writing this book, go to therapy, think about renting a summer house. Why, you might plausibly wonder, am I thinking about renting a summer house if I'm also thinking about killing myself? Because for a moment I have an image of myself as someone stronger than I am, able to stand on her own two feet, do the things grown-ups with advantages like my own do. I see myself sitting in a little cottage near the water, reading, writing, entertaining friends, taking walks. But what if I wake up unable to move on a Saturday, the way I do here in the city? What if I lack the requisite energy to fill the fridge, stock up on paper goods? What if no one visits me? What if I resent the friends who do visit, wonder why they don't offer more of a helping hand?

And then, of course, I've never learned how to drive. A skill most people master by the time they're in their teens has eluded me. (In my mid-thirties I embarked on a series of driving lessons and was doing well when I suddenly canceled the next lesson in a panic and never continued.) Recently, in one of my rare fits of forward-lookingness, I ordered a *Driver's Manual* from the New York State Department of

Motor Vehicles. It is an attractive booklet, with a brightly colored cover featuring three blue cars going along a Z-shaped black road with a broken yellow line (p. 47, "Single broken line: You may pass other vehicles or change lanes if you can do so safely and not interfere with traffic"), but I've barely glanced at it. Learn to Drive: it is part of my unmastered list, like Learn to Live.

34

I have always felt adrift in the city on summer weekends, like someone who's been left behind while everyone else has gone off on some merry outing, but it is only now, in ripe middle age, that I have made my way to taking part in this peculiarly Manhattan rite of passage of escaping the city. First there were the years I relied on my family's house in Atlantic Beach, where the screen door was always slamming, hectic barbecues were officiously presided over by one of my brothers-in-law, and Zoë's excitement at the prospect of spending time with her many cousins was palpable. The place had been sold within five years of my father's death, over my ardent protests, and in those intervening years I took on the role of a peripatetic houseguest with young daughter in tow. I sang for my supper by bringing cunning little gifts, pretending to love Scrabble, and trying to fold the dinner napkins just the way my hostess liked them.

Finally, about six years ago, I stopped turning to others to provide escape hatches and decided to try devising some of my own. I began looking at summer rentals, despite my certainty that I wouldn't be able to afford anything I actually liked. In the end, I chose a whitewashed cottage—part of a complex of former servants' quarters for estates in nearby Southampton—in a hamlet called Noyack, four miles from Sag Harbor. The house had its own little slip of bay beach and picture windows everywhere, even in the bathroom. I thought that renting it would make me feel more expansive, like someone whose life had added up to something, who had the wherewithal to host weekend guests and entertain them with games of croquet in between serving up bounteous breakfasts. I wanted to be such a person, even though I did not drive and was easily overwhelmed by basic housekeeping chores. The house itself felt like a snug little boat, but although Noyack was officially located in Southampton, the only places to walk to were a slightly rancid-smelling grocery store, a pizza parlor, and a liquor store.

After two summers in Noyack I switched to a rental in East Quogue, a tiny blue-collar village you can sail through in five minutes, situated between the far more beautiful Quogue to the north and the more bustling Hampton Bays to the south. Its tiny stretch of a main street was home to several auto-body parts shops, two delis, a nail salon, a minuscule sushi restaurant, a Chinese takeout, and a wispy store or two selling T-shirts, canvas bags, and dried flowers. With the exception of a market that carried reputedly excellent meat and upscale items like imported dried pasta and handmade chocolates, I found there was little reason to walk into town, other than to catch the Jitney home. Then again, the rents were correspondingly cheaper there than they were elsewhere in the Hamptons, which was what had drawn me in the first place.

I never took to this house, despite its having a big garden and pool. I hated its arid, pseudo-Zen décor but didn't want to risk hanging up any pictures on the bare walls, lest I leave a mark. The house's interior, which was a one-story, made me feel both claustrophobic and isolated, whether I was there alone or had visitors. The only time I really felt content was on weekend afternoons, when the sun was still out but no longer so high in the sky, and I'd read or tan in a lounge chair; the darkening of my pale skin felt transformational, as it always had. There was a chicken coop on the property that had been rented out by the owner to a neighboring farmer and over the course of my time there, I went from finding the squawking of the chickens an annoyance to a companionable backdrop.

That was the summer my mood began to tank, and by August everything was taking on a more ominous cast. It had been unusually hot, and my antidepressant medication heated me up on top of my natural tendency to feel hot wherever and whenever: I felt as though I'd spent the past two months sweating profusely. Beads of perspiration gathered on my forehead and began to trickle down the sides of my face while other people just looked faintly flushed. Embarrassed by my visible overheatedness, I was constantly dabbing at my glistening skin with tissues.

As August progressed, I felt myself literally slowing down, both in my thinking and in my speech. Sentences took more time than they should have to form; I felt impatient with my own halting words. I didn't allow myself to think beyond the immediate present, because to project myself any further into the future would have caused too much anxiety. For a while now I had been practicing keeping the idea of suicide off the table—trying to live as though there were no other option but to get on with day-by-day existence. I felt determined to keep this downswing under control, not to let it bloom into some extended process in which I ended up in a semi-vegetative state, but wondered if I had the strength to keep it at bay.

Meanwhile, Zoë had helped me rearrange the few pieces of furniture in the East Quogue house to create a little work area in the bedroom, and I faithfully carried out a new, lightweight laptop every weekend, but I mostly avoided sitting down at the desk. There was nothing preventing me from working on my book there (*this* book, to be exact) except me. I was assailed by all the familiar demons of self-doubt: Who was interested in what I had to say? I had never quite gotten to the point, even after decades of writing, of believing that I was, in fact, a professional writer—much less that there might be an audience for my work. It wasn't so much that I doubted my ability to write enticingly as that I was chronically unable to envision enticed readers at the other end. I had no trouble, on the other hand, imagining a panel of disapproving critics ready to pick apart my every word and accuse me of all the potential hazards of writing autobiographically, from self-absorption to self-pity, with stops along the way for excessive candor and unsightly narcissism.

Then, too, I was worried about the whole matter of what I could, and could not, say in a memoir of the sort I had embarked on. Although I was aware that I'd acquired something of a reputation over the years for being the kind of writer who divulged personal details—sometimes embarrassingly personal details—without apparent difficulty, the reality was far more complicated than it appeared to be. When it came to writing about my family, I had always left a lot out, especially as concerned my five siblings, whose privacy I didn't want to intrude upon.

This tactical selectivity had worked well enough in my long-ago novel and in the personal pieces I had written for *The New Yorker* and *The New York Times Magazine* in the intervening years, but it didn't make much sense any longer. Observing my mother's strangely embracing response to psychological dysfunction in some of my siblings, particularly as it occurred in the form of debilitating depression, had colored my view of my own vulnerability in this area. I had learned that being a verifiable basket case had its rewards for all of us; it got my mother's wholehearted attention the way nothing else did, and it brought out in her a maternal solicitude that she rarely showed otherwise. It wasn't just me, in other words, who had stumbled badly on the road to adulthood, but how to describe an entire malfunctioning system without betraying the code of silence that enveloped the public façade of my family? I had always looked on at writers who spilled the beans without apparent regard for the pain or damage they might inflict on those closest to them with a mixture of admiration and unease, but I knew I didn't quite have their steely resolve.

When I wasn't getting agitated about how and, indeed, whether to get on with the book about depression that I had been contracted to write by three successive publishing houses over the course of more than a decade, I tormented myself by studying the Hampton giveaway glossies, of which there were any number—more, it seemed, with each passing week. These featured glamorous couples and local celebrities who took up creative and remarkably remunerative hobbies in their spare time when they weren't attending candle-lit charity soirees. All the women were, needless to say, thin, even if they had recently given birth. The husbands were uniformly prosperous-looking, with slicked-back hair and well-cut blazers; many of them sported loafers or suede driving shoes without socks. I would lie in my bed late at night and actually ponder the lives of these people, what their families of origin might have been like, how they had become couples, whether any of them liked to read books.

One Sunday when I had a couple and their young son as guests we drove into Quogue for brunch at a café that also carried take-out items. I ordered a pound of lobster salad to go without asking the price, feeling like one of the people I read about, at ease within a luxe universe that existed precisely for my delectation. But when the bill came to $90 for the lobster salad alone I immediately requested that the order be changed to half a pound, to the visible annoyance of the woman, dressed in a white apron and possibly the creator of said lobster salad, who was helping me.

In the back of my mind I felt my mother glaring at me from the grave. My mother, who never bought enough fruit—or, indeed, food of any kind—on summer weekends so that by Sunday morning there was a forlorn peach or two left and the tiniest bit of smoked salmon that was saved for my father's lunch. Who did I think I was, I could hear her say, with my wild spending? Didn't I realize that I was to look but not touch, that money existed in plentiful supply for some but not for me? I had never established a clear sense in my own mind of my intrinsic value, and when it came to the material world I vacillated wildly between covetousness and paranoia. Was this object worthy of me? Was I worthy of it? Was I getting a bargain? Or was I being duped? Even something as simple as buying Sunday lunch could suddenly feel fraught with peril.

As the days passed, I tried to bat away the doleful thoughts that had started up in my head again, as familiar as they were anxious-making. My father, for instance: Why had he had so painfully little interest in me? My brooding about my father's indifference had been going on while he was alive and had continued since he had died. It had been fifteen years since I had rushed home from Hong Kong, where I was staying at the swanky Peninsula Hotel with an eight-year-old Zoë at the end of a week-long cruise, cutting short a trip *The New Yorker* had sent me on as their resident movie critic, so as to get to his bedside before he breathed his last. Had it mattered? Should I have bothered? Had I done it for him or myself—or, as was more likely, for my mother?

On some level I fully subscribed to William Faulkner's famous edict about the past ("The past is never dead. It's not even past"), but on another level I understood that in real life people moved on, or at least pretended to move on, lest they end up like doomed characters in a play by Tennessee Williams or Eugene O'Neill—characters, like Laura in *The Glass Menagerie*, whom I closely identified with. I hated my own stuck key of a refrain, but didn't know how to unstick it. Not for the first time I wondered if I might have done myself a favor by undergoing ECT when it was pushed on me the last time I was hospitalized, instead of resisting it with all my might. Maybe it took something as primitive as shock treatment—I didn't care how much the treatment had been refined and made more palatable over the years, I still thought of it as primitive—to set an obdurate mind like mine on a new course . . .

My shrink was also out of the city, but we spoke regularly on the phone; he was wonderful that way, willing to go above and beyond what had always struck me as the arbitrary rules of his profession, trying to remind me that he was in the picture even if he went away to a house on an island off the coast of Maine for two months every summer. I had been seeing him for two years and felt that he was the sort of thoughtful ally I had almost given up on finding—or perhaps, more to the point, could only now make use of. With him in my corner, there was the possibility that I would let go of the terrors of the past, give up on the fantasy of the warm Jewish family I had never had, and face up to the cost of being my mother's "chosen" child—the one who only had eyes for her and was possessed by her in return.

Still, I had trouble holding on to him in my head as a real person—as someone who retained me in *his* head. It was as though I fell off the end of the earth the minute I wasn't in the presence of another person—or perhaps I meant that the other person fell off the end of the earth, or that we both did. However the process worked, everyone seemed to dissolve, and I was left to wander around in a moonscape bleached of reliable human connection.

I got through the end of that summer by drowning myself in books: memoirs, biographies, novels. There was a mesmerizing true-crime account set in Tokyo, *People Who Eat Darkness*, that I read in two nights from start to finish, too afraid to turn the light off when I put the book down, lest something or someone evil creep up on me under cover of darkness. And when I finished one book, I would pick up another. What was the point of brooding? *Shut up*, I told myself. *Shut the fuck up. There's a big world out there, outside your obsessive little brain: pay attention to it, for a change.*

The last weekend I spent out at the East Quogue house I packed the kitchen up with Zoë; the two of us, hoarders by nature, argued back and forth about which itty-bitty item of food or half-finished beverage could be dumped as opposed to being dragged back to the city in a jumble of boxes and shopping bags. I was more relieved than anything else that it was time to be going—that I had gotten through August without crashing to a halt. The end of the summer had always made me sad in years past, but this time was different. I would miss the garden and the talkative chickens, would miss closing my eyes and giving myself up to the sun, but not much else. I had tired of perusing the Hampton glossies and walking through the shabby little town on my way to the Jitney, wondering why I had traveled two and a half or sometimes three hours only to land here. And although the fall didn't precisely beckon, there was always a chance things would take a turn for the better once I was at home.

I arrived back at my apartment and was glad to be among my familiar companions, my thousands of books, again. They called to me from the bookcases, old and new, suggesting all manner of directions I might roam in. For a moment everything felt freshly come upon, as though my depressed self had stepped back in honor of my homecoming, giving me room to move forward. I had forgotten what it was like to be without its smudgy imprint, and for a moment I floundered, wondering how I would recognize my life without that telltale darkness.

35

I go on a Thursday evening to see my psychopharmacologist, a preternaturally young-looking man who trained as a neurologist. We have struck up something of a friendly relationship beyond the confines of the patient-doctor interaction; we will sometimes share a taxi across town, for instance, if mine is his last appointment. I have sent a bunch of people—ten or twelve in all—to him who mean a lot to me, so convinced am I of his skill and understanding. And yet I don't believe in his expertise when it comes to my own predicament, mutter darkly about the guesswork and hit-and-miss character of medication (*Why does no one know how, exactly, any of these pills work?*), insist that what ails me is not biochemical at all but rather hinges on a lack of vital nurturance when I was young.

"It's not either/or," he explains once again. "It's susceptibility. Not everyone who went to war or gets raped develops post-traumatic stress disorder. But etiology makes no difference at this point. What happened, happened."

Is there to be no undoing, then, no way of going back and putting myself—my chemistry—in order? If what happened, happened, what front am I fighting on? Between us we hold an ongoing forum on the nature-versus-nurture debate, the plasticity of the brain, and the efficacy of therapy as opposed to pills. For one thing, if this were the fifties or sixties, when nurture was all the rage, I probably wouldn't be seeing a psychopharmacologist to begin with; the spotlight would be on the psychological dynamics. But now that the biological view of emotional illness is in the ascendant and insurance for psychotherapy is practically nonexistent, the environment is given short shrift.

The real point, beyond the fluctuations of a given cultural moment, is this: if there is a propensity for depression in your family history, there is a 50 percent chance you will develop a depressive illness. But if depression doesn't run in your gene pool, your childhood might be Dickensian and you might all the same not develop a depressive illness. Although it is difficult to hold on to both the nature and nurture sides of the situation, depression comes about because of a confluence of genetic propensity *and* the triggering circumstances. The latest research on schizophrenia suggests that it involves no less than 108 genes; it's unlikely that depression will ultimately involve one gene or just a few.

I have explained to Dr. M. more than once that I don't see my family as particularly "loaded" for depression, despite the incidence of it among my siblings. By this I mean that neither of my parents suffered from it, and that although there have been instances of depression on both sides, they don't suggest a more-than-usual occurrence in a Jewish Ashkenazi family of European origin. Hell, look deeply into *any* family's background and you'll find a melancholic uncle here and a clinically depressed second cousin there. All of which suggests no more than a 50 percent chance that I would have developed a bad case of the life-long blues.

I tell him I am tired of the struggle. "I should be dead by now," I say. "I appreciate all you've done but this isn't what I want." ("This" being life.) "I've stayed around long enough." He insists that this is my depression talking, something apart from me. "You have a major depressive disorder," he says regretfully, as if this were the first time he'd come to this conclusion.

"Do I?" I ask. "Are you sure?" The truly strange aspect of my so-called condition is my own difficulty in believing in it as a condition, a disorder, a verifiable illness. Much of the time I make light of it, dismiss it, the same as everyone else does, try to prod it into submission. *Pull your socks up, stop thinking about your feelings*, that sort of thing. I am deaf to my own pleas for tolerance, unforgiving as a Midwestern accountant of what I know on some level to be a disease written into my bones, a cancer of the psyche, in addition to whatever my personality flaws may be.

Dr. M. tells me he has seen me worse than I am today—that the first time I consulted him, some years ago, when I had gone off all medication at the suggestion of the therapist I was then seeing, I could barely speak. "You looked terrible," he says, "like someone underwater." Today he decides to go up on one of the pills I am on—Abilify. The problem with Abilify, not that anyone will state it upfront, is that it makes you put on a significant amount of weight. I was once a relatively slim person—thin enough to pass muster, at any rate—but this is no longer the case. I have often wondered whether the thirty to forty pounds I've gained since I added Abilify to my regimen of pills some years back has deepened my sense of despair about myself, given how important the mandate of thinness in women has become in our culture. A friend of mine, a younger woman with a highly developed regard for her own looks and a bipolar disorder, went off Abilify precisely because of this unwanted side effect and immediately shed many pounds. "They fell off," she announces happily.

There are other drawbacks to both Effexor and Abilify, none of which have been spelled out to me by Dr. M. beforehand but which I discover as time goes by. These include a rise in my blood sugars and liver count; the latter is so high that I had a liver biopsy done two years ago to try and assess what was causing the problem, with nothing much determined other than that I had a fatty liver.

All the same, I sense some hesitancy on Dr. M.'s part connected to the use of this drug, although I can't precisely put my finger on it. I wonder whether there is the unspoken possibility of my eventually developing the symptoms of tardive dyskinesia, which can occur as a side effect of taking antipsychotic medication, also known as neuroleptics. This is a disorder that involves involuntary movements, especially of the lower face—such as grimacing, tongue-thrusting, and repetitive chewing—which are hard to reverse and can become even worse with time. You occasionally see people with tardive dyskinesia on the subway, looking as though they can't fit in their own skin.

"Is there something wrong with Abilify?" I ask.

"No," he says, "but it *is* an antipsychotic."

"Meaning?"

"You don't want to prolong your stay on it."

"I see," I say. I entertain a vision of myself as an elderly woman in a dragging coat, screwing my face up wildly, frightening strangers left and right.

"Would *you* take it?" I ask, thinking to ensnare him.

"If I had your condition and it helped, I would," Dr. M. answers.

Once again I am left being me, with my particular past—"What happened, happened"—when this is so transparently not who I want to be. Sometimes, for minutes on end, I forget who I am in Dr. M.'s cozy office, imagine us both as intergalactic fighters, familiar with the evil forces of Planet Depression, as he calls it, and all they entail. At those times I feel valiant, like someone who has determined not to surrender to an enemy most people can't even see.

36

In a few weeks I will turn the age Virginia Woolf and Deborah Digges were when they committed suicide. It is by now well documented that nonlinear creative types, artists and writers in particular, often suffer from depression; whole books have been devoted to exploring the high incidence of both unipolar depression and bipolar depression in this group. Anywhere you look, there they are, the unhappy poets and painters, drinking or drugging themselves into a stupor, cutting their wrists, hanging themselves, shooting themselves, jumping from buildings, and driving off bridges. It is a matter of some amazement to me that I am still here, given my recurrent desire not to be. In that way I've surprised myself: not giving in to the undertow.

But perhaps I've all along underrated the pull of life itself, slyly offering up its enticements. I tend to give short shrift to these enticements when I'm sinking, but they are very real. They would include but are not limited to the supreme diversion of reading and the gratifications of friendship, the enveloping bond of motherhood and the solace to be found in small pleasures, such as an achy Neil Young song or finding the perfect oversized but not voluminous white shirt. Not to overlook my (mostly) inextinguishable sense of curiosity; a certain pleasure I take in beautiful things and aesthetic experience generally, such as a filmy, dun-colored scarf, or the cerulean shade of sky on a late summer afternoon, or listening to Vivaldi's *The Four Seasons* played as if it were newly composed one May evening in the Sainte-Chapelle in Paris. And, yes, the tug of love, when I allow myself to feel it, for all those who help tether me to this world.

Still, how many times have I shoved off thoughts of suicide, walked myself around the wish to die, back to some kind of truce with life? How many times have I explained my suicidal frame of mind in a slow, halting voice to a therapist who first threatens to call 911 and then asks me to put off killing myself at least until the next session, as though he were asking me to postpone a decision to get a haircut? I agree for the interim, give my word that I won't act on my lethal wishes, at least for the moment. All the same, how long can you flirt with suicide before embracing it? Spalding Gray, whom I never saw in performance but whose journals I devoured with the avidity of one who recognizes a fellow desperado, listed "suicide victim" as one of nine alternate identities for himself (along with "a Zen monk" and "a movie star") years before he finally called it a day and jumped off the Staten Island ferry.

In my fantasies of suicide, I never write suicide notes—with a few exceptions they strike me as, on the one hand, gratuitous, and on the other, slightly melodramatic—but of late I have been thinking I would owe my daughter, at least, an explanation. And an apology, for all the good it will do. (In *Death Becomes Them*, in the chapter "The Art of the Suicide Note," there is oddly no mention of children as the potential recipients of such notes: "Suicide letters have been addressed to siblings, husbands, wives, lovers, bosses, friends, fans, mentors and enemies.")

I have heard all the terrible statistics about the children of mothers who kill themselves, the lingering harm it does; I think of Nicholas Hughes, the zoologist son of Sylvia Plath and Ted Hughes, who was an expert on "stream salmonid ecology" and hanged himself in 2009, when he was forty-seven. He was reported to be suffering from depression, and I glean from what little information is out there that he was something of a loner, but would he have killed himself without such a ready maternal model at hand?

Then, too, my daughter has been dealing with the reality of my depression for so much of her life that I'm convinced it half bores her, like a story that's gone on too long. On the other hand, I worry that my relentless misery has taken away her right to assert her own unhappiness as legitimate, equal in seriousness to mine. Not to overlook her *happiness*, a capacity for which I fear I may also have thwarted. She is a creature of many moods but she keeps most of them to herself, as if to keep her distance from my own tendency to spill my emotions—my "rawness," as she calls it, with a note of disdain in her voice—all over the place.

The only exception to her disinclination to talk about herself is when she has had too much to drink, which she sometimes does at social gatherings. Then she opens up like a flower, becoming giddy with merriment, pleased to confide her innermost secrets to perfect strangers instead of merely being the ready listener. You can see at those moments the person Zoë was meant to be, engaged with the world in a free and easy way. Once, when we were attending a family wedding together, she got the rather closemouthed man sitting next to her to divulge his sexual loneliness in the wake of his wife's death by virtue of her gentle probing. At other times, though, the effect of drinking is more troubling— leaving her sodden with sadness. Then she will call me in a slurry voice to tell me how tragic everything is, and I fear this is the true inner Zoë. My one consolation is that she seems willing to be talked out of her gloom, at least until the next go-round.

I think of how much more Woolf had done by this point in her life than I have in mine—all the books written, the founding of the Hogarth Press with her husband, Leonard, her intense rapport with so many people by way of conversations and letters. It's not that I have accomplished nothing—I have published three books and written hundreds of thousands of words for a wide-ranging assortment of publications, been a passionate if not always reliable mother, a caring sister, a good friend, and a devoted aunt—but that it falls so short of what I once hoped for.

I suppose you could say that the mere fact that I'm still banging around is itself a triumph of something—strength, fear, indecision—but I wonder whether it isn't also a failure to keep my word to myself. I have promised myself suicide the way other people promise themselves a new car, gleaming and spiffy. It is something I think I deserve, a reward for bearing up under what feel like intolerable conditions, the dreary dailiness and balefulness of existence coming at you again and again. I understand that taking one's own life is not in itself a positive thing, of course, that it represents a turning on the self of the most radical order, but I also think it is possible to look at it as a kindness, a way of paying utmost attention to one's own utter bereftness.

Then there is this: I have always secretly believed that suicides don't realize they won't be coming this way again.

If you are depressed enough, it seems to me, you begin to conceive of death as a cradle, rocking you gently back to a fresh life, glistening with newness, unsullied by you. If you are depressed enough you are prepared to jump off the ledge of dailiness and into the embrace of oblivion—in the private and entirely unprovable knowledge that oblivion will yield to an expanse of green field, dotted with wildflowers, where you will run and run, unencumbered by the heaviness you have been carrying with you for what seems like forever.

This secret conviction bears some resemblance to religious faith, although it demands nothing and offers nothing back except its own irrationality. Because I suspect myself of harboring this dubious and childlike belief, I have written down a quote from Rilke's "Ninth Elegy" that tells me otherwise, in which the poet acknowledges that while happiness barely exists except as a prelude to unhappiness, this world is all the same our one and only ticket. If I could heed the poem's unsentimental message and last the dark season out—and the next one—there might be something durable, a more permanent holding:

> But because *truly* being here is so much; because everything here
> apparently needs us, this fleeting world, which in some strange way
> keeps calling to us. Us, the most fleeting of all.
> *Once* for each thing. Just once; no more. And we too,
> Just once. And never again . . .

Somewhere along the way, I've apparently internalized this message enough to have scribbled my own version of it while looking out at the Long Island Sound one summer, committing it to memory like a prayer: O *My Lord, what a tragic and terrible, weird and slightly wonderful life this is. My one and only, our one and only, hold it close, away from the worms, live it through, give it every chance you've got.*

•

Despite my pronounced habit of losing things, I still have my Virginia Woolf doll roughly forty years after first receiving it, having managed to hold on to her through at least four moves. She is, admittedly, a bit worse for wear, my Virginia: she is missing one black sock as well as the miniature envelopes that once nestled in a pocket. But she is still dressed in the clothes she first arrived in, that knitted maroon cardigan over a gray wool skirt. This Virginia is resilient, would have gone on to write many more astonishing books, would have sat in the garden with Leonard as the sun went down and their hair turned white and the latter half of the twentieth century came in.

Would Virginia Woolf have lingered longer if she had been properly diagnosed and put on the right medication? Can it really all be a matter of tweaking the serotonin uptake level here, and upping a dopamine infusion over there? Or is this just the latest fashion in wishful thinking? The history of antidepressant psychopharmacology is a relatively young one, about a half century old, and the ways in which the complicated circuitry of the brain affects mood is still a matter of informed conjecture. Undoubtedly the increasing number of people who look for cures to what ails the psyche in the chemistry of the brain and who refer the vicissitudes of emotional development (or "affective disorders," as they are called) back to inherited temperament would say they could have set Ms. Woolf right.

Others, who look less to cut-and-dried biochemical answers and a bit more to a complex interaction of proclivity and life experience, might choose to hedge their bets, given the traumatic loss of her beloved but elusive mother when Woolf was thirteen, followed less than seven years afterward by the loss of her beloved half-sister, Stella. Not to overlook the sexual abuse she suffered at the hands of her stepbrother, George Duckworth, or the effect of living with an eccentric and fiercely demanding father at the tail end of a repressive and misogynistic age. But even with the most advanced treatment—some ideal combination of medication and therapy—there is always the possibility that Virginia might have chosen to commit suicide eventually, one or two—or ten—years later. These things are hard, if not impossible, to gauge. "Life is one long process of getting tired," Samuel Butler said. There will always be people who feel that although everyone else is tired, they are too tired, have waited long enough, and that it's time, now, to get going.

37

There is something I want that I cannot have, a redress that will never come. No one is going to make anything up to me—not now, not then, not ever. This can't be so, but it is so. This simple truth enrages me—I will not make do with such thin gruel!—but there is nowhere for my rage to go. If you're a socialized person, you can't go spewing your anger at the nearest available target. You must learn to live with it, sublimate it somehow, or work it out in a counterproductive fashion, by eating or drinking or drugging too much. No wonder I am so fascinated by serial killers, staying up late at night to watch their biographies on TV and reading up on them, everyone from Ted Bundy to John Wayne Gacy, stopping on the way to acquaint myself with the British and Russian variety, fashioning an expertise that would make me a useful addition to Quantico's serial killer profiling unit.

These days I am in need of reading glasses, and more recently I have been diagnosed with diabetes and have to take medications to keep my blood sugar under control. (I am not sufficiently committed to good health to stop eating sugar and pasta, however, and I've taken to hiding cookies from Zoë—who is protective of my health in a way I fail to be—so she won't confiscate them.) Then there are my knees, which have gone arthritic on me, sending shoots of pain down my legs whenever I walk up or down a flight of stairs. Also: I am vain when I am not too depressed to care about how I look, so there is also the possibility that one of the injections of cosmetic fillers I occasionally indulge in will go astray and occlude some crucial artery, causing blindness if not death. You see, I have grown old—older, despite the fact that I have dreamed of killing myself since I was a young girl, leaning out the seventh-floor bedroom window and imagining myself jumping soundlessly to the street, away from everything that was wrong with my family and away from my incessant tears. There is a line in Jean Rhys's unfinished, posthumously published autobiography, *Smile Please*, that states the dilemma exactly: "Oh God, I'm only twenty and I'll have to go on living and living and living."

I pretend, that is, that I understand the basic scaffolding of adult life, where one is called upon to look assiduously after one's own well-being, when the fact is I don't care about my well-being except in the most superficial, narcissistic sense of not letting my hair go gray and of trying to stave off the more onerous signs of aging by the application of eye cream and moisturizer. Other than that, flirting with death as I do and still longing for the parenting I didn't get, I generally ignore my physical health until such moment as it causes me immediate discomfort or pain. I don't mean to suggest that I abstain from the tedious rituals of daily hygiene—I brush my teeth, take showers, and wash my hair on a regular basis—but even here I sometimes feel resistance coiling up within me, demanding to know the purpose of this upkeep, why things need to be done over again and again. Let your teeth rot and your hair hang stringy and be done with it. Sometimes the malaise wins out: I haven't had a mammogram in over fifteen years, although one of my sisters has had breast cancer. I guess it's my own defiant little form of Russian roulette: catch me if you can.

And yet here is where you'll find me, come summer, despite my intermittent suicidal longings—that "almost unnameable Lust," as Anne Sexton described it in a poem: I'm lying on my back in the swimming pool in the garden behind the small but inviting house I have rented on Long Island, very much alive. This is the fourth house I have tried and the one most suited to me, since it is within walking distance of the village (I still haven't learned to drive and at this point it looks like I probably never will) and is compact enough so that I don't feel lonely when I'm alone. It has taken me a while to get used to renting a summer home, to feel comfortable with the planning and stocking up and inviting, not to mention paying for someone else's choice of furniture and dinner plates, but I am finally beginning, in fits and starts, to get the hang of it.

I have not been back in the hospital for eight years, although I have had some very shaky times, when all the negative feelings pop up again, robust as can be. I once dreamed of conquering my depression for good, but I have come to understand that it is a chronic condition, as much a part of me as my literary bent. To this day I can't figure out if it qualifies as a full-fledged disease, like cancer, but I've learned the hard way to give it, ephemeral as it may seem, its due. So although I fantasize about going off medication for good, I continue to pop my pills prophylactically, the side effects notwithstanding, and I continue to see a shrink, a combined approach that works as well as can be hoped for. If I can't quite declare victory over my depression, I am giving it a run for its money, navigating around it, reminding myself that the opposite of depression is not a state of unimaginable happiness but a state of approximate contentment, of relative all-right-ness. Perhaps depressives expect too much of life when they're *not* feeling depressed, have too exalted an idea of what the standard is. One night last winter I heard myself repeating to Zoë, much to my surprise, something my friend E. has told me, over and over again. "Life is a gift," I told my daughter, and then, to underline the point, I added: "A great gift." I expected Zoë to roll her eyes, especially at this kind of semi-pious sentiment coming from me, but instead she looked intrigued.

When I first heard my friend say this, it went over my head, like the maxim I spotted on a list in a store window as I was walking along Madison Avenue: "Activate self-esteem." What, I wondered, could that possibly mean? You either were possessed of self-esteem or you weren't; it wasn't something you simply "activated." It in turn reminded me of a statement I saw stitched on a bright Jonathan Adler pillow: "Hope is chic," as though hope were the new navy, decorative rather than essential. Although I'm not sure how much I believe that life is a gift (if only because no one asks whether you, in particular, desire to be born before you tunnel your way out of the womb), I very much want to believe it. Perhaps it's a sign of growing older, but anything else seems ungrateful—even to me.

I close my eyes and float where the water takes me. It is a lambent Saturday afternoon in July, not intolerably hot, with a slight breeze stirring the leaves on the trees. The two

friends I have invited for the weekend are reading on deck
chairs and Zoë, who has been expected all day, is predict-
ably late. It is not an exceptional scene but it is one that I
cannot imagine having arranged until relatively recently,
one that requires me to take the helm instead of hoping that
someone else will manage things for me. I stand up in the
pool with the intention of doing a few laps when suddenly
somewhere in the sky I could swear I feel my mother's presence, more benign than not. For a moment I feel her loss
intensely, and when I'm sure no one is watching I look up
and give her a little wave, just in case.

After swimming back and forth vigorously a few times,
I get out of the water, wrap a towel *tallis*-style around my
shoulders, and sink down on a chair next to my friends. They
are discussing whether or not they believe in psychics;
J., who is very logical, is explaining why she considers them
to be con artists, while L., an editor for one of the magazines
I write for, insists on keeping a more open mind. I pick up
the book I've been reading, *KL*, an eight-hundred-page
history of concentration camps—my typical light summer
fare—that is both heartbreaking and riveting, when Zoë
suddenly appears in the entrance to the garden, dressed in
her usual floppy clothes and carrying a bulging backpack.
"There you are," I say, "I was giving up on you."

In an hour or so the four of us will take a walk to the
shabby pizzeria-cum-Mexican-restaurant I have taken a
liking to, frequented mainly by locals rather than summer
folk. Later we will watch TV or play word games while eating tubs of pale ice cream from the Candy Kitchen, and
Zoë will pick an argument with me before the night is
done, as if on cue—something to do with the way I wash
dishes or host guests that is intrinsically objectionable. As

we are going to bed, she'll remind me to take my evening meds. Then, just before I am about to turn off the light, she'll come into my room, lean over, and give me a quick, barely-there kiss.

After she leaves, I'll lie in the dark and think about the small group of family and friends I've gathered under my borrowed roof, peopling a life I have often found difficult to bear but that right now, at least, seems like one worth claiming. I root around in my head for the usual sense of insufficiency, a clamorous lack waiting to be filled, but, for the time being, anyway, it is nowhere to be found.

The room feels cozy and I pull the fluffy comforter closer around me against the pleasant chill of the AC. Tomorrow presents itself as a glimpse of sun and water, hours to read in, shared meals and wandering conversation. As my eyelids start to droop, I suddenly recall a favorite line of poetry, by Charles Olson: "I have had to learn the simplest things / last. Which made for difficulties."

Whoever thought I'd be this close to happy?

ACKNOWLEDGMENTS

A book such as this draws on material that is inherently difficult and on aspects of myself that are inherently fragile. It has required the support and nurturance of any number of people, including some who've read early drafts of the manuscript. For their discerning assessment and input, I'd like to thank, first and foremost, Elaine Pfefferblit, who has been there from the original iteration many years ago to the final one; Carol Gilligan; Chip McGrath; Honor Moore; Deb Garrison; and Susan Squire.

For general life and writerly counsel, I extend my gratitude to Andy Port; Nessa Rapaport; Anne Roiphe; Jorie Graham; Dina Recanati; Joy Harris; Brenda Wineapple; Deborah Solomon; Jami Bernard; Bethanie Alhadeff; Lev Mendes; and Stephen Drucker.

Ileene Smith, my editor, has believed in my ability to finish this project despite rumors to the contrary. Over the years her probing questions and nuanced suggestions have been immeasurably helpful. Markus Hoffman, my agent, has been an invaluable source of both constructive criticism and unwavering encouragement. My publicists, Lottchen

Shivers and Sandi Mendelson, have been persistent in their advocacy.

Closer to home, my two sisters, Dinah Mendes and Debra Gerber, have consistently urged me on despite what may be the fraught nature of the material. My assistant, Anne-Marie Mueschke, has valiantly kept me organized and proved to be a deft reader. My friend Alice Truax has helped me move beyond the darkness and realize my intentions with her unerring psychological instincts. Finally, there is my daughter, Zoë, who prefers not to read what I write, but whose infusions of love and wisdom keep me afloat.